C# 3.0:
The Complete Reference

Chapter I—WHO OWNS THE EARTH?

We Look at American Soil and American Farmers of 1940

Cultures Are Characterized by Their Use of Natural Resources

IN THE DAYS when the major role of asphalt was to catch saber-tooth tigers, asphalt could hardly be called a resource. But it had become a resource in the days of paved roads when oil-minded Edward Doheny saw this same black oil-soaked "brear" which had caught the saber-tooth tiger. Again, though from another angle, oxygen in the air is not named among a nation's resources, though all men use it. Oxygen in the air has not been "developed" through human activities; it is a universal and a "free" raw material. What we commonly reckon as a country's natural resources are those raw materials in the earth possessed by the country which her people have learned to use; and use, in most resources, demands some development, some work done to the raw material. Indeed, the characteristic ways of developing and using raw materials form a pretty good description of any people's culture.

The Stone Age, for instance, means the stage of culture in which men developed tools from the natural resource of stone. Iron was in the earth, more of it then than now, but unworked. When people finally learned to use this great natural resource, their culture took on utterly new characteristics which are indicated in the general term "Iron Age." And along with people's use of these two great natural resources went characteristic food and housing habits, habits of protective social groups, habits of group or private property, habits of beliefs in infinite variety. All these work habits, play habits, belief habits were strongly influenced, if not actually controlled, by the people's physical environment and the ability to use it for their own ends. So it would be of outstanding importance to have the right to use natural resources. Presumably, in very early times, the strongest man got the best stones for himself or for his group. If so, these primitive people lived by the economic principle that "might makes right." And in accepting this economic disposal of natural resources, they also accepted the social consequence that the weak would suffer or die off. In other and bigger words, the use of natural resources in any

3

culture must be seen against the background of social institutions and economic system believed in, or at least sanctioned by, that culture.

What are the habits characteristic of our present-day culture in the United States? What are the American food, clothing and housing habits of today? What are our road habits; that is, how do we get from place to place? What natural resources do we use in order to live according to these cultural habits? And through what kind of work, what kinds of human relationships are these resources being developed? Have we substituted any new economy for the early one of "might makes right"? What social institutions, what economic system is sanctioned—believed in—in present-day United States?

Begin with food, which everyone through his own stomach recognizes as a basic need. The man in the Stone Age met this food need by a cultural pattern which depended on seizing food with his own bare hands or killing with traps or stone tools; the man in the Iron Age, by another pattern in which he helped his bare hands by primitive metal tools. The modern Chinese farmer meets his food need by still another pattern in which irrigation, terracing and care of the soil of his rice fields supplement his handwork. The man in present-day United States is fed by still another pattern distinctive of what we call modern Western culture. Take, for example, a typical American city dweller. Observe him in his everyday habit of sitting in a chair eating a piece of bread and butter. What natural resources lie back of this simple act? What work processes are involved in getting him his bread and butter and his chair?

The chair: wood (forests; soil, rain; lumber mills); nails (iron mines); perhaps cloth (wool—sheep—or cotton; soil, climate)—all produced through an elaborate series of processes involving machinery and power, which again involve more natural resources: metals, coal, oil or water; transportation (roads—again a whole series of resources and work processes from raw materials through factories—and fuel—probably coal, more mines); a chair factory, store, advertising, salesmen, probably other middlemen, and finally delivery to the house.

Bread: wheat (rain, soil); processed to flour (machinery, metals, power); transportation—again the whole complex of machinery and raw materials; cooking—more machinery and fuel—utensils, which bring in another string of natural resources and work groups.

Butter: cows (grass, soil); again a chain of processes, each one trailing directly or indirectly the use of innumerable raw materials.

This city dweller sitting in his chair munching his buttered bread is what the economists call a consumer—which is to say, he is using up things. What is he using up—what is he consuming? Directly and

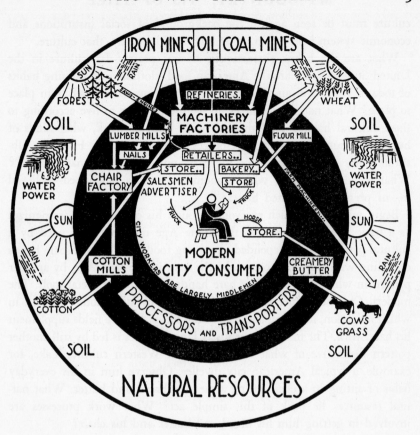

IRON MINES | OIL | COAL MINES

FORESTS

SOIL

WATER POWER

SUN

RAIN

COTTON MILLS

COTTON

SOIL

REFINERIES.

MACHINERY FACTORIES

LUMBER MILLS

NAILS

RETAILERS..

STORE..   BAKERY..

CHAIR FACTORY

SALESMEN ADVERTISER

STORE.

MODERN CITY CONSUMER

CITY WORKERS ARE LARGELY MIDDLEMEN

PROCESSORS AND TRANSPORTERS

NATURAL RESOURCES

WHEAT

SOIL

FLOUR MILL

WATER POWER

SUN

RAIN

CREAMERY BUTTER

COWS GRASS

SOIL

MODERN INTERDEPENDENT PATTERN

City dweller sitting in his chair munching bread and butter is also consuming factories, railroads, workers and natural resources. Charts of his housing, clothes, or road habits would show similar patterns.

obviously he is consuming the chair, the bread and the butter. Indirectly, but still obviously when you stop to think of it, he is consuming—helping to use up—factories, railroads and the work of the men who make them run. He is also consuming natural resources. He is, above all as a food consumer, consuming the natural resource upon which most living things depend—soil. It is a queer picture. There he sits chewing his buttered bread all unconscious of the chain of workers (and we have mentioned only a few of them), of whizzing factory wheels, of puffing engines, of waving wheat fields, of cows and forests, which eventually link him with faraway patches of soil, watered by the rain and warmed by the sun.

The picture becomes well-nigh bewildering when he takes his place as only one of 130 million people in the United States, each one eating or wishing to eat three meals a day made up of a multiplicity of foods; each connected with a shorter or longer chain of workers, machinery, animals or plants: back, back to a nearer or farther-away patch of soil. And if our gentleman wiped his lips with a cotton napkin (another cultural habit), he would add another chain of workers and work processes back to cotton plants and so to more workers and more patches of soil.

Two striking facts characterize this food pattern: first, an amazing number of man-made machine processes are involved; second, the whole chain of processes starts with soil—a natural resource.

A "machine culture"—the "age of machinery"—an "industrial culture." Such are the names often given to that complex of cultural habits by which the Americans of today meet their basic needs, of which food is only one. And these names are just. Even the people who work the land for their own needs depend upon machines of some sort; for who in America now fashions his own plow or spade, not to mention wagons or forks or clothes or a hundred and one machine products found in the poorest and most remote homes? Yet these names, by stressing the man-made contraptions, tend to lessen the significance and value of "God-given" resources, of "the good earth" which starts the whole chain of processes. Even our machine culture cannot feed itself or clothe itself, run its railroads or even its coal mines without SOIL.

NATURAL REGIONS. WHAT THEY DO TO PEOPLE AND PEOPLE DO TO THEM

Where, then, are the people who work to feed us? Where is this precious soil in which the food for 130 million Americans must grow? Where are our wheat lands, our cattle lands, our cotton lands, our forests? What do we, as a nation, do to keep our soil healthy and productive? What do the farmers, the guardians of our soil, do for it? Have they made great fortunes from developing the products of our soil? Are they a wealthy and honored group? How do they live? The newspapers, magazines and bookstores are full of conflicting reports about farmers, the "farm problem," the program of the Department of Agriculture. Geographies are full of talk about "natural regions" mysteriously outlined in red, sprawling in unexplained shapes across the familiar state boundaries. Many an American is using the newest of our road patterns—the automobile—to see for himself (and so to believe in) some of the great regions of his country, with their individual work patterns and people.

Big and little cars, with or without trailers, bowl over our vast network
of highways (another road pattern). Buses carry an army of sight-seers
from coast to coast. Why not join the procession and see the regions of
America's great natural resources in a humble Ford? First should come
the farm lands!

THE DRY HIGH PLAINS: A REAL "COW COUNTRY"
AND A FALSE WHEAT LAND

Thus began our personal adventure. With a rumble well stocked with
geology maps and physiographic charts; with books, magazine and newspaper clippings on agriculture, farm economics and social conditions;
with thermos bottle, raisins and crackers always within easy reach, we
had been heading east. We knew that our days in the Rockies and in
the vast plateaus to the west of them were almost over—carefree, ex-
clamatory, neck-craning days with the top of our little Ford down. Even
so, we were not prepared.

Suddenly, before us lay the great plain. The engine was boiling from
the steep climb behind us as we pulled over to a resting place. And there
below us stretched the plain. It was breathtaking, this first glimpse of a
boundless flatness, opalescent and shimmering to the horizon. We had
become used to gorges, canyons, towering rocks; to wilderness views of
unused rock deserts; to small mountain meadows. Then here, on a
sudden, was a new world beginning with unbelievable abruptness at
the mountains' edge and stretching to the far horizon. The High Plains,
most western and elevated part of the Great Plains. The short-grass
region. The "cow country."

Down we plunged to where the mountains ease into the plain, down
through the band of luxurious tourist and health resorts. We knew that
to the north, at the mountains' feet, rose oil derricks or culm heaps of
coal mines. Not for us now. Now we were determined to see for ourselves the lands that grow America's food (and our own), the lands
that grow her cotton and her trees; to see for ourselves the farmers and
their work.

Down we went past the "hogbacks," those hard ridges of tilted strata
which run parallel to the great mountains. We smiled at the local humor
and pride which had given the name of Mount Washington to one hump
rising an insignificant 200 feet above the plain, since it is just the height
above the sea of New Hampshire's famous peak! Down, down, and out
into this new world, the first of the lands we had come to see.

Enough of anything is impressive, even thrilling. The flatness was

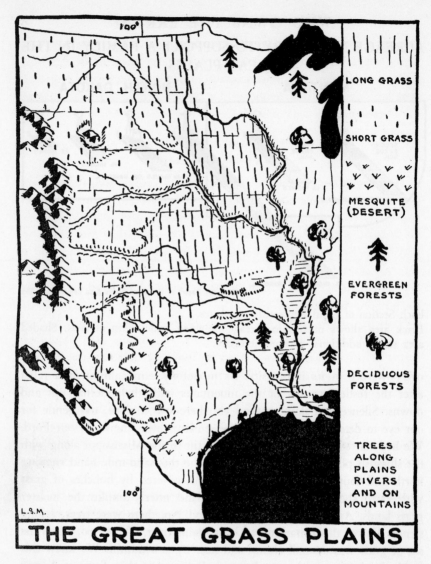

THE GREAT GRASS PLAINS

The High Plains are outwash plains from ancient mountain erosion, lying like a veneer on top of the Great Plains. Overgrazing and the plowing of this short grass region for wheat gave us the Dust Bowl. The High Plains are a fine grazing land if properly used; but their soil is easily eroded, they get less than 20 inches of rain a year (often much less), and they are marked by violent storms, tremendous strength of winds and wide fluctuations of temperature. "The Plains are the classic ground for last stands—bison, Indian, bad man, cowpuncher having in turn faced their final destiny there. And now the dry farmer . . ."

ACREAGE NECESSARY TO SUPPORT A FAMILY IN THE GREAT PLAINS

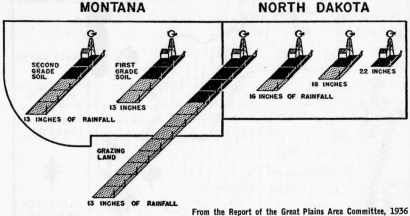

From the Report of the Great Plains Area Committee, 1936

Each Section of Land Represents 160 Acres.
Black area shows maximum acreage provided under existent laws. Shaded area shows additional acreage necessary.

overpowering in its immensity. Its monotony came almost as a relief after the restless variety of the mountains with their eternal ups and downs. Silence and flatness. And yet there was a slope, too gentle for our eye to detect, but evident to the sensitive little engine in our Ford. We had started on the 600-700-800-mile tilt to the Mississippi along with the sluggish plains rivers. We were on the thousand-mile band running north and south from Mexico to Canada, covered by bunches of grass with earth showing between, a grass land utterly unlike the moister grass lands. And not a tree all that way! No, there were trees, a long slender line of them marking a Great Plains river. There, too, across the sea of grass was a small clump and near by a windmill. We knew this marked a house, too low and too small to see at this distance. A cow needs about 70 acres to get a living from this short grass in the driest region near the mountains. A family needs 2600 to 4000 or more acres to live on. No wonder the houses are far apart! What family could stand the strain of being alone with itself and grass and flatness? We looked across to the place where we knew there was a house. What woman looked out from those windows? Was she one of the many who lose their mental balance in this monotony and isolation?

The cow country. Where were the cows? I thought of the great herds I used to see from the train window when, as a child, I crossed this country many times a year. There were real cowboys then with sombreros and lassos, such as one seldom finds nowadays except in "Westerns"—movies or novels. Off on the horizon there were still the familiar horned profiles. Often we were near enough to see the white faces and red bodies of the plains cattle. But they seemed mild. And though there are actually more than formerly, they no longer dominate the scene. For now they are largely fenced, in big mile-long stretches, to be sure, but not wandering in the fenceless, thousand-mile-long expanses of the past. Why?

The answer lay all around us, growing in force as we moved ever down the gentle tilt and the grass grew a little longer, as the average yearly rainfall increased inch by inch from 10 to 20 inches, and the soil grew a little darker. For now we could see the overturned soil. Tilled fields lay around us where the cattle used to roam. Yes, we were in the land of dry farming. Here in this land of scanty rain, the sod had been broken and plowed deep: a desperate attempt to distribute the rare and precious moisture which had soaked into the earth, and thus to keep the topsoil from becoming too dry and caked. Queer tilled fields: most of them without crops. Now the houses that we passed were often empty. Where were the eager homesteaders of a few years ago? Gone. One hundred and fifty thousand of them moved out between 1930 and 1935. For the topsoil had gone, gone with the wind quite literally, and with the rains since the plowing under of the sod. Three hundred million tons of topsoil blown off in a single wind storm! In places one can find great stretches of scoured hardpan, blown clean of the soil that had slowly formed over the detritus which millions of years ago had been washed down from the old mountains in great flood plains and deposited as the High Plains on top of the Great Plains—soil which was built at the rate of an inch in five hundred years! Gone the free range, its few watering places and best grass lands claimed by the homesteading farmers. Gone the grass, which had fought for many centuries to get a firm footing in this land of little rain, grass which could grow when there was rain and lie dormant when there was none, nutritious grass for all its shortness—gone under the hard hoofs and hungry mouths of the too many cattle and sheep crowded on the range, gone under the plows of the homesteaders. And now the very soil itself—gone with the wind, gone with the rare but torrential rains. In place of the old free grassy range, bare subsoil, deserted wheat farms, and High Plains farmers on relief.

What had brought people to this dry land in the first place? Cowboys,

then farmers. Out came our history books. But we found, of course, that
though this region is so markedly different from the rest of the United
States the use to which its soil was put grew out of the history of the
whole country; that to understand the use we have made of the High
Plains in our present machine age, we should have to go back to the
happenings and psychology of the days when our young country thought
in terms of agriculture. This sweep of history we must postpone until
we have seen the other farm lands of today.

Up and down the High Plains we went. The story is not always the
same for the farmers in this land of extremes. Some years there is more
rain, and then, in places, the wheat still waves—wheat, alas, which may
not find a market. In these wet years the grass still shows a dusty green
where the plow has not turned it under, and great herds of cattle are
packed into cattle cars and shipped to the corn lands for fattening on
their way to the great packing houses of Kansas City and Chicago.
Sheep one finds too, close cropping the growing tips of short grass with
their cleft lips so that the shallow roots die. But there are also drought
times in this land of uncertain rain, when the emaciated cattle die by the
thousand before they can be driven to the trains and shipped to greener
lands. There are times when the wheat seed is blown from the ground
before it takes root, and lies in drifts along the fences or piled up against
heaps of drifted topsoil. For this is the Dust Bowl. This onetime greatest
cow country of the world is now the Dust Bowl of America.

A strange sequel to the high hopes and gallant endurance of the last
of our land pioneers! A strange sequel to the million-year-old soil made
from the mountaintops. A strange sequel to the use of Public Domain—
first given away by a lavish government but in sections unwisely small
—ruined, much of it abandoned, now gradually being returned to the
government for painstaking restoration. A shocking, if not strange, sequel
to World War demands for food, to tearing more and more millions of
these once grassy acres into plowed strips of wheat fields, exposing the
dry soil in a region of blistering winds and, by 1937, making five hundred
thousand farmers dependent on federal grants.

THE GRASSY GREAT PLAINS: A REAL WHEAT LAND

And where has the soil gone? Drive a little farther. Drive east until
you reach the cliffs which mark the edge of the High Plains, from Texas
to the southern edge of South Dakota. Go down off the High Plains to
the lower level of the Great Plains with its darker chocolate soil, to a
land east of the 100th meridian that has more rain—20 or more inches on

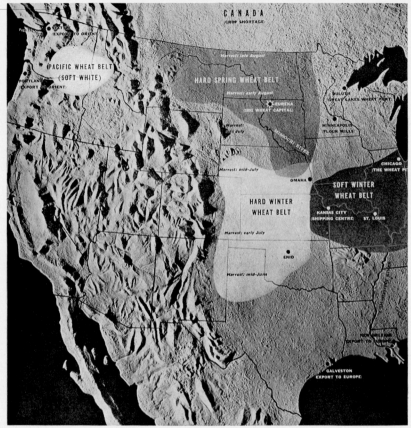

WHEAT LANDS

Compare with map of Great Plains (page 8) and map of erosion (page 14).
Note that the 100° meridian runs through the hard winter-wheat belts. The
Dust Bowl is west of this meridian, which is roughly the line of 20 inches
rainfall, and largely on the High Plains—the western portion of the Great
Plains.

the average—a land still covered with the nutritious short grass, here a
little longer, a little more abundant than on the doormat of the High
Plains. Here, too, the plows of the homesteaders cut up a great range
land. And here, too, the farmers are leaving; or if they stay, remaining
on relief. For they are first in the path of the dust blown from the
wind-eroded High Plains.

On the western horizon appears a darkish cloud. And every man or
woman springs into terrified action. Quick! Close the doors and windows

with newspapers in the cracks. Call the children, quick! Why don't they run faster? The cloud is nearer; it is darkening the sun. The wind hits the flimsily built house. And with the wind comes the dust. Fine-powdered grains which sift under the doors, gather on the window sills, find every crack in roof or walls. The children begin to cough. Tie up their mouths and noses with gauze. Put on your own mask. Try not to cough. Pretend to the children that you don't feel strangled, that it will soon stop blowing. Try to cook dinner. Grit in every pot, grit in your eyes, grit in your teeth. In the twilight of the room the children sit on the floor and try to play. But what do they play? That father is lost in the dust storm? That they help dig out bodies after the storm is over? They stop to cough. They say they can't eat, it tastes of dust. Will it never end? Yes, it will end, sometimes after a few hours, sometimes after three days. Yes, it will end. And when it is over, your little room will be knee-high with dust. The drift against the side of your small house will be perhaps six feet high. And your wheat fields? Why look at them? No hope of a crop this year. Why did we ever come? Why did the others off there to the west, up on the higher level ever come? Shall we go to California? They say there are jobs there. Or can father loan us enough to get back to the farm in Michigan? To be sure, we left there because we couldn't make a living. But at least we would have a roof over our heads and *something* to eat. Mother would take us in.

Yes, this Great Plains region just east of the High Plains is where the soil from the onetime cow country is blowing to. This is still the Dust Bowl—a name which covers both the High Plains land from which the dust blows and the Great Plains land to the east on which so much dust settles. Under this far-blown dust and local dust, farms are ruined.

Not all the soil blown from the wind-eroded High Plains settles so close to the spot from which it started. The future, the far future, would not look so dark if it did. To be sure, much of the land which has lost its topsoil is damaged beyond recovery within the span of time for which we can think or plan. But the drifts of good soil that settle might eventually produce a sod cover if left unplowed. Indeed, this is the way loess, one of the most fertile of soils, is made. The Russian steppes and much of our own grass land were originally made this way, by a layer of rich topsoil blown from other land. But the finer, more powdery grains of soil from the High Plains rise high in the air and get caught in the upper currents and drift for hundreds, even thousands, of miles before they fall. There have been times when New Yorkers have looked up above their skyscrapers and wondered what made the sky look so yellow. *Soil from*

EROSION

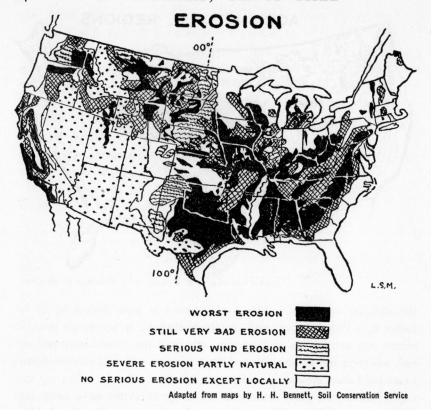

WORST EROSION

STILL VERY BAD EROSION

SERIOUS WIND EROSION

SEVERE EROSION PARTLY NATURAL

NO SERIOUS EROSION EXCEPT LOCALLY

Adapted from maps by H. H. Bennett, Soil Conservation Service

A map of erosion shows little by itself except the vast extent of seriously eroded land and the small extent where erosion is negligible. (In this small-scale map finer gradations have been omitted.) If, however, an erosion map is studied with a topographical map (see end papers), its significance increases. Note that slight erosion is practically confined to the flat lands, except in New England.

The relation of erosion to crops is also significant. Here the human element of care of agricultural lands enters. Note that wind erosion is in dry region west of 100° longitude. Note cotton and worst erosion (and see chart on page 122).

the High Plains. The dust from these farms is swept up from the floors of the White House in Washington; it falls on the decks of steamers far out at sea; it falls, alas, tons and tons of it, on the sea itself and is lost for mankind at the bottom of the Atlantic Ocean.

Erosion. The word has entered into the vocabulary of the newspapers, the movie newsreel, and so has filtered through to ordinary conversation. Geologists, too, talk about erosion. They tell us natural erosion gave us

AGRICULTURAL REGIONS

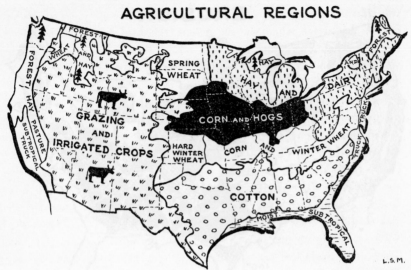

Adapted from maps by O. E. Baker, U. S. Department of Agriculture

the skeleton of our soil. Man-made erosion is now destroying it. Or rather it is dislocating it, and thereby destroying it for man's use. Go where you will in this vast country, wherever the plow has turned the sod, wherever the ax has chopped the trees, you will find erosion. Sometimes mild sheet erosion in which rain has removed only a thin top surfacing; sometimes gully erosion in which great ravines have eaten into the cultivated fields and left only carved skeletons of the subsoil. Here no crops will grow, at least not for hundreds of years. The hardiest of primitive plants can be made to take root; they will grow, die, add their decaying bodies to enrich the robbed earth so that less and less hardy plants may find food; and bit by bit, with unimaginable slowness, a layer of humus will be built in which the crops needed by men again will thrive. Drive east from the Great Plains; drive through the winter wheat belt; drive north from there through the spring wheat belt; drive through the whole stretch of the Central Lowland, through the corn and hog belts which are, naturally, the same. Drive through the cotton lands stretching in a great arc from Texas around the Gulf of Mexico and up the Atlantic plain and the Piedmont hills at the foot of the Alleghenies. Drive wherever farmers of America have been plowing the good earth. If the idea of erosion lies in your mind, your eye will see it everywhere until you nervously begin to wonder whether there will be enough soil left in this vast country to raise the food fuel for its 130 million human engines. You see the soil running away in every muddy river you meet;

you scan every road cut, every hillside, and sigh with relief when you reach a flat stretch where the silt gathers, thankful if it is not in a reservoir. The disease of water erosion is taking three billion tons of United States soil each year. No one who has ever seen the Dust Bowl can ever get the fear of the disease of erosion out of his soul.

Yet, apparently, even this stricken land is not hopeless if we have energy and skill. In the *New York Times* on Sunday, June 25, 1939, appeared this startling headline: LIFE RENEWED IN DUST BOWL. The article was written by H. H. Bennett, Chief of the Soil Conservation Service. He reported that "in the Texas Panhandle, farmers and elevator men are predicting 15,000,000 to 25,000,000 bushels of wheat. In the worst drought season, 1935, the area yielded only 4,000,000 bushels and the area then was larger than this year." And this is in the heart of the Dust Bowl.

This startling change in yield from four million to fifteen or twenty-five million bushels is not due merely to rain, that incalculable element over which men still have little control. It is due in a large measure to change in farming techniques. Wrong techniques can destroy life—no visitor to the Dust Bowl can ever doubt this—but right techniques can also renew life. They can, at least, if the damage hasn't gone too far. How? It is a part of the Soil Conservation Service to teach the farmers how. And through their teaching they have reduced the area exposed to wind action in scattered tracts in the Dust Bowl from sixteen million acres to eight hundred thousand acres!

The point is to make full use of what rain does fall. This is done by the simple trick of contour plowing. Plow up and down a hill and you make a trough for the rain to run down. Plow around a hill and you make a terrace which holds the rain. Where some soil is left, vegetation will again appear if the water is held. If enough soil is left, it will even yield crops. At least six and a half million acres of land plowed largely for wheat should never have been plowed. They should be turned back to the cows. That still leaves large areas for farming. The farmers who are left in these parts of the Dust Bowl have learned their bitter lesson. Contour plowing is spreading fast. Life is being renewed.

Moreover, not all of the wheat lands need medical care. Not all of them are eroded. The Great Plains are so vast that one catches oneself saying —yes, and thinking—they are limitless. And with the sense that there is always "plenty more" comes almost the sense that it is unnecessary, even paltry, to be concerned with the waste of the soil on what is, after all, only a small part of this enormous region. If we, with the detachment of visitors, with the definite purpose of seeing each region as a part of the

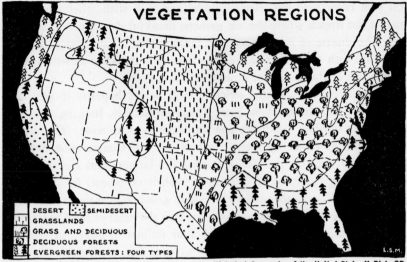

VEGETATION REGIONS

DESERT · · SEMIDESERT
GRASSLANDS
GRASS AND DECIDUOUS
DECIDUOUS FORESTS
EVERGREEN FORESTS: FOUR TYPES

L.S.M.

Adapted from C. O. Paullin's "Atlas of the Historical Geography of the United States," Plate 2D

national food problem, caught even a breath of this attitude, what must have been the temptation to people coming to the wheat lands as pioneers? Again we needed the sweep of history as an explanatory background for the present.

And the people, now? What kind of lives do the wheat ranches give them in those uneroded parts which still yield great crops? Nothing gives more of a sense of security than a great growing crop. Mile-wide fields of wheat ripening into successive harvests beginning in the south and moving north with the lengthening days of the summer sun. How can a farmer manage a great seasonal crop like wheat? There are mammoth tractors to be handled, there are reapers and threshers and hauling to the stations for shipment. Sometimes there is hot, wet weather and then he has rust to fight. Sometimes there is dry weather and the crop withers before his eyes. Sometimes there are grasshoppers to be fought, pests which darken the sky, settle on the fields and leave only upstanding straw. Sometimes there is hail. No, life on a wheat ranch is not so secure as it looks from a Ford window.

Even in the good years, life is fairly hard going. To be sure, in those years the army of workers who move north as the harvests ripen find plenty of work. And the impressive wheat elevators towering over every small station store great quantities of threshed wheat in their gigantic bins. But what happens inside the houses even in bumper-crop years?

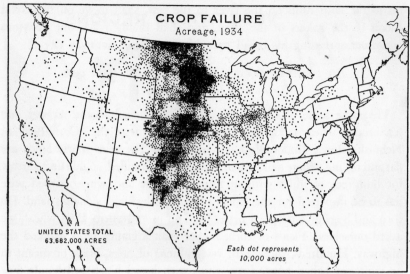

CROP FAILURE
Acreage, 1934

UNITED STATES TOTAL
63,682,000 ACRES

Each dot represents
10,000 acres

U. S. Department of Agriculture—Bureau of Agricultural Economics

Drought in 1934 was of unprecedented duration and extended over most of the country between the Rockies and the Appalachians north of the Cotton Belt. This drought was especially severe in the Great Plains. In the northern plains it had been preceded by several dry seasons, which helps to explain the magnitude of the crop failure in the Dakotas. In 1924 and 1929 there were roughly 13,000,000 acres of crop failure; in 1934, 63,682,000 acres.

As one sits down at the clean kitchen table on which the farmer's wife or daughter places homemade bread, milk and cold pork, one somehow senses that these people are nearer the pioneers in thinking and in habits than most Americans. The frequent radio, telephone and glass-doored bookcases; the big farm machinery under the shed or greased and standing in the open, show that the early days of struggle are over. Yet here is nearly one's old conception of democracy—few rich and few very poor, almost no illiteracy (seven-tenths of one percent among those of native parentage and only one and four-tenths percent including children of the foreign-born). Hard work, great respect for the school and the church —or rather for the churches, of which there are many denominations. A determination to succeed in the face of shrinking income which is taking away both comforts and an even more prized privilege—education.

And after the harvest is over and the army of seasonal workers has moved on, the farmer returns from the fields for five months of enforced leisure. In the meanwhile excited bidders on the Chicago Produce Exchange set the price of his wheat and decide how much of it shall move

on to the flour mills on the river to the east, shall move on the Great
Lakes to the bakers of the cities, and shall finally reach our oblivious
consumer spreading his bread with his butter in a faraway city.

THE STONELESS CENTRAL LOWLANDS: WHAT HAVE CORN AND HOGS DONE FOR PEOPLE?

The same sense of fertility that we had enjoyed in the moister and
less eroded wheat lands characterized the farms of the "Corn Belt" of
Nebraska, Iowa, Illinois, Indiana and Ohio. The real prairie lands are
flat and rolling, where a plowman, if he were so minded, could run a furrow
for hundreds of miles without hitting a stone and where barbed wire
has to be imported for the fences of this treeless and stoneless land. Do
corn and hogs give people a better life and more security than wheat, we
asked ourselves? Fields of corn, higher than a giant's head, flanked the
highway. Hundreds, thousands, yes, millions of hogs, black or meant to
be white, or belted hogs, dirty white with broad black bellybands. For
corn turns most profitably into hogs. And into cows, too. Here at the
corn cribs of the corn country west of the Mississippi were the onetime
lean range cattle, now eating themselves fat and fit to be turned into
meat at the great slaughter and packing houses of Kansas City and Chicago. Perhaps it was well to die fat and contented, at any rate!

Many other crops, too; more as we moved east from the natural grass
lands of the prairie states, where originally trees grew only along the
rivers, into the natural meadow and woodlands, where trees had been
cleared for farms. Fields of purplish quivering oats, of vivid green alfalfa
and grass ripening into hay made a magic color pattern. More vegetable
gardens for home use; though pork and potatoes, served with gravy of
skimmed milk thickened with flour, still appeared as the usual dinner in
the tree-sheltered farmhouses. Huge red barns with round silos, and
barnyards filled with the cheerful cackle of chickens, and sleek fat cows
returning from green pastures at milking time—quite different creatures
from their wild, gaunt cousins of the range. Yet, when we stopped for
a glass of milk, it was often skimmed! The cream had gone to the
near-by creamery to be made into butter. At one farmhouse two children
had broken into the creamhouse and stolen some cream. But this unac-
customed luxury had made these farm children sick.

Cream to the creameries. Fodder corn to the pigs, and sweet corn to
the children and the corn-canning factories. Women to the corn can-
neries, too, when the season is on. Here is a chance to eke out the slender
incomes. So many a housewife from the Middle West small towns sits

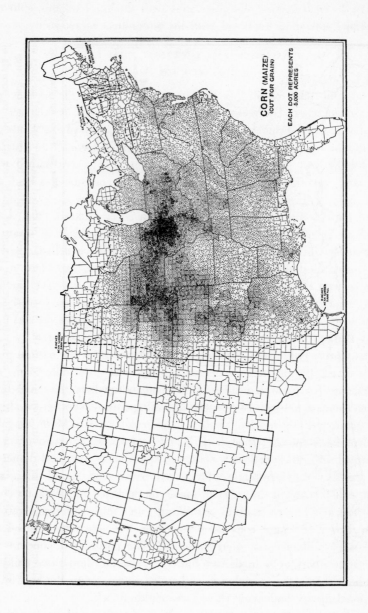

CORN (MAIZE)
(CUT FOR GRAIN)

EACH DOT REPRESENTS
5,000 ACRES

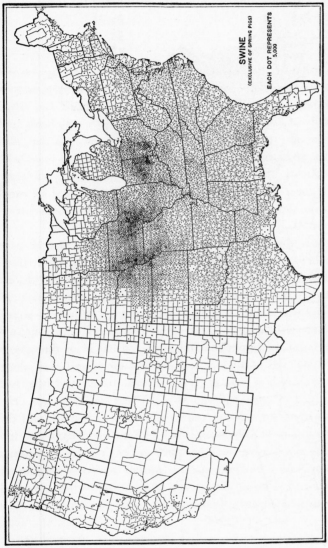

SWINE
(EXCLUSIVE OF SPRING PIGS)

EACH DOT REPRESENTS
5,000

Three-quarters or more of our corn is fed on the farm where it is produced and is marketed as hogs or cattle. As a southern Senator once expressed it, "Why, suh, a hawg is nothin' but cawn on foah laigs!" About 6 pounds of grain and 6 pounds of hay produce one pound of lamb, live weight; 10 pounds of grain and 10 pounds of hay produce one pound of beef; and 5.6 pounds of corn make one pound of pork.

hours a day in a cannery husking corn, or stands in the steaming rooms where the corn is cooking. At home the oldest girl takes care of the younger children, cooks and puts the corn, pork, potatoes and flour gravy on the table. Yes, the machine age has certainly entered the farms of the Corn Belt.

THE DAIRY LANDS AROUND THE LAKES: FARMERS SERVE THE CITIES

And north around Lake Michigan were more cows. Unbelievably fat and friendly were these dairy cows, who gave their milk to their masters twice or three times a day. Herds of big, slow-footed, black and white Holsteins. Herds of mild-eyed, deerlike Jerseys. Herds and herds and herds! It was not surprising to read that Wisconsin's cows gave 240 million dollars' worth of milk in 1930. Near by was always a corn field, and a silo was always attached to the barn. Big hay fields, and even larger pastures. How green they looked after the High Plains! And on every hand were cheese factories and butter factories where we could always get fresh buttermilk.

Yes, throughout the Middle West, farm buildings and crops all gave the sense that here was "good earth." Yet in the midst of this fertility, in Missouri, Iowa, Wisconsin, Indiana, Ohio, appeared the land disease we had learned to watch for—erosion. Here it was water erosion. In places, the topsoil was washed in a thin sheet from the surface. In places, whole farm slopes were gone in great gullies. The trees were gone, not only the great forests of Minnesota and Michigan but in or throughout the meadow woodlands of Illinois, Indiana and Ohio, and even along the river beds of the wheat country. Who cut these trees? And what had the country gained by their cutting? What it had lost was clear. The muddy rivers we crossed, coming from these cut-over regions, told the same story of a runaway soil. Along the Ohio and the Mississippi and the Missouri we were shown the high-water marks of floods. Sometimes these were painted on a building in the center of a town with dates of floods after them. Floods and erosion and past cutting of trees. We had learned from our newspapers at home to link them together.

Yet these Middle West farms looked like story-book farm pictures— "good earth" and homes that looked comfortable to eyes filled with recent dust from the Dust Bowl. But the story-book farmers always owned their farms. There is a close emotional tie in most minds between ownership of land and the working of the land. We do not feel this tie between the ownership of a city house and its occupant. No one feels that it is somehow un-American, against democratic habits, to rent a house. But there is an American voice heard sometimes on the street, sometimes in the press, sometimes in the halls of Congress, protesting that a man has a right to do what he wants with *his own land*. Government regulations of crops? Government supervision of farming methods? No, answers this protesting voice. That is not democratic. No one must stand between the farmer and the land he farms. A farmer needs to take the full responsibility for the use of his farm. Surely, he can be trusted to take care of *his own land*.

His own land. Is it his own? Quite literally, who does own the land that the 1935 census tells us was worked by six million, eight hundred thousand farmers? The simple answer is that 2,865,000 or 42% of all American farmers were then tenants, the largest proportion we had ever had. These figures, however, do not tell all. For tenancy is not necessarily an evil. Tenancy used to be thought of as just one step towards ownership. Young men without the capital to buy farms could start as tenants, and after they had saved enough money could buy farms. This was not an untypical situation in the Middle West up to the time of the World War, although to climb the ladder to ownership became more difficult as the supply of free land went down and the prices of land consequently went up. Then with the World War came a tremendous boom in land prices because of wartime food demands. The Middle West farms, always dependent on a cash crop the price of which is set in a world market, were violently affected; whereas New England, where the crops are largely consumed on the farm, felt the war-boom prices but slightly.

At this same time prices shot up in the things that farmers had to buy —farm machinery and the hundred things that the family needed. To keep in the running with these expansion prices, farmers increasingly had to borrow; and most of them had only their farms to offer as security. So, more and more, they took out mortgages on their farms—first, second and even third mortgages. The banks were glad to take mortgages on these midwestern farms. Most of their depositors were farmers. Besides, they thought the farm lands were good investments. Farmers and farm communities (and the rest of us, too) believe deeply in land. The good earth. It can't run away. (Only it has! Look at the map of erosion.) It must be a good investment; it is the ultimate source of the food of the world. (Only here we were to find that even good land may not yield a living wage.) So the farmers mortgaged their farms and thereby got the cash they needed for boom times; and in the bad times that followed, individuals, the government, banks, insurance companies and other corporations became absentee owners of farms they did not farm. In large sections of the wheat and corn lands, this absentee landlordism grew to alarming proportions. For wartime prices did not survive the war. When Europe once more began raising its own foods, demand for American wheat and other crops collapsed. Farm income collapsed. Land values collapsed to the point where the money that a farmer had borrowed on his farm often equaled its market value. The debt burden thus carried once affluent farmers down to the plight in which we found them. Thus tenancy in the Middle West became not a step towards ownership but a step away from ownership, even to the tragic sequels of foreclosures and evictions.

Go into many farmhouses in these regions; talk with the farmer, with his wife. "Yes, I was born on this farm but we don't own it now. The bank does. We mortgaged the farm, but we thought we were going to make enough to pay it off—and more, too. But everything seemed to cost more. Then we took out a second mortgage. But the bottom seemed to drop out of everything after the war. We didn't make enough out of our crops to make ends meet. . . . We couldn't pay the mortgage interest. Finally the bank foreclosed. No, we weren't evicted. The man down the road was. Yes, we've had riots hereabouts. You read about them in the eastern papers? Well, they were real enough. I never thought I'd see farmers rioting. But we farmers have to stand together even if it means fighting the law. A farmer somehow has a right to *his land*."

So, many a farmer is now a tenant on the old farm he used to own. He pays rent. The fields no longer belong to him. Though his crops are big, the prices they bring are low. His income is small. Shall he fertilize the fields? They need it. Shall he buy a new tractor? He needs it. Shall he paint the barn? It needs it. But he doesn't know how long he can stay on the farm. The average occupancy of farm tenants is about two or three years as compared with the average owner occupancy of about fourteen years. His lease runs only for a year. Better postpone until times are good again. So the farm runs down. He is caught in a vicious circle. The farm gets poorer, so the farmer gets poorer. The farmer gets poorer, so the farm gets poorer. The farmer is getting less and less income. There comes a time when he can't even pay his rent. The bank or other absentee owner is nervous. The farmer must go, be turned out, be evicted. Then, sometimes, his neighbors get excited. They are all more or less in the same fix. Their time may come next. And they know a farmer must have land to farm. They resist. They even fight officers of the law. And the eastern newspapers come out with headlines about riots in the farm lands. The farmers must be getting red!

This, with variations, all through the great farm lands of the Mississippi slopes. This, in what used to be the richest farm land of the United States! Sometimes it was taxes that could not be paid and then the farm was lost to the state. Sometimes it was lost to an insurance company, sometimes to a bank. Here in the wheat and corn lands the tragic sequels read: In war-boom years: high price of farms + high costs → mortgages. In postwar depression years: high mortgage debts + low income = tenancy → impoverished land → impoverished farmers. A sorry picture—in its way, as sorry as the Dust Bowl.

Yes, the present is easy, tragically easy to read. But how had it really come about? We were plagued with "whys." Why all this talk about war boom and collapse? Had farmers been so much better off before the first World War? If so, why, in nearly twenty postwar years, had they not been able to recover those conditions? Would history give us an answer? More and more the present seemed inexplicable, paradoxical taken by itself. More and more these farmers on the dry High Plains, in the wheat lands of the Great Plains and in the corn and hog lands of the Central Lowland seemed to us caught in a national economic jam. Their problems turned not merely on richness of soil and size of crops, but on markets, on incomes and expenditures, on standards of living, on that strange intangible thing which we call present-day American culture. More and more we felt that we should never understand the "farm problem" without understanding the past of our country. But again it seemed well to postpone history until we had seen the next great farm region. It was time to turn to the cotton lands. For the South, with its own regional expression of the farm problem, still lay before us.

THE COTTON LANDS: DEPLETED SOIL AND DEPLETED PEOPLE

And in the cotton lands, what did we find? We came first to the newest of the cotton lands in Texas, for cotton has marched steadily west ever since its white fluffy bolls first ripened on the southern Atlantic seaboard. Our little Ford made good time over the vast level stretches of good road. The roads themselves were interesting. Sometimes oiled surfacing—for Texas is a land of oil discovered in the midst of its cotton fields. Sometimes, towards the south, gleaming white surfacing which turned out to be broken oyster shells. For Texas has a long seacoast arching in a great curve around the warm Gulf waters. We clicked off the miles by the hundred, on roads so good that they came to seem in-

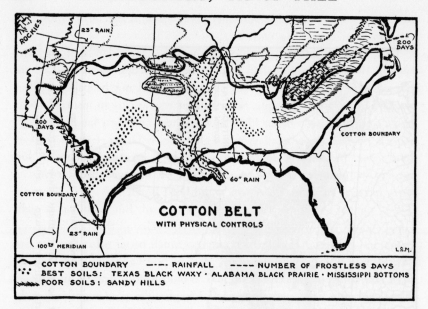

COTTON BELT
WITH PHYSICAL CONTROLS

~~ COTTON BOUNDARY   —·—· RAINFALL   ---- NUMBER OF FROSTLESS DAYS
∴∴ BEST SOILS: TEXAS BLACK WAXY · ALABAMA BLACK PRAIRIE · MISSISSIPPI BOTTOMS
⟩⟩⟩ POOR SOILS: SANDY HILLS

Every curve in the cotton boundary is explainable by some physical control. Western limit is controlled by dryness (23 inches of rainfall, roughly the 100° meridian), by Edward's Plateau and the Llano Estacado (the Staked Plains). Northern limit is controlled by summer temperature (200 frostless days), the Ouachita Plateaus and the Ozarks, the Cumberland Plateau and Blue Ridge Mountains. Southern limit is partly controlled by wetness (60 inches of rainfall) and marshes. Heavy rains beat down cotton. This area is used for rice.

congruous. Slender paved lines, bespeaking a wealthy nation, running through a land whose poverty deepened the farther east we went.

We sped through the Cotton Belt from Texas through to Georgia, noting all its variety of topography, of native vegetation running from different kinds of grasses to dense forests, its differences in density of population, in proportion of Negroes and innumerable other characteristics. Yet we felt the likenesses in the cotton lands as well as the local or regional differences. What made *cotton* dominate this enormous stretch of country roughly 1500 miles from east to west, from the Carolinas to Texas, and 300 to 400 miles from north to south? What had made southern farmers plant 42 million acres in cotton in a single year? Was it climate? In a way. For we discovered by a little study of our maps that the southern and western limits of cotton were set by rainfall, in one case too much and in the other case too little. And the northern limit was set by temperature. As for soil, apparently cotton will grow in almost any soil. The

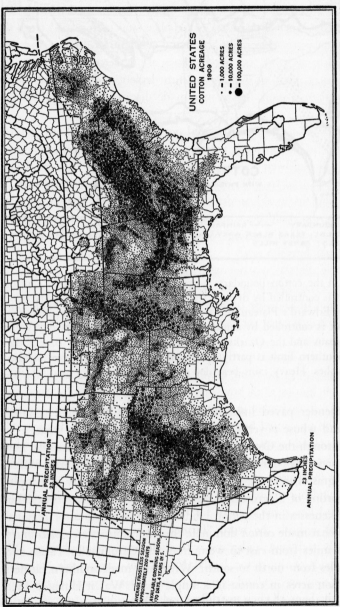

From the "Atlas of American Agriculture," 1918, Part V

Heaviest cotton acreage in 1909 coincides strikingly with best soils. Later maps show increased acreage towards the western limit and in hilly and sandy parts to the north. History (page 63 and later) suggests other reasons in addition to soil depletion.

quality of soil, however, does partly determine the size and quality of the crop.

What had cotton done to the many million acres of good earth that it had covered? Much. For cotton is a robber crop taking food from the soil in large measure. Cotton lands demand constant fertilizing. And they have not had it—at least, not enough. They are depleted soil, yielding less and less per acre. Here in the cotton lands depletion and leaching of the soil are added to erosion. Three man-made diseases. Verily, the soil has been mined.

But these physical characteristics did not explain another kind of unity which bound the cotton lands together and gave them a common problem. The land had been a good land once; would even be a good land now, if it were cared for. Why did the farmers of the South not care for their soil? And the world needed cotton. What was the matter with the farmers? No one could be a moment in the South without seeing that something was radically wrong. Why should not the cotton lands "flourish," as the old histories say?

The trouble plainly was not with the physical stage set—the soil, the climate, not even chiefly in the waste of soil. The trouble lay in the human drama. Indeed, the tragedy in the human lives was made more grim by the goodness of the land. What kind of lives were being lived in the cotton lands?

Everywhere the houses were unpainted. Most of them never had been painted. Apparently the paint brush now seldom stroked even the fine old plantation houses—and how rare these pillared mansions were, considering the role they play in popular imagination based upon romantic literature. The unpainted South! But paint came to seem a luxury, relatively unimportant except as a symbol. There was more than paint which separated these cotton farms from the comfortable farmhouses and big silos of busy farmyards of the Middle West, and from the small white farmhouses and big red barns of New England. These roadside shanties that we passed never *had* been fit for farm families.

We had to rethink the word "farmer." This was true even on the incongruously well-kept highways, with their neatly painted signs. Who used these roads of the cotton lands? Visitors, in comfortable "through" buses or fast touring cars, and every now and again farmers on the move, carrying with them all their worldly goods. We stopped to look and to talk. Every kind of object that could run on wheels—coughing Model T's, old touring cars, wagons drawn by a cadaverous mule. Inside, the family—farmer, wife and children numbering from one to seven—furniture tied on at strange angles—perhaps a bed and patched mattress and a few chairs, a stove, sometimes a pig and a few chickens in rickety crates wedged in with a few pots and pans and strange-shaped bundles. Nothing more. Was this a farmer? Where were his farming tools? Was this a farmer's wife? Where was her china, her glass? Where were her curtains, her rugs, her sheets? Where were the children's mattresses? Where were their clothes, their shoes, their toys, their books? I was haunted with visions of city vans on moving days, of trunks of clothes and boxes of innumerable household goods, loved and lived with; other visions of the treasures of a New England farm attic and well-stocked cellar which come to light on the rare occasions when a Vermont farmer moves. Could this be *all* a farming household had? Were those flour-sack and, sometimes, potato-sack clothes all the children ever wore? Did they go to school in them? Barefooted? And how did a man farm without tools?

When we stopped at some of the poorer houses, we got some of the answers. Often the children simply didn't go to school, or went only for a few months a year. Sometimes this was because of lack of clothes, particularly shoes; sometimes because the schools had simply closed for lack of public funds, or because a faraway consolidated schoolhouse had replaced the old and near-by one-room school and then the community had been too poor to run a bus for the children; sometimes because the children were needed to work in the cotton fields. They had no toys except corn-cob dolls which they put to bed under scraps of potato bags. They had no books, no magazines, seldom even a newspaper.

The furniture in place looked even more meager than piled into the old wagon or Ford. Usually the farmer and his wife had some kind of bed and at least one pair of sheets, but the children slept on the floor—three, four, five—up to nine in a room. The stove was often made from an old oil drum in which wood was burned on cold days. But nothing could keep the wind from blowing through the cracks or the rain from streaming through the roof. Many of the houses had no glass windows—only wooden shutters which reduced the inside to darkness on rainy days. No closets—but then there were no clothes to hang in them. A lean-to, usually, with a rickety kitchen stove. What was cooked on this stove? Corn meal, with turnip greens and cheaper cuts of pork fried in lard for good days. Molasses, gravy of lard and flour, yams, a few eggs. Seldom milk. Seldom green vegetables. Why did not they have their own vegetable gardens? Wasn't there time to raise vegetables?

Couldn't a farm family afford a cow? Story-book farms always did! Yes, we had to rethink the word "farmer" in this land of the three M's—Meal, Molasses and white Meat.

Around the house on the hard-trodden dirt scratched a few scrawny chickens. Often a few razor-backed hogs, wild and swift, finding their own keep. An old mule sniffing out stray blades of grass. We looked around for the water supply. A well in the yard. Seldom running water, even in the kitchen. Outside privies or none at all. In a survey of one Mississippi locality it was found that 61% of white families and 85% of Negro had no privies. In one county of North Carolina, four-fifths of the Negro families and more than half of the white families lacked privies. We found many schools, for that matter, with no privies. Was this America, the land of plenty and opportunity?

Always our questions led us back to the relation of the farmer to his land. *His* land? Oh, no! Over half of all southern farmers are tenants; 73% of the farmers growing cotton. Two-thirds of the tenant farmers in the South are white; one-third are Negroes. Among these tenants are "renters" and "share-renters" as they are called. But 39% of the tenants don't even *rent* their farms. They don't even own the one old mule, the plow and other tools. They don't buy their own seed, fertilizer, feed. They are sharecroppers, owning nothing but their labor and that of their wives and children and the few possessions we had seen packed into their old cars or wagons. White and Negro croppers are about equal in numbers. All of what a sharecropper raises goes to the landlord. And in return the landlord does two things. First, he "furnishes" the sharecroppers with house and farming equipment. Second, he pays back to the sharecropper half of what the crop brings after all expenses have been deducted.

The following quotation from the *New York Times* on April 21, 1935, gives some concrete details of what the sharecropper agrees to do in return for "furnishing" and half the crop:

The independence of the sharecropper may be determined from some of the clauses of a lease form much in use in Northeastern Arkansas. Under it the sharecropper agrees:

"To prepare the land and to plant, cultivate and harvest all crops, and to do and perform all other work and services under and in accordance with the direction and full supervision of the first party.

"To pick and deliver all cotton to the gin of first party at ———, Ark., and to gather, or harvest and deliver all other crops to any place which shall be designated by first party.

"To cultivate land close up to all ditches, fences and turn rows, and in plowing to throw the dirt away from the ditches and to clean out and

COUNTIES IN WHICH AT LEAST HALF OF THE FARMS
WERE OPERATED BY TENANTS AND CROPPERS

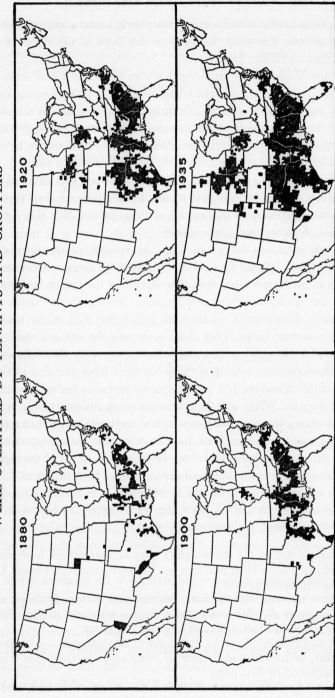

From "Farm Tenancy," the report of the President's Committee, 1937

Counties where at least half the farms were operated by tenants or croppers increased in number from 180 in 1880 to 381 in 1900, and further increased to 585 in 1920 and to 890 in 1935. Nearly all the counties in the Cotton Belt in 1935 had more than half the farms operated by tenants, and there were substantial numbers of such counties in several corn- and wheat-growing states of the Middle West.

cut all weeds and shrubs along and in the ditches, fences and turn rows, during the period, or periods of time to be designated by first party.

"To do and perform all other work or services of whatever nature, which may become necessary for, or which may be required by, first party in carrying out the terms of this agreement."

The sharecropper agrees also that any failure on his part to perform "any duty required by this contract" shall result automatically in a forfeiture of his right to go on living in his cabin and immediately give the landlord the right to harvest his crop, charging the expense to the account of the hapless tenant. Title to all crops is vested in the landlord.

But this is only part of the picture. Go into a store where a sharecropper or his wife is buying sugar or shoes or overalls. What do you see? You see a raggedly dressed woman pulling out a "doodlum book" and paying in certificates. You see the storekeeper keeping the account of these purchases and balancing them against what the landlord owes the tenant. For the store is the landlord's. And the accounts—both what he owes the sharecropper and what the sharecropper owes him—are in the landlord's keeping.

This economic and social system, smacking both of feudalism and of slavery, has been the background of many happenings. Even if the lurid tales of these happenings as they filter through to sympathetic northern ears were reduced by half, they still remain amazing and shocking. Negroes, as an "inferior race," are not accorded the rights or protection of American citizens. The law does not really protect them. An infuriated white mob can still string a Negro to a tree and light a fire under him, and few questions are asked. Lynching of Negroes may not be actually approved of in the South, but it is condoned—accepted as inevitable. Read the descriptions told by an eyewitness, James H. Street, a southern newspaper reporter, in his *Look Away*. Negroes are not allowed to vote. They are prevented by the simple device of a poll tax which they are too poor to pay. Shaking hands with a Negro, calling him "Mister," writes one down as a socialist or communist—the most damning name that the South can call one.

And no wonder these names are infuriating to the southern landlords. For socialists and communists were among those who actively encouraged the organization of the Southern Tenant Farmers' Union in the summer of 1934. To the amazement of the whole South in May, 1936, about 5000 cotton choppers and day laborers, members of the Union, struck for higher wages. They were then receiving from 60 to 75 cents per day, working from sunup to sunset. They demanded $1.50 for a ten-hour day.

Their organization and their action ran against all inherited southern prejudices. The Union treated white and colored laborers alike—even called the colored men "Mister." The Union presumed to question wages, hours and living conditions. The Union even engaged legal counsel to test the rights of sharecroppers in the courts.

The southern landlords responded with their historic weapons. Evictions. In five counties of Arkansas over two hundred sharecroppers were summarily evicted in midwinter for the crime of belonging to the Union. Night Riders fired upon the house of the man who had dared to become the Union's legal counsel. Sympathizers—particularly those from the North—were run out of town.

The fight is on. Each side believes it is right. Read this quotation from the Imperial Wizard, head of the Ku Klux Klan, that secret society of masked night riders:

I know—and I make the statement with full knowledge of its import —that the Klan is stronger today than it has ever been before. . . . Why are we so intolerant of races, sects, and colors? The answer is that we are *not* intolerant. . . . Our attitude towards the Jews in America is simply that this is a Christian country and that he is not a Christian. This, we hold, is not intolerance, even of the religious variety. . . . The Catholic question is different, except that the Klan's attitude is not based on religious intolerance . . . its [the Catholic Church's] dogma of authority is intolerable in a free country. . . . Our attitude towards the Negro race is not based on racial hatred, nor on the question of native birth or religious belief. It is based simply on breeding principles.

The Imperial Wizard states that the Klan as "a patriotic organization" is "going to meet all the problems which affect the welfare of the native-born American citizen." (By which he means someone who is neither a Jew nor a Catholic nor a Negro.) We all know *how* the Klan meets these problems—by terror and violence, even to lynchings—all this, because America is a "free country."

Read almost any southern newspaper on the iniquity of the antilynching bill that came up in Congress in the winter of 1938, and which would hold communities legally responsible for lynchings occurring there. Keep your eye on future newspapers. For the end is not yet come. It is more than an economic war that the Southern Tenant Farmers' Union is waging. It is a social war. History will show us how deep are its roots.

But the farmers of the Great Plains, the Central Lowlands and the South are not the only farmers of America. The farmers on both the

Pacific and the Atlantic coasts present a very different picture. California is the greatest of the farm states judged by value of its produce. Its reputation for fine climate, rich soil and many jobs sent thousands and thousands of down-and-out farmers to California a few years ago. The climate and soil reputation was justified. But these onetime farmers found few jobs in California. They form the great homeless group, living in automobiles and tents—one of California's chief problems. This unemployed army in California are not counted as farmers. Of those enumerated in the Census as farmers in this state, 21.7% are tenants. The Middle Atlantic states, land of the great truck farms, have 16.2% tenant farmers. And New England, historic home of the Puritan and the self-contained farm, has only 7.7% tenant farmers. These farming areas bring down the percentage of tenancy in the United States taken as a whole to 42%. Even that reduced figure is startling. Almost a half of all American farmers are tenants. Again we said, "Why?" And again we said that later we must look to their past to find what has given New England one pattern and the South such a different pattern.

Our adventures in the farm regions were nearly over. Images crowded upon us. Visions of the dry High Plains, the cow country turned into the abused land and abused homesteaders of the Dust Bowl, now being painfully and expensively restored by government help. Visions of the vast grassy Great Plains with great tractors moving over mile-wide wheat fields, and farmers looking in vain for a market for their wheat, interspersed with deserted tracts covered with dust from the High Plains. Visions of the stoneless Central Lowlands with wondrous corn fields, and fattening hogs and cows, and farmers mortgaging and losing their farms. Visions of the cut-over Northwest, cows now grazing where trees once stood and farmers shipping vast quantities of milk to the cities, interspersed with eroded areas whence come our floods. Visions of the cotton lands of the South, one of the world's greatest staple crops raised by listless sharecroppers and spindle-legged children, always in debt, always on the move, always near starvation. Visions of California, abundant and wonderful, with thousands of unwelcome homeless people seeking jobs. Visions of New England, trim and thrifty, turning into summer camps or back into forests.

More than images crowded upon us. We were haunted by a sense of what, for lack of a better word, may be called the psychology of the regions, an attitude towards their work, an attitude towards their fellow beings. It is a curious fact, supported by both past and present history, that people justify, really believe in, a social order that jumps with their own

Farm Security Administration—Photo by Lange

ABANDONED HOUSE IN THE GREAT PLAINS

A small farm, too small to yield a living in southwestern Oklahoma.

DURING A DUST STORM

AFTER A DUST STORM

Farm Security Administration—Photo by Lee

A CORN BELT TENANT FARM

Improvements like this barn and silo are possible under good tenure conditions. In this case the operator rents from a member of his family.

interests. And for the common run of men, this means with their economic interests. Few individuals and probably no groups are uninfluenced in their sense of what is *right* for the other fellow by what is *good* for themselves. This almost universal tendency goes far to explain the tolerance of a region or of a group for what look, to an outsider, like intolerable conditions. It goes far towards explaining, for example, the attitude of one part of the South towards the rest: labor, Negroes and "poor whites."

It is unquestionably an economic advantage to the landlords to have the farmers dependent on them. (An economic necessity, many of the landlords insist.) By a vicious circle of reasoning, the very inability of the sharecroppers to buck an impossible situation is advanced as evidence that they are not worth helping. "They are shiftless good-for-nothings. No use bothering about them." Such has been the traditional southern attitude towards Negroes before and after slavery, for economic reasons. Such has been the traditional attitude everywhere towards the "lower" classes. For "lower" is defined by the "uppers" in terms of dependence upon them. This gradually gets shifted to the earmarks of dependence in a series of lacks—either lack of money or lack of education or breeding which are difficult to sustain without money. Such is now the attitude of the landlords extended to the white sharecroppers whose "lacks" now place them in a position of economic dependence.

Along with this traditional attitude of superiority on the part of those with power go other attitudes, which appear with some historic regularity. The old master, when he was a kind one, "looked after" his slaves. He tolerated no questioning of the way he looked after them. To be sure, his standard of living for his dependent labor was a pretty low one; nevertheless, he felt that his slaves owed him not only service but gratitude and loyalty in return for being cared for. The southern landlords, a few years ago, met the government's experiment in crop control by this "hands off" attitude. They resented the Agricultural Adjustment Administration. They said they would look after *their* sharecroppers. How they did it was nobody's business. Only by taking this regional psychology into account can one understand the kangaroo courts, the lynchings, the exclusion of Negroes from the polls. Surely, history must still be living in regional psychologies. We must look to the past to explain these psychological "historic lags."

Yes, the world over, the "haves" have opposed organization of the "have-nots." A union obviously gives the have-nots a power which the

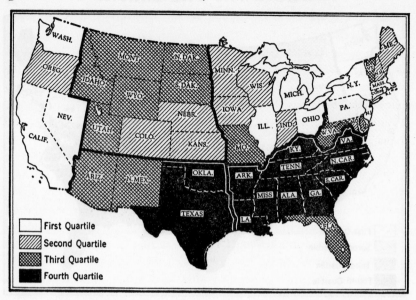

First Quartile
Second Quartile
Third Quartile
Fourth Quartile

THE RELATIVE STANDING OF THE STATES IN WEALTH

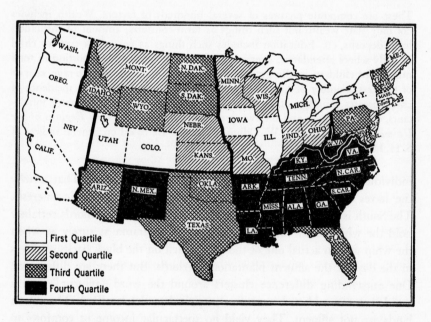

First Quartile
Second Quartile
Third Quartile
Fourth Quartile

THE RELATIVE STANDING OF THE STATES IN
EDUCATION

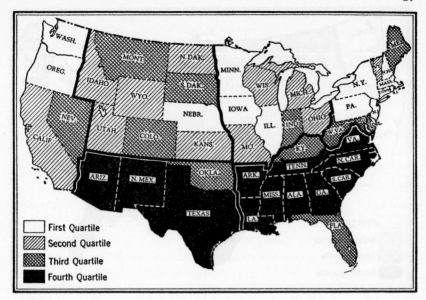

First Quartile
Second Quartile
Third Quartile
Fourth Quartile

THE RELATIVE STANDING OF THE STATES IN HEALTH

These are composite pictures of several hundreds of factors. Wealth includes
not only state wealth but such things as farm comforts, amount of insurance,
bank deposits, etc. Education includes such things as per capita cost for child
in daily school attendance; average number of school days; proportion of total
number of children in the grades, high schools, and colleges; average salaries
of teachers; number of libraries, etc. Health includes death rates, incidence of
chief diseases, number of physicians and hospital beds per thousand inhabitants, etc. (This map and the two preceding are from *Southern Regions of the
United States* by Howard W. Odum, 1936, and are based on general indices of
S. H. Hobbs for 1930.)

individual lacks. That is why the have-nots want a union. That is why
the haves do not want it. It is a conflict between economic interests.
The South is opposed to unions. And no wonder! The landlords certainly
hold the whip handle in the present-day farm drama as surely as when
the whip was an actual one of thongs and fell on the black backs of slaves
in the days of the affluent plantation overlords. But there are differences.
One outstanding difference clusters around the word "affluent." It is a
word that can seldom be accurately applied to the landlord. The cotton
lands are not affluent. They yield no spectacular income or comforts to
anyone. Compared with the sharecropper, the cotton landlord is indeed
fortunate; compared to the old plantation owner, to the Middle West

dairy farmer, to the average of the group of "owners" to which he belongs, he must be classed as unfortunate.

The whole South lives on a lower standard of comfort, of health, of education than do the North and West. Low standards in one lead to low standards in all. The three M's inevitably crowd out the three R's. The North in its city tenements and the West in its migratory laborers can match the South in poverty. But the South can nowhere match the North and West in great fortunes, in their leisure classes and their broad middle-class comforts. The "Solid South"—solid because all are caught in a vicious circle which involves not only unbelievable poverty and the loss of all democratic rights for millions of its colored people, but involves also a philosophy on the part of those in the saddle which justifies such a condition. The North, with its own psychology of regional superiority, is prone to forget how much its own post-Civil-War exploitation of the South is responsible for these conditions. So, too, many persons, indignant at the plight of the southern workers, forget that the landlords themselves are caught in a regional dilemma.

The Middle West, too, has its psychology; the banks, insurance companies and other nonoperators that now own one out of three Middle West farms have their psychology; New England has its psychology, and California has its psychology. For each region has its own economic interests. And these interests subtly determine what each considers right in human relations!

Historic Lags

Such, then, is the present that we saw and anyone can see in our great farm lands of today. A picture quite different from the "story-book" farming that exists so often in imagination, so seldom in fact. More and more we were impressed with the misfit of habitual attitudes and present ways of living.

The farm problem split itself into two main aspects: (1) Wondrous soil grievously damaged. What practices and what psychology led to this spectacular waste of the greatest of our resources? (2) Farmers not making enough income out of the land to sustain a decent standard of living. Regional expressions of their situation, but all sharing certain common characteristics. Outstanding among these characteristics is absentee ownership of farm lands, farmers being tenants. In the High Plains the government bulks large as an absentee owner. In the Middle West the banks and insurance companies often play this role; in the South the relatively well-off, neighboring landlord. Everywhere farmers on relief or being

WHO OWNS THE EARTH?

WHO OWNS THE EARTH?

helped by some government agency. Everywhere people wanting to leave the farms. What practices and what psychology led to this even more spectacular waste of human resources?

The farm problem is the Nation's problem. Not only because the farm population is a fourth of our entire population, but because food and raw materials for clothes are basic in any culture. Our present-day food and clothes patterns conform with a machine culture, the raw materials passing through many processes and many middlemen on their way to the faraway consumer. But the raw materials still start the whole process going. And our farmers produce the raw materials.

Out of what did the present come? What of the past still lives in "historic lags"? This is more than an intriguing academic question. It is a question vital to the understanding of the present dilemma of the farmers. It is our next approach to the farm problem. We need history to help us understand our present economic whys and to explain inherited psychologies. To the past, then, to see if through history we can better understand the present—and, eventually, the future.

Chapter II—DAMAGED SOIL AND DAMAGED LIVES: OUR INHERITANCE

History Lives in Present Soil

Natural Resources of the United States Are Discovered Slowly

The Regions Set Their Patterns. From Colonies to Independence

The Yankee Merchant and the Southern Overlord Fight Their Mother Country

The Pioneer Spirit Attacks More Natural Resources. From Union to the War between the States

We Build a Nation. But at What Cost? From Civil War to World War
  Farming Becomes a Business

The World-War Boom and Its Aftermath

The New Deal in Agriculture

The Future of Farming

History Lives in Present Soil

Natural Resources of the United States Are Discovered Slowly

America was not discovered in 1492. Innumerable tribes of red men had known and used the whole of the vast country we now call the United States for untold years. But they never discovered the wealth of natural resources upon which we have built a nation. For they did not know how to use them. If the Indians had had a Natural Resources Board, its report would have covered the same regions as did the report of our Board in 1934. But the Indians' report would have told only of where, in the dense forests, most deer or bear or turkeys lived their wild lives; or of where, on the vast flat grass plains or over the rolling hills, roamed the largest herds of buffalo. Or what streams contained most fish. Or where grew the supplest wood for bows, or the strongest pliable grasses for baskets. Or where in the mountains grew the lodge-pole pines for the tents of the Plains Indians. Or where the best clay for pottery, or shells for wampum, were to be found. The report might have included some slight discussion of how to cultivate corn, with fish as fertilizer, and potatoes and tobacco. It would surely have noted the value of berries, nuts and roots and the healing power of herbs. No mention of farms, of animal breeding, of mines, of oil. No abuses of the land or its vegetation, unless perchance a wondering if the constant burning of the grass of the plains in the buffalo hunts might be the cause of their treelessness. Mostly hunters and mostly a hunting culture, discovering and using only the wild animals and plants, molding their culture to the products of the natural regions and leaving their happy hunting grounds little modified by thousands of years of use.

But the hunter-redmen and the wild animals they hunted left trails through the wilderness for the white men's feet to follow.

Nor did the explorers really discover America. They were looking for wealth according to the cultural impulses of their day and failed to see the riches that lay in the wilderness lands. The early explorers whose little ships went nosing up and down the Atlantic coast would have described this land of incredible resources as a disagreeably large obstacle blocking their way to India. Inadvertently they discovered the harbors and rivers. And the later explorers who finally took to the land, following the Indian trails or floating down the wilderness rivers looking for gold, inadvertently discovered pelts and souls, commodities valued by trappers and missionaries! The natural products of animals and "heathen" (according to the white man's culture) were the first natural resources to be used by white men. French trading posts and the Christian cross rose side by side on the inland river roads. And political ownership, French, Spanish, English, Dutch, was marked on strange distorted maps. Though these explorers for European crowns, these trappers and missionaries left diaries telling unbelievable true tales of this land, the white men had not yet really discovered how to use this country. They came to subdue, to make, to build, to teach, to give. But not for that alone. They came to America to grab something—gold, pelts, souls—and to return whence they came.

Then came homes into the wilderness, white men and women from Europe rearing children and asking that the land give them a livelihood. The first homes were nearest to Europe. And in particular nearest to England, whose small ships carried most of these first homeseeking pioneers.

Up and down the Atlantic coast spread these English pioneer homes, from rocky, hilly, tree-covered New England south over the flat coastal plain to Spanish Florida. Little colonies clinging for life to the edge of a New World, facing east to the Old World. The Old World with its old soil; its land all possessed; its privileges all possessed; its ways of working, of thinking, of human relations all inherited. The New World with new soil and unowned land, new freedoms, new ways of working and thinking, new human relationships yet to be determined. All pioneers have something of the bargain hunter in them. New World land looked like a bargain. Land hunger consumed them. For land they were willing to endure almost unendurable hardships. Little by little the land behind them, the land to the west where only Indians were masters, burned into their consciousness. The land must be theirs!

Thus the homeseekers began their discoveries. Bit by bit these English homeseekers moved in pulsing waves back from the coast, halted by each natural regional boundary, until they found a way to break through each barrier or a way to live in the next western region. At first, towards the south, they were checked at the "Fall Line." For this rocky cliff at the edge of the rolling Piedmont, over which the rivers from the mountains fell in waterfalls, stopped their little boats—and so their homes. Pioneering souls moved up the cliff and into the rolling fertile hills, only to be checked again by the long line of mountains. But they would look behind the mountains. Again pioneering souls sought and found ways through the mountains, and homes appeared in the Great Valley of many names, crossed by many streams. Gradually pioneer farm homes stretched in a a thin line from the Hudson Valley in the north through the Lancaster and Shenandoah Valleys to the Tennessee Valley. One more barrier had been conquered. One more region had been discovered.

But beyond the valleys and ridges rose the abrupt cliff of the Allegheny Front, the edge of the Appalachian Plateau. They would look behind the Great Wall. How get through? In the north was the one great natural break in the thousand-mile-long mountains: where the Mohawk River flowing from west to east joined the Hudson flowing from north to south and made, then as now, the one "water-level" route to the west through the mountains. But here, in the flat valley, lived the Five Nations, the fiercest of the hostile Indians. That way was barred. Two other ways, old Indian trails, wound through the mountains: one a difficult path over the mountains to the trading post at Pittsburgh where the Monongahela and Allegheny rivers joined to make the Ohio; the other an easier path through the Cumberland Gap. The pioneers went through where they could and came to the lands that the passable routes led them to. The northern route, which started from two different points, led them across a broad stretch of the Appalachian Plateau. Pittsburgh itself was a plateau town. The Cumberland Gap route led them over a narrower prong of the Plateau. For the most part, however, the early homeseekers passed the Appalachian Plateau by. Not yet had they any use for the great layers of coal lying under the poor topsoil. Over beyond the wild rough plateau, one procession of homeseekers came to the cane land, "Kaintuck." But no thoroughbreds grazed on the nourishing blue grass in those days. Only buffaloes. And down the Ohio from Pittsburgh floated another procession to the meadows and forest of the Central Lowland. But then the corn was scanty and no hogs fattened on the land, except as the homeseekers brought them along.

North America has a simple continental build, propitious for nation building. Once past the barrier of the eastern mountain systems, the going was relatively easy all the way to the barrier of the western moun-

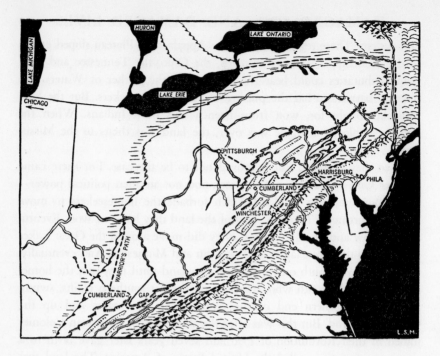

EARLY FRONTIERS AND EARLY TRAILS

Frontiers

The first settlers were checked by the cliff where the Piedmont (foothills) meets the Coastal Plain, known as the Fall Line because of the waterfalls on the rivers. When the settlers crossed the Piedmont and the Blue Ridge Mountains, they found the Great Valley. They were next checked by the flat-topped hills of the Folded Mountains and by the Allegheny Front, called by the early settlers the Great Wall.

Early Trails

(1) The Hudson–Mohawk route skirts around the Allegheny Plateau and finds nearly level land from New York to Chicago.

(2) The route to Pittsburgh from Philadelphia (which becomes Forbes' Road) crossed the Great Valley at Harrisburg, wound through the Folded Mountains and up the Allegheny Plateau to Pittsburgh, where early settlers floated down the Ohio.

(3) The Cumberland Gap route followed down the Great Valley to the break in the Allegheny Front, crossed the Allegheny Plateau where it narrows and is called the Cumberland Plateau.

Anthracite basins lie in the northern tip of the Folded Mountains (see map, page 152). Note Cumberland, where the early soft coal from the Allegheny Plateau was brought in wagons and floated down the Potomac River. Harpers Ferry lies where the Potomac cuts through the Blue Ridge Mountains.

tain system. These regions beyond the Appalachian Plateau sloped gently to the Mississippi. Great river roads, the Ohio, the Tennessee and their many tributaries could bear the pioneers to the Father of Waters. No physical barriers to bar the pulsing waves of homeseekers. But the land must be fought for, won from French and from Indians. When the seven-year bloody struggle was over, the land was theirs to the Mississippi!

Or so they thought. But it proved not to be the case. For there came another kind of barrier—not physical, and not an alien political power—but a mandate from England which forbade the homeseekers to move into the Northwest Territory, part of the land they had just won. Eventually, by slow and bloody progress, they did move around the Great Lakes and up into the forest lands of Wisconsin and Minnesota. And eventually, too, they moved south on the Central Lowland until they met the homeseekers from the south who, traveling on the flat southern plains, swung around the southern end of the Appalachian Mountains and up the Central Lowland. But this was after the thirteen little American Colonies joined in their Revolution of 1776 and seven years later gave birth to a strange new nation called the United States of America. The land was theirs from Atlantic coast to the Mississippi.

Beyond the Mississippi stretched the French possessions: west across the long-grass Great Plains, west across the short-grass High Plains, up into the Rockies from Montana to Colorado, south through the Mississippi Bottoms to the mouth of the great river that drains two-thirds of our present country and formed the western boundary of the nation. The land across the river looked good to the young nation, to whom land and ever more land had become the symbol of success. Besides, it held the mouth of the Mississippi, the great road of those days. This land, too, must be theirs! And so, in 1803, the twenty-year-old nation bought "Louisiana," 827,987 square miles, from Napoleon; and the homes moved across the Mississippi into a new and strange region of limitless grass where trees grew only in narrow lines marking the plains rivers. Prairie land, new patterns, new problems. More of America's soil resources coming under the young nation's culture.

Eager possessive eyes now turned to Florida, held by Spain. More good land, and important for defense, touching the young nation's southern boundary. This, too, must be theirs! Better this land of Florida, thought the young nation, than a claim that they had to Texas, a vast

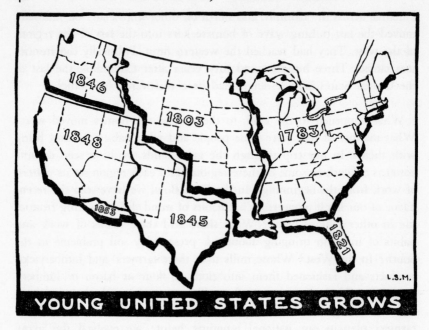

YOUNG UNITED STATES GROWS

tract of western land coveted by Spain. A bargain was struck and Florida joined the United States.

And yet the eyes turned still farther west. A new vision: a nation that sweeps from ocean to ocean. Why not? In the north on the Pacific coast lay the wondrous forests, broad rivers running down from the mountains through fertile valleys to the good harbors on the coast. A good land, too, but shared with England. The young nation decided that its "title to Oregon is clear and unquestionable." It was willing to fight England again for this good land; but England had had her fill of wars. The two nations, the young and the old, came to an agreement, and the United States touched the Pacific coast.

But there was still more good land which homeseekers of the United States were looking at. Those Mexican possessions called Texas lay between them and the Californian Pacific coast where another fringe of Spanish homes had long existed. By war, by intrigue and a little money, the United States got this vast tract from Mexico, three years after part had come voluntarily as a separate republic of Texas. But the greatest of all regional barriers lay between the Great Plains farm region and the newly found gold and the wonder valleys of the California and Oregon coast—a thousand miles of mountains and deserts. The homeseekers and gold seekers would not be balked. First on wagon trails or on ships to

Panama, across the Isthmus, and north on other ships; later on railroads, moved the last pulsing wave of homeseekers into the last of the regions of the west. They had reached the western limit. Politically the frontier was closed. Three hundred and fifty years after Columbus, the last of the United States land resources had been discovered for homes.

What happened to the land, to the soil, as the homes moved west? What manner of folk were these people and what habits did they bring with them? In our trip through the farm lands we have seen definite patterns of work in some of these regions. Did each region set its pattern of work from the beginning? In the Dust Bowl we have seen the recent havoc of our latest pioneers. What habits of mind did pioneering frontier life in other regions breed? What share had these habits of work and habits of mind in bringing about our present-day soil problems in the South? In the West? Whose mills took these farmers' and lumberjacks' products and fashioned them into cloth or flour or bacon or lumber? And how did the interests of the millowners who took their products affect each region as homeseekers moved into it? What role did the farmers play in our national economy before we evolved the many middlemen who now separate them from the city-dweller consumer? What was the government's policy as it acquired one land kingdom after another?

These are the questions which we would ask of history. Their answers lie in the past, but their consequences survive in the present. History must reveal more than the growth of political boundaries. It must reveal the growth of habits of work, of human relations, of standards of living; it must show us how our land, our resources and our people came to be what they are today. It must interpret the tragic sequels of the Dust Bowl, the mortgaged Middle West, the sharecropping South; or at least it must show the steps by which these regions moved into their present-day problems.

Back then to our first homeseekers on the Atlantic coast for a few snapshots of them at work in the colonies of the North and of the South. What happened to the *people* who first asked that American soil yield them a living?

THE REGIONS SET THEIR PATTERNS. FROM COLONIES TO INDEPENDENCE

Early, on to the New World stage in northern New England, stalked the Puritan. Solemn of face and solemn of clothes, he braved the terrible hardships of the voyage in small English sailboats and sternly endured a life of near-starvation in an alien "heathen" culture. Why? He would be his own master. He would worship his God his own way; curb the lightness of his women in his own way, with the ducking stool and other salutary devices; bring up his children to abhor pleasures and to condemn all who differed from them.

But being right and being righteous were not by any means the sole occupation of this New World Puritan. He turned hunter and shot the wild turkey and the frightened deer. He turned lumberman and felled the forest trees for his log cabins. He turned farmer, and in the cleared land he planted seeds of pumpkins and tubers of the New World potatoes, and Indian corn wrapped in bundles of fish. Later he fashioned boats from the trees and took to trading and to whaling and to salting the cod he pulled from the sea. He turned merchant and shipped pelts and fish and logs back to England.

Back from the coast and up into the rocky hills he pushed, paddling up the rivers to small isolated inland valleys. It was a stern land of thin soil and harsh climate, this region of New England in which the Puritan found himself. But there he felled the trees, painfully gathered the stones from the cleared fields and piled them in long walls, and lived his life with his family far from the seacoast world of men. He turned Jack-of-all-trades. And so did his wife—or perhaps she was Jenny-of-all-trades! Water, food, clothes, houses, lighting, all depended upon his own activities and those of his family. Class distinctions were pale; "hired help" were neighbors' boys and girls. His farm was self-contained, self-sustaining; nearly the pure pioneer pattern of work, with closely knit family and town units. He survived through ingenuity, through hard work, through thrift. In short, he turned into a Yankee.

And those who stayed on these isolated self-contained farms remained and still remain Yankees—thrifty, ingenious, conservative, intolerant, independent, generation succeeding generation on the same land. But land hunger reached these Yankee farmers; and streams of them left to people the West, as difficult ways through the natural barriers were opened. But the story of these western homeseekers belongs to the better farm regions to which they went.

What did the Yankee farmers do to the land from which they wrested sturdy characters and a thin livelihood? Little that constitutes a present-day farm problem. The problems of present-day New England lie in the manufacturing and trading areas. These developed early, too. New England was early the home of traders. And America's first mills appeared

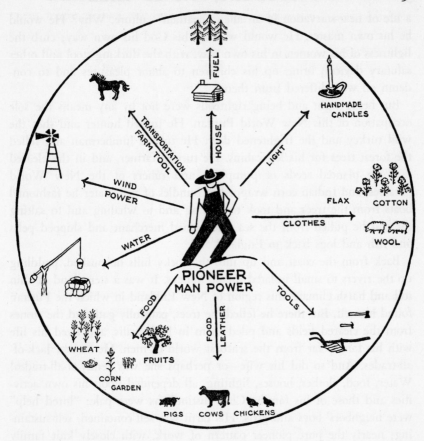

PIONEER SELF-CONTAINED PATTERN

The pioneer went directly to natural resources and did his own processing and transporting. This pure rural pattern persists only in isolated regions. It was this pattern that made the Yankee. Contrast with southern feudal pattern (page 53) and modern interdependent pattern (page 5).

on the waterfalls of her many rivers. Europe sent a stream of workers to work in these mills, workers who later spilled over into New England farms. Their history belongs with the history of industry rather than with soil.

The problems of New England are not primarily those of erosion, depletion or leaching of the soil, nor are they those of tenancy. Farmers have long been disappearing in the remoter parts of New England, not so much because the land has been abused as because it has always been poor. If England had happened to be opposite California, the New England hills might never have been farmed and the Yankee might never have been born! New England farmers have never been able to compete with those on the western lands. Indeed, they never tried to. On these small self-contained farms, they consume more than half of their product —except milk, which now feeds the babies of the crowded cities of New York and Boston. Here, indeed, is the story-book farm which so many city people, curiously enough, still think of as typical of all farms. Now as the farmer moves out, the summer tourist and the forest move in. New cultural patterns—what is called the recreational industry—and nature herself are fairly well taking care of the soil of New England and its future use. And on the farms that have not been abandoned "the rugged individualist," lineal descendant of the Puritan, still living largely by the pioneer, self-sustaining, Yankee pattern, hardly a part of America's farm problem, is making his last stand.

While the solemn-faced Puritan was stalking on to the New World stage in New England, other and different Englishmen were arriving on the New World stage to the south. Here came the cavalier, seeking possessions for himself and for his king or queen. He was neither so stern of face nor so stern of clothes nor so stern of conduct as the northern Puritan. And he found a less stern land. He, too, must needs be hunter and lumberman in the early days. But when he turned farmer, the land and the climate gave him a pattern of his own. Flat, easily tilled land and a warm climate would grow large stretches of single crops. Great fields of indigo, rice and tobacco—more and more tobacco, till the South Coastal Plain waved with the big-leafed precious weed of the New World. For whom? Not for those who lived on the plantation. How could the pipes of the few colonists of Virginia, and of the Carolinas, smoke all the tobacco from these great fields? No, the crops were raised largely for the mother country across the Atlantic. It was English gentlemen who smoked most of the New World weed, and English mills that took their indigo. The single-crop pattern had begun. The southern plantation owner throve on a distant market, as he was later to suffer when a distant market declined his product. Part of the stage for our present farm problem was being set.

Nor did this southern farmer till his own fields, except at the very beginning. His imagination and his farming job quickly expanded beyond the limits of his own work. Over the wide plantation fields bent many backs; many hands picked the big leaves and hung them up to dry; many strong arms loaded them into the waiting ships. Whose backs?

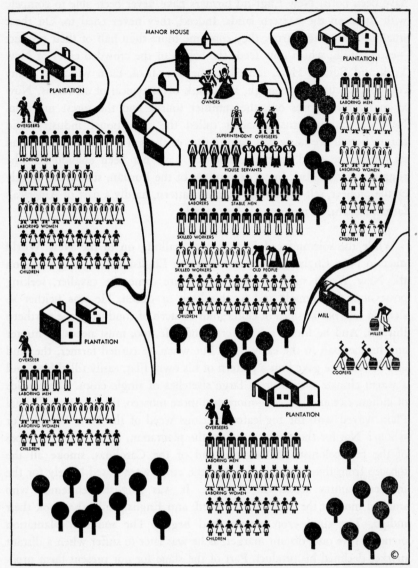

From Hacker, Modley and Taylor, "The United States: A Graphic History,"
Modern Age Books, Inc.

Whose hands? Whose arms? They belonged to anyone whose labor was
cheap. In the early days they often belonged to "indentured servants,"
who sold their labor for a term of years in return for passage from old
Europe, so eager were they to get to new America with its promise of new

land and new freedoms. Sometimes they belonged to the unsuccessful pioneers who could not set up a plantation for themselves. For not everyone succeeded in this "land of opportunity." Later they belonged to Africans seized in their native land and sold as slaves to enterprising Yankee traders. Unfree labor. And keeping the backs bent and the hands moving stood the overseer, taking orders from the owner and giving orders—even with the whip—to unfree labor. The feudal system in the New World: overlord giving orders to overseers, overseers giving orders to unfree labor. The caste system, begun in tobacco days, flowered in the later days of cotton. Around the stately, many-pillared, white plantation house clustered the slave quarters, and inside lived the hospitable southern gentleman and his gracious wife and beruffled daughters and gallant sons. A gay life full of music, of pleasure, of leisure supported by unfree labor and the early need of English gentlemen for their pipe tobacco and cigars and the later need of thousands of English and New England mills for cotton. On the tidewater southern plain the southern overlord had been born. And with his birth came another important part of the stage set for our modern farm problem.

What did the average plantation overlord do to the land which gave him his social prestige and a good income? Much. Year after year he planted and raised his crops. Year after year the soil gave up its store of plant food. For tobacco is one of the great robber crops and quickly exhausts the soil it grows in. Year after year his crops grew smaller. Should he follow the careful Old World methods? Should he restore the soil? Should he fertilize, plant rotating crops? No, that was costly; that was unnecessary. No picayune methods in the New World! For unused land was to be had for nothing or next to nothing, to the west. The plantation owner's investment was not in land. It was in his unfree laborers. For had they not been bought from the northern traders with hard-earned money? Did he not have to build them rude shelters, provide them with enough food to keep them in working condition? Pack up and move west. Cut down more trees; plow up more land. Keep big plantation crops growing. Ship the big crops overseas. That pleased him and it pleased the English smokers across the sea. Thus began the pioneer psychology which was to flourish so tragically in the cotton days to come, the psychology of "Why bother to save when there is plenty more?"

What happened to the depleted lands out of which the plantation owner and his cheap labor moved? They were left to the rains and to the unsuccessful. What tobacco began, cotton was to carry further. Erosion. Waste of soil and waste of human effort. Depleted land and depleted human beings. The South had begun its tragic pattern.

THE YANKEE MERCHANT AND THE SOUTHERN OVERLORD FIGHT THEIR MOTHER COUNTRY

Before settlers from the eastern settlements surged across the Mississippi into the Middle West wheat lands and the southern cotton lands, the thirteen little coastal colonies had joined in their historic fight for independence. Traders and small self-sustaining farmers in the North; plantation overlords in the South. How could people whose cultures were as unlike as the Yankee North and the feudal South join in a common cause? What had they in common that made them wish to cut the silver thread of dependence and loyalty which tied them to their common mother—England?

They had what seems to be the strongest of human bonds—common grievances, which eventually reached the intensity of a common hate. At first the silver thread to the mother country had been a life line to the daughter colonies. This was before they had learned to make the land yield them even raw food, according to their food habits and standards of living; far less, yield them manufactured goods—tools, weapons, clothes, house furnishings and even building materials. Without supplies from England, the early settlements perished—literally starved or were killed by the Indians. And for a longer time, all comforts came across the sea. No wonder that the early pioneer faces were turned to the east, whence came the little ships bearing supplies.

But in return for her supplies and protection the mother country demanded a price from her daughter colonies, a price which affected the northern traders one way and the southern planters another, but which came to seem intolerable to both. Over in old England, new patterns of work were evolving. Workers were being taken from their farms and from their simple home industries, were being assembled into groups to tend the new machines. Factories. New inventions. The Industrial Revolution. The beginning of the world's machine culture.

England could not use all the goods she manufactured. She must find people to buy them. Her colonies: they must buy her goods. That was part of the price the colonies must pay for her protection—buy her goods. That meant they must not manufacture goods themselves. They must remain agricultural. And they must buy goods from no other country.

That followed as a matter of course. That was another part of the price. Her colonies must sell their raw products to her and to no other country. They must ship their goods in English ships, not in ships of their own making. Another part of the price. Her colonies must pay taxes to help England pay for colonial government. Another part of the price. And all natural enough for a mother who thought of her children as young and dependent upon her and owing a loyalty that would always see their mother's interests as their own.

But there came a time when this silver thread of dependence and loyalty to the mother country no longer seemed a life line to the daughter colonies. Rather it seemed a galling tie that bound them to serve England's interests and kept them from developing their own. The daughters had reached adolescence. They were ready, practically and spiritually, to set up for themselves.

More had happened to them, in both North and South, than a mere change in the location of their homes. For they had been getting the feel of this great new country, had more and more been getting the sense that they *belonged,* had more and more been developing their own patterns of work and of thought, had more and more ceased to look east across the ocean whence they had come, and had more and more looked west to the new country they were discovering year after year. They no longer even needed soldiers to protect them against the Indians. They knew better how to fight in their country than did the "Bloody Coats." Why should they pay for what they no longer needed? Neither did they need England's manufactured goods—not if they could get them from other countries more cheaply. What they needed was cheap goods. Why should they not buy molasses direct from the French West Indies when they could get it 25% to 40% cheaper than from England? Why should they not buy cloth direct from Holland instead of through a British trader at a higher price? And why, too, should they not sell their tobacco to the highest bidder? France wanted great quantities of tobacco for snuff. Why sell through England and let England get the profit? Why pay taxes to England—horrid taxes that made them lick a stamp for every commercial paper? The colonies seethed with indignant whys. The southern planters were indignant about the restrictions that sent up the prices of things they bought and lowered the prices of things they sold. The northern traders were indignant at the restrictions upon their trade. Why should all the spoils of trade go to England? Then, too, the North was troubled by a new dream. They looked at the great new country and found it good. It held not only limitless forests and wondrous soil for their pioneer farms. It held water power. Why should they always buy things made in English mills? Why not have mills of their own? Why should all the spoils of industry go to England?

So North and South became more indignant, each in its own interests. The land must be *theirs!* Not only for homes and farms, but for mills; for factories; for trade; for cheap tools, cheap cloth, cheap molasses, cheap tea. They would not live their lives to serve England's interests. They would not be held to the pattern of agriculture. Dreams of industry and of trade consumed them.

And so they fought, side by side, these thirteen differing little English colonies. Together they cut the silver thread of dependence. Together they wrote their creed of human relations, first in the Declaration of Independence, and after their victory in the Constitution of the United States. The land from Atlantic to Mississippi was theirs, to plan for and to use for themselves.

The Pioneer Spirit Attacks More Natural Resources. From Union to the War between the States

Common grievances, a common fight and a common government. Yet none of these things obliterated the differences that had developed among the onetime colonies. Their lands remained different; their work habits, which sprang from the use of the land, remained different; and their economic systems and social philosophies, which sprang from their work habits, remained different. These pioneers did not want the same things from the vast new land which they now possessed together. They wanted such different things that within eighty years of the time when they had fought side by side for their independence from England they were fighting among themselves. The Civil War, it was called by the North to show that it was an internal rebellion within a *nation;* the War between the States, it was called by the South to show that the *States,* not the United States, should determine their own destinies.

What did the South want from the land? It wanted fresh soil, ever fresh soil, for cotton, the crop made possible on a great scale by the newly invented cotton gin, the crop that was soon to cover the southern land and soon to absorb southern interests. For King Cotton was coming into his own!

First on the south coastal plain the fluffy white bolls supplanted the long leaves of tobacco. The many backs now bent over cotton plants; the many hands, more and more of them black hands, now pulled the fluffy white bolls and stuffed them into bags trailing behind; the many strong arms now bound the bales and loaded them into the waiting ships bound for overseas or for northern ports. For the new machines of England and of the North asked for more and more raw cotton. The southern lands responded. The pioneer psychology—"Why bother to save when there is plenty more land?"—which started in tobacco days, prevailed in cotton days. For cotton, too, was a robber crop and quickly used up the soil it fed on. Pack up the slaves and move west. Cut down trees; plow up more land. Keep big cotton crops growing. As mills in Europe and in the North grew, so grew the cotton lands; so grew the belief that in cotton and in cotton alone lay the future of the South. So cotton began its western march, felling trees before it. It marched around the Gulf. When Louisiana became ours (1803), it marched up the Mississippi Bottoms. When Texas became ours (1845), it marched on to its vast grass plains, ever west until there was not enough rain. But before it reached this limit, plantation owners had been robbed of their slave labor.

For cotton throve on the backs of the slaves even more than had tobacco in its day. The southern overlord, born on the tidewater Atlantic plain, throve as cotton throve. The feudal system—overlord to overseers to unfree labor—was even more the dominant economic order. Thus the southern landlords, during the eighty years between Revolution and the War between the States, wanted from the new nation, of which they were a part, new lands for cotton; they wanted slavery; they wanted a European market for their cotton. All these desires rested upon the nature of their lands and on the farm system which best exploited land and labor in their economic interests, which bound them to King Cotton and the single-crop pattern of dependence upon faraway markets for the sale of their raw materials. These were their wants as producers. As for the things which they needed to buy from others—manufactured goods—their desire was to get them cheap. And since the more they bought from Europe the more would Europe buy their cotton, they looked to English mills for their manufactured goods. These were their wants as consumers. On both counts, as producers and as consumers, their interests came into conflict with those of the North; also with those of the West as the new western regions grew in power and developed interests of their own.

And the North? What did Northerners want from the new nation which had been born after the Revolution? What did they want from the vast new western lands which the new nation possessed? Some had fought as traders, some as small independent farmers, some with the

vision of turning the new nation into an industrial as well as an agricultural nation. What did these three groups ask of the nation or of the land
in the eighty years after independence which brought them into open
war with the South?

The small independent farmers did not ask much—not those that
stayed at home. For their self-contained pattern by its very nature kept
them from relations with the rest of the nation. They had little to sell.
They did not go into politics. Those who were not satisfied with life on
their isolated farms moved west—great processions of them. And in their
new homes in the new western regions they enter into the picture. The
Yankee farmer had no need of unfree labor. His land led to small diversified farms; his habits of work led to conceptions of equality and of
freedom. There was, on the New England farms, no economic urge to
approve of slaves. Northerners were free to condemn the southern slavery
system. And they did. They became ardent abolitionists. Conflict number
one.

The northern would-be industrialists and the traders had certain things
in common. At the waterfalls of many-rivered New England rose mills,
mills that took the southern cotton, spun it, wove it into cloth and sent
some of it back to the South whence it had come. More mills that wove
woolen goods; more that made shoes and food and lumber products
and iron pigs and other mineral products. More manufactured goods to
be sent to the South. Trade and industry worked hand in hand, and both
profited by the market of the agricultural South.

But industry was bound to have a hard time getting started in a new
country. It was older in Europe, especially in England. European goods
undersold those made in America, even with the added cost of the journey across the Atlantic. "We need protection against cheap foreign
goods," argued the struggling industrialists. And they got it. By means of
tariffs which raised the price of foreign goods, the new nation protected
her "infant industries." But this meant that Southerners had to pay these
higher prices both for northern and for European goods. They did not
care to develop, to protect, the northern millowners—certainly not by
paying more for their goods. Cheap goods: no tariffs. Protect infant industries: high tariffs. Again agricultural South against industrial and
business North. Conflict number two.

The traders looked to the West. Here were new lands, new raw products. Wheat had left the early Middle Colonies, the "bread colonies" as
they had been called when there was no West, and was spreading over
the great grassy stretches across the Mississippi. Where should it go? Down

the Mississippi to New Orleans led the great river road of the Nation. Down the Mississippi went a procession of rafts and boats carrying goods to the South. This troubled the northern traders. The West must connect with the East—not with the South. The West must buy northern goods. The industrialists saw a new market. Yes, the West must connect with the East. But how? Canals and highways were one answer. Railroads, 30,000 miles of them, were beginning to be the new answer in 1860. Railroads built by the North to steal the trade of the West from New Orleans, from the South. Conflict number three.

And the West itself? Where did it stand in these conflicts between business-minded North and cotton-minded South, between the northern partners, trade and industry, and southern planters? What happened in the West in the eighty years between independence and civil war? Amazing, incredible things that were the wonder of Europe and the pride of the young nation. Not only had we acquired first Louisiana, then Florida, then Oregon, and then Texas, so that our political possessions were more than three times as large as at the time of the Revolution. We had acquired people as well as land. Europe had begun its dramatic march to the United States. In 1790 we had less than four million people. In 1860 we had nearly thirty-one and a half million. The center of population marched west as the frontier pushed west. In 1790 most of the people were farmers, lumbermen and fishermen. Over two-thirds of the whole population lived within fifty miles of the Atlantic coast. By 1860 the eastern industrial towns absorbed many workers in their mills and factories (New York City's population was already over a million); the farmers and lumbermen were scattered as far as the Pacific coast. Amazing, incredible things, indeed, in growth of territory, growth of population, growth of an industrial dream in the northern East and along the gateway to the West, growth of a new agricultural empire in the West.

But even this was not all. For the West was not really born until after a new social philosophy had been declared in the New World. It was a philosophy each region interpreted in accordance with its self-interest, that is, in accordance with its economic interest, as is the way of human beings. When the thirteen colonies needed independence from England to develop their economic interests—agricultural in the South, commercial and industrial in the North—they developed the doctrines of freedom, of self-help, of *democracy*. No more eloquent statements of the rights of the individual have ever been drafted than those by which we justified the cutting of the silver thread that had tied us to the mother country. In the next eighty years (and after) we needed people. We were long on land and short on workers. So we gloried in being the "land of opportunity." We welcomed millions into our land of "unlimited resources." For such we conceived it to be. This attitude had a profound effect upon our use of our natural resources of the West. For it was to the lands beyond the Alleghenies that eyes were turned.

The pioneer psychology of the southern overlord who used up his cotton land and moved west to fresh soil prevailed everywhere in the West. Get people on to the land at any price. Get people to use the soil, the water power. Bribe them through gifts of land. Our resources are limitless. Cut the trees; till the soil. Our destiny lies in expansion, in development. Thus spoke the pioneer spirit in individuals and in government.

But the West, though peopled from the East as well as from Europe, possessed regions utterly unlike the eastern regions. The West developed its own work patterns, its own social philosophy, its own problems. The loneliness and danger of frontier life and the vastness of the land around and ahead left deep effects in western character. If the people lacked the protections of the East's law and order, they were also free from its restraints and conventions. Life was apt to be rowdy in the far-spaced towns where men could congregate. Timothy Dwight early expressed the persistent attitude of conservative Easterners. "The class of pioneers," he said, "cannot live in regular society. They are too idle, too talkative, too passionate, too prodigal, and too shiftless to acquire either property or character." It was true; the West was full of the country's malcontents, of people in whom the impulse to move on never rested. A settler who moved in 1819 from Virginia to Ohio, in 1825 from there to Indiana, and on to Wisconsin in 1835, wrote in 1849: "I have reached the Pacific, and yet the sun sets west of me, and my wife positively refuses to go to the Sandwich Islands, and the bark is starting off my rails, and that is longer than I ever allowed myself to remain on one farm."

Yet behind the restless and rowdy frontier there gradually grew up settled farm regions in the wide flat lands of the lowlands and plains. Both North and South, of course, wanted to get the West on their side. Who succeeded? Neither. The natural earth forces made the decision— regional topography and climate. The famous Mason and Dixon line was not merely a political line separating Pennsylvania from Maryland. It was the line of temperature separating northern crops from southern; the line separating northern hilly land from flat coastal plain; the line separating diversified farms, which did not depend upon unfree labor, from the cotton farms, which did depend upon unfree labor. The western states developed work patterns according to their regional characteristics and split clearly into northern and southern patterns, with "disputed states," borderland types, in between. Those of the southern West developed cotton and needed slaves just as the old South did. They had the same economic interests as the South. They were slave states and joined the South. Those of the northern West, raising varied products, at first had important trade ties with the South. Down the Mississippi to the cotton states went grain, meat and other foodstuffs. But with the building, in the North, of a great system of canals and railroads, this great natural link was broken. By Civil War times the northern West was already joined to the northern East in trade. Grain, meat and other raw products moved east; manufactured goods from northern mills moved west in return. The states of the northern West were no-slave states. When war came, they joined the Yankees.

This fight of the regions was on in Washington before it was carried to the battlefields. In Congress the South prevailed and had since the days of the first president, the Virginian, George Washington. Steadily for thirty years a southern Congress had reduced the tariff which protected the northern infant industries. But in the Supreme Court the northern influence was uppermost. For that great tribunal of our Democracy was then, as now, composed of human beings. And the mere donning of a white wig and black gown did not do away with their regional sympathies and beliefs, which were then so closely lined up with national policies. Then in 1860 the North gained a political victory. Abraham Lincoln was elected. The crisis had come. Four years of terrible war followed.

The North triumphed. At least it won the war. The Union was preserved; slavery as a legal economic institution ceased to exist. But the differences between North and South did not cease with the stilling of their guns. The differences in their work patterns and in the trailing psychologies persisted. And to these historic differences of North and South was now added a third—the West. It was a complicated pattern of interests and habits that called itself the United States. The price for the northern "triumph" ultimately proved heavy not only for the impoverished South but for the whole nation—which, perhaps, is the way of all wars.

We Build a Nation. But at What Cost? From Civil War to World War

Fifty-five years passed after the surviving blue-coated and gray-coated cripples went back to their homes and to what work they could find, or do if they found it. Then another group, this time khaki-clad, maimed or shell-shocked, returned from another war, this time overseas. Again amazing things had happened to the still new nation in this brief period between Civil War and World War. For we were still young. What is a hundred years in a nation's age?

The impoverished South went back to its cotton fields. Four million freed and bewildered slaves turned to the land. Could they own land? Would it yield them a living? And many longed for the days when "old Marser" had fed them, and clothed them, even though he had also beaten them sometimes and had sold them and their children on a market block. The onetime rich plantation owners went back to their stately houses. Poverty in the midst of past splendor. Silence where music had been, bitter aristocratic women trying to do the work that many black hands had done for them before. The paint peeled from the plantation houses and the weeds grew in the gardens. How could the fields be tilled? How could the cotton be picked? For cotton still ruled their minds and held their hopes. And the small plantation owner, too, was robbed of the only way he knew how to work. A single-crop system in a hot land—and the feudal system of working slave labor suddenly cut from under it. What happened to the land? What happened to the people?

We have seen these lands and we know. The land itself, the good earth, had already suffered deeply in the days when cotton marched steadily west, leaving in its wake depleted soil. The trees and natural vegetation had gone, but the rains continued year after year. First little rivulets carried off thin sheets of topsoil. Then larger rivulets cut small ditches in the empty fields. Larger streams, bigger gullies eating into the banks. Fields where once big cotton crops had grown tumbled into great gullies. Barns, houses, followed. The land was gone—not with the wind, but with the rain. The richer, more energetic plantation owners had gone too, to fresher lands. The poorer, less successful farmers were left on the eroded, depleted lands. We have seen the lands; we have seen these farmers. Both were the heritage of the intrepid pioneers who served King Cotton.

Such was the land to which bewildered Negroes and broken plantation owners turned after the Civil War. And now there was little new West to go to. Cotton was approaching its limit where the dry West was to stay its march. Did the broken plantation owners and the newly freed Negroes turn to and restore this abused land? How could they, either of them? The South was poor. And it had no way to get back its wealth. But it was still cotton-minded. Painfully the depleted land was asked to yield its crops. The size of plantations dwindled. The landowner, unable to till his land, leased parts of it to Negroes and to even less successful white farmers, "the poor white trash." The one-mule farm appeared. The renter, the share-renter, the sharecropper. Legalized slavery went in 1865. A new slavery took its place. And still the fields were not fertilized; still the children, colored and white, worked in the fields. The South, impoverished and embittered, adapted to new poverty, a new economic version of the feudal system. The southern farm problem, born in early plantation days, had moved to fuller expression. The World War was to add still another phase when it came.

Not so the North. Northerners had fought the South for business; they had fought for industrial expansion; they had fought for western markets, western trade, western expansion. And now it was *their* day. More amazing incredible things now came to pass, born of their new power in a new world of new machines and new natural resources. The men who made these incredible things come true were pioneers—but not homeseekers, like the early American pioneers or those who were even then pushing the frontier west. They, too, were bargain hunters, but their bargains lay not in soil alone. They were pioneers in industry; they carried the pioneer psychology of "unlimited resources" and "Why save when there is plenty more?" into new natural resources, into new earth gifts. They opened mines. Coal, first soft coal lying in many layers under the great stretch of the Appalachian Plateau, then anthracite or "stone" coal lying in the narrow basins of northern Pennsylvania; iron and copper lying close to the surface in the Northwest, conveniently near Lake Superior for shipment. They pierced the earth for oil pulsing in thick black streams from underground pools. "They built a hundred cities and a thousand towns. But at what a price!" They built the railroads, so that gleaming tracks finally stretched from ocean to ocean. They built colossal fortunes, and their ruthless genius cast gigantic shadows on the workers of the new land and on the natural resources by whose exploitation they mounted to dizzy financial success. Their genius brought forth an economic system new in America—monopolistic control of prices by the few possessing most of a given product. Farmers, of necessity, worked by free competition and had individually no way of influencing prices or total production. And our early farming culture had built an air of sanctity around the word. Competition. Freedom. They were closely allied in the early American psychology. Now came this new order. Much of its history lies with the history of coal and oil which follows. But the shadows

it cast were too great not to fall on the soil itself. For the interplay between industry and agriculture is organic, and the farmers and farm land
throve or languished as industry took on new patterns. And railroads
were the line of life to the West.

Along the north Atlantic seaboard, at the river waterfalls; through
the Mohawk Valley, level gateway to the West; around the Great Lakes,
rose the smoke from the new factories. Still farther to the west lay
new soil waiting for new homeseekers who would grow raw materials
for these smoking factories and buy the factories' goods. What happened
in the West in these fifty-five years when southern plantation owner and
freed slaves were trying to start their cotton fields anew, and the northern
business and industrial barons were building their gigantic enterprises?
What happened to the soil of the West? What happened to the people
who worked the soil?

"Turn thine eyes unto the West whence cometh our help." So might
the people of America and their government have paraphrased the Psalm-
ist in these years. A land of unlimited resources. Open new lands: the
old can take care of itself. Thus the pioneer psychology still spoke. Bargain hunters were still ready to endure new hardships. So the frontier
marched west.

The West. What was the West? Always the land that lay beyond the
homes—always the new land waiting for the homeseekers. Grants had
been made by states and even by England when she still owned the land.
But most was unpossessed public domain. Floating down the wilderness
rivers on roughly built rafts, tramping, the women often on their bare
feet, over the rough trails, a stream of "squatters" had squatted on land
of their own choosing. By such a strange new pattern had the private
ownership of much of the land extended roughly to the Mississippi before
the Revolution.

After the Revolution the frontier marched into the Northwest Territory. But now it marched under a law passed by the new Congress. The
Northwest Ordinance, though passed before the war, could not be put
into effect until the Territory was owned by the new nation. Now for
the first time the land was divided into townships, and townships were
divided into sections and quarter sections; and the quarter sections (160
acres) sold for $80. Settlers from the East responded, and soon New Eng-
landers and Scandinavians and Germans were buying from government
"land offices" and making new homes. Rough and difficult were those
frontier days, with ever-active rifle, ax and plow, the three frontier tools.

Rough log cabins in the midst of hostile Indians and a little patch of cultivated soil. In spite of land offices, the squatters continued to squat; and who was there to prevent them?

Then came another new pattern in American land, and a bright idea it was, too, from the business point of view. Why not make money out of the frontier lands? Buy up big tracts—not for homes—but to sell again to the homeseekers. The government, too, thought it a bright idea—anything to get people onto the land. So the government sold huge tracts to big land companies at a lower price than to settlers. The Ohio Company bought 1,500,000 acres, the Scioto Company bought 3,500,000 and other companies bought a million apiece. American soil had become a commodity. Land to be sold at a profit, not land to be worked for production. Thus from Ohio west through the Northwest Territory began the speculation in land which has now helped to reduce Middle West farmers to tenancy.

More new lands. Louisiana, then Texas. The frontier marched into one new West after another, now spurred by government Homesteading Acts. For these new western empires beyond the Mississippi belonged to the government. And after the Civil War the government was Republican; that is, under the control of the North, whose interests looked to the West for trade and for markets. By the Homestead Act of 1862 the new tracts were to be sold, again, on the quarter-section basis, a size that had proved suitable for a farm in the moist lands of the earlier west. In drier regions this was not enough land. But the frontier marched on.

It marched to the northern West, too. Lumberjacks attacked the forests, and the trees of northern Minnesota floated down the Mississippi to New Orleans. When the trees were felled, the lumberjacks left and erosion began its deadly work. The soil went and the floods came. But the lumber companies had made their money. The new nation was proud that it was growing rich.

The frontier marched into the stoneless belt where the prairie grass stretched for miles and the only trees hugged the river courses. A land strange to eyes that estimated the goodness of the earth by the trees it could support. So the first homeseekers cut the few trees and lived close to the rivers, and left the prairie sod unturned. It was tough sod, not easily turned by their frontier plows in any case. Then came the tempered steel plow; the tough grass roots yielded, and homes crept out over the prairies. North in western Minnesota and the Dakotas, sod houses appeared in the treeless lands; and inside lived lonely hard-working Scandinavian women hoping that some day there might be a school near

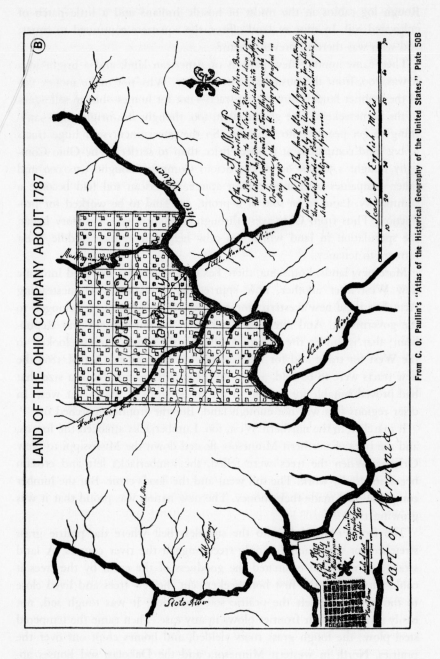

LAND OF THE OHIO COMPANY ABOUT 1787

A Map

of the federal Territory from the Western Boundary
of Pennsylvania to the Scioto River laid down from
the latest information and divided into Townships
and fractional parts of Townships agreeable to the
Ordinance of the Hon.ble Congress passed on
July 1785 —

N.B. The small black squares in each township
from the site actually by the United States for what is —
those eighteenth sections always herein has planned to give
School, and Religious purposes —

Scale of English Miles

From C. O. Paullin's "Atlas of the Historical Geography of the United States," Plate 50B enough for the children. In winter a desperate land where the steam from the kettle turned to ice on the kitchen walls and did not melt for three months, where the family washed by rolling in the snow and the cow grew lean and dry. South, in Kansas and Nebraska, more Scandinavians attacked the tough prairie sod, and more hardy men and lonely women and wild spindle-legged children battled in a new kind of world. Until, in time, mile-wide wheat fields ripened in the summer heat. By then, the frontier had moved still farther west.

It marched across the wheat lands, and herds of white-faced cattle, from Texas to Montana, sought their own food on the unfenced short-grass High Plains. Cowboy days when cattle were rounded up once a year and driven east on the hoof to be fattened in the corn lands on their way to the markets of the North. These cowboy frontiersmen did not own the land their cattle used. The herds grazed on government land, on the Public Domain. And who was there to prevent too many cattle from being crowded on the sparse grasslands? Apparently Congress was worried. For in 1878 they asked Major Powell to report on the use of this grazing land. And a fine report he made, almost as good as the report of the National Resources Board fifty-five years later. But apparently Congress was not sufficiently worried to read the report they had asked for. And it was quite forgotten by 1916, when the Grazing Homestead Act sent homeseekers into the cowboy land and speeded up the Dust Bowl.

But long before that time the frontier marched west over the mountains. A new lure. Gold! Gold in the California mountains, found in 1849, just a year after our conquest of Texas was complete. The forty-niners, with pick-axes and pans, swarmed across the wide dry plateaus and alkali deserts, and up into the Sierra creeks. Companies washed the soil from the mountains with huge hoses to tear out the glittering nuggets of gold. And when the gold boom was over, many a disappointed prospector turned farmer in the wonder valleys of California. More settlers followed. By 1890 the last West had been settled.

At first the frontiersmen pushed west on the natural roads of a young country—rivers and trails. A long procession of lurching covered wagons had plowed through mire, swum the plains rivers, lost their way on a trackless alkali desert. Land ahead, land as free as air! They must reach it, no matter what the hardships. But as the frontier marched west, the earlier wests began to yield crops which must reach a market. It was for these crops that northern business men had urged western expansion.

Some better swifter way must be built to these ever-growing homes of the West, some better swifter way to get the crops to the mills and traders of the northern East. First came canals and highways. Then steamboats on the rivers. Then came a revolutionary invention—new swift engines that ran on shining rails. These new engines must wind through the Alleghenies; they must cross the Allegheny Plateaus; they must cross the plains; they must climb the Rockies; they must span the desert and climb the Sierra; they must connect Atlantic and Pacific across the whole proud width of the young nation's possessions. But how? Who could afford to build the costly railroads?

The government answered. We are rich in land. We will pay in land, and we will lend money to those who will build us railroads. And so the railroad barons were born. Business men of the business-minded North spread their gleaming tracks over the young country with incredible speed. They began in 1830, with short runs near the Atlantic; by 1869 the golden spike had been driven into the tracks near Ogden, where the eastern and western rails met. Railroads had spanned the continent. Their tale lies with the history of coal and oil. But their tale also concerned the land and the workers of the soil.

Nearly 168 million acres of public land were given to the railroads either directly or through the states. Naturally the railroads profited as much as they could. There were mineral and timber resources to exploit, and money was to be made also by withholding the land from settlement while its value mounted.

These generous grants and the speculation which followed were characteristic of the way in which public lands turned into private property. The government, well past its early stage of land sales to meet a desperate need for revenues but still glad to have cheap means of handing out favors, busily gave away land as fast as possible—to reward war veterans, to encourage the building of schools and colleges, to promote the reclamation of swamp lands, to hasten road building. All these gifts, with the easy terms on which farms were sold under the Homestead Acts, were part of a program to get people on the land. The railroad era at last accomplished this in a way that belied the wildest dreams. About 1830, estimates by government officials as to how long it would take to settle the country ranged from 500 to 1000 years. By 1900 practically all good land was in private hands.

Not all became immediately productive. For example, the proportion of improved land to total farm acreage has never exceeded 55%. Unim-

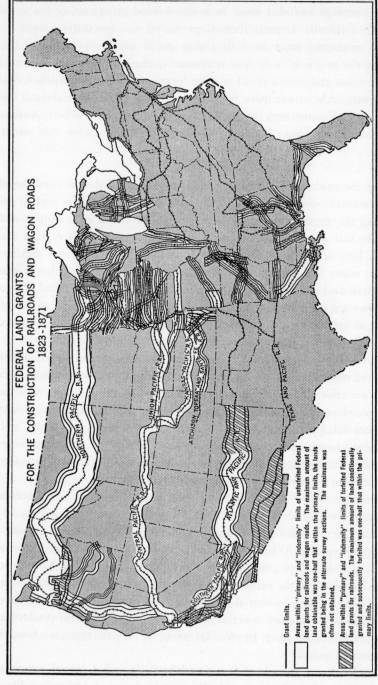

FEDERAL LAND GRANTS
FOR THE CONSTRUCTION OF RAILROADS AND WAGON ROADS
1823-1871

NORTHERN PACIFIC R.R.

CENTRAL PACIFIC R.R.

UNION PACIFIC R.R.

KANSAS-PACIFIC R.R.

ATCHISON TOPEKA AND SANTA FE R.R.

ATLANTIC AND PACIFIC R.R.

TEXAS AND PACIFIC R.R.

SOUTHERN PACIFIC R.R.

Grant limits.

Areas within "primary" and "indemnity" limits of unforfeited Federal land grants for railroads and wagon roads. The maximum amount of land obtainable was one-half that within the primary limits, the lands granted being in the alternate survey sections. The maximum was often not obtained.

Areas within "primary" and "indemnity" limits of forfeited Federal land grants for railroads. The maximum amount of land conditionally granted and subsequently forfeited was one-half that within the primary limits.

From C. O. Paullin's "Atlas of the Historical Geography of the United States," Plate 56D proved acreage included more than was needed as pasture or for wood supply. Evidently farmers themselves shared the speculative urge. To many, acquiring more land than they could use seemed a good bet. Though it might be a burden temporarily, chances were that it would rise in value and yield a profit at some future sale. Most frequently it did! However, such an extensive farm layout made much more difficult the huge task of connecting the scattered farms with their markets. Anyone who has driven over "back" roads even today knows what this meant.

FARMING BECOMES A BUSINESS

The use made of American earth, farming included, was conditioned fundamentally by the fact that the United States was on the way to becoming the greatest industrial nation in the world. Plains, ranges, and wonder valleys of the West, together with older farm lands of East and South, became the lunch box for ever-increasing millions of city dwellers and a source for the fibers machine-spun to make their clothes. Great industrial and commercial metropolises, as they grew up, reached out 50, 100, then 200 miles for their milk; 1000 miles, perhaps, for bread flour and meat; as far and farther for their major supplies of vegetables and fruits. Not only city people grew dependent. Farmers also began to look to faraway factories and mail-order houses for clothing, tools, power, and a hundred other things they required for everyday living. Increasingly they put their efforts into cash crops and bought what they needed with the income, depending even on food processors nearly as much as city dwellers did. Farming became a business! For the most part, where "self-sufficient" farms exist now—that is, where farmers are growing things for their own use more than for sale in the market—it is on lands that are too poor to make farming commercially successful.

America's success story, chapter 1860–1915, stands written in fabulous figures. Wheat production in 1859 was 173 million bushels; in 1909, 683 million. Corn cut for grain increased from 839 to 2552 million bushels in the same period. While production of these great crops trebled, that of cotton doubled: 5,387,000 bales in 1859; 10,649,000 in 1909. Acreage in farms doubled, but the value of farm property in 1910 was five times what it had been in 1860. Industrial development was even more startling. Iron and steel were the chief material of the new industrialism, so production of pig iron tells the story. In 1860, 821,000 tons; in 1910, 27,304,000 tons, or 33 times as much!

This headlong growth of farms and factories—what special constellation of forces brought it about? What and who made America? First, *millions of years.* The source of everything was American earth—fertile, seemingly endless, loaded with potential fuel and metals. Second, *the world's inventors.* The commercial use of natural forces was conditioned by new machinery, new power techniques. These, although in a way they had already been at hand for many a decade, waited upon other influences for full fruition, one being the growth of the population. So, third, *millions of people.* The riches of American earth might have stayed in the ground for decades more if the United States had remained sparsely peopled. Farmers, miners, lumbermen, construction hands, mechanics— all kinds of workers were needed to spend their labor and to spend their wages: for great industries do not develop without great markets. American families grew sons and daughters at a goodly rate. Besides, 27 million immigrants entered the country between 1860 and 1915. The 1860 population of $31\frac{1}{2}$ million grew to nearly 100 million by 1915; practically all farm lands were settled; great cities grew more rapidly than ever before or since. At no other time and place could Chicago have grown from a hundred thousand to two million in fifty years. Here was a great junction of industry and agriculture. Fourth, *roads.* Commercial growth of factory and farm alike depended on a new system of transportation: on the iron horse and his iron roadways, which both speeded and cheapened traffic, and made the union of the states a physical reality. Fifth, *social inventors.* To organize the energies of many people in gigantic enterprises, a great social invention—the corporation with limited liability—was taken up and adapted to new needs. Forms of organization, and legal permissions, developed in such a way that capital could be drawn from ever larger and more widely dispersed groups of investors, while control of the growing corporate empires became more and more strongly centralized. Sixth, *European money.* To build the railroad network and all their marvelous industrial plants, American business men needed large supplies of capital in the form of money. Profits were already beginning to accumulate. Yet if these had been the only funds available, development would have been slow. Europeans, however, were ready and eager to invest in every kind of new enterprise here. Over 3 billion dollars' worth of American securities were held abroad in 1900.

To pay for imports of goods and capital, a nation must export; and in more than one sense American industry was built on American land. Agriculture, from 1870 on, was yielding more than enough meat animals and grains, as well as cotton, for domestic needs. Great surpluses were sold abroad. Farm products, until after 1910, made up the greater part of the value of the nation's exports, which in total more than balanced visible imports and so made possible the gradual repayment of debts to Europeans.

This had important consequences for the farmers. It meant that the welfare of thousands upon thousands of them depended not only on the weather above their own heads but on the skies over Europe, South America, India, Australia. Bumper crops anywhere lowered prices everywhere, but bad weather overseas was the American farmer's good luck. It also meant that for the thousands whose income changed with sudden factors abroad, like weather and wars, longer trends might become decisive. If India, Russia, Australia, Argentina, Canada, should greatly expand farm production—as this country was doing—American agriculture might have to change its direction: turn from an increasingly competitive world market and grow more diversified crops for home use. However, this was only a possibility, one not imagined in the days of expansion.

If international traffic was both boon and bane to many farmers, so were other forces in the nation's growth. Long after the worst hardships of pioneering were over, and long before the wholesale catastrophe reflected in today's talk about "the farm problem" descended, farmers had difficulties to meet. What were the chief ones?

For one thing, American earth, though rich, was not quite Eden. The great new farm region between Mississippi River and Rocky Mountains was subject to extreme weather violence. Drought, hail, torrential rains, and fierce cold could bring sudden ruin to crops. Even in milder regions unseasonable frost frequently spoiled fruit and vegetables; floods drowned the fields; or sudden wind storms mowed the grain prematurely. The man-made difficulty of soil depletion pressed harder on farmers as fresh land became scarcer. Besides, even fresh soils varied extremely as to chemical composition and suitability for particular crops. Knowledge of this is only recent. Back when farm lands were still in demand, a farmer might pay a fancy price for acreage next to a productive wheat farm, only to find that for mysterious reasons his own grain came up scraggly and poor. Little was known about the nature of growing things, about plant and animal selection. Pests and disease made frequent inroads: boll weevil in the South, grasshoppers and wheat rust in the plains, hoof and mouth disease among cattle. The ravages of all these need not be exaggerated: farm production did increase. The point is that when such catastrophes struck, farmers, isolated, were almost defenseless. No limited liability for them! And every planting was an uncertainty, destined to bring anything —complete failure, a bumper crop, or something in between. In 1894 the nation harvested 171 million bushels of potatoes. Two years later, with nearly the same acreage, the yield was 252 million bushels (not entirely a blessing to the farmers, however; for the value of the larger crop was $20,000,000 less than that of the smaller). Examples could be multiplied endlessly.

A second difficulty was moving the crops once they were grown. Railroads were a happy event in that they opened great markets for farm produce, but the iron horse has always looked to farmers more like a beast of prey than a faithful Dobbin. Such sudden expansion as the country experienced could hardly happen without growing pains: freight rates were bound to be high until traffic increased. Greed, graft, and haste pushed them higher. Every little producing community had visions of a railroad coming to its door. Groups of promoters were glad to make promises, to sell stock. Rival communities bid against each other for a rail connection; rival promoters fought each other for franchises. Many projected lines never were built. Those that were frequently failed—because there was not enough traffic, or because of rate wars or of unskillful or unscrupulous management. Mergers, and pools whereby rates were held up and traffic apportioned between competing roads, resolved some of the chaos. But too often these meant arbitrariness in giving and withdrawing service, discriminatory rate-fixing by means of secret rebates and drawbacks, the maintenance of unsound branches as feeders for the trunk lines, and a constant effort to keep rates high enough to cover interest and dividends on overvalued capital. Freight rates, it is true, declined remarkably between 1870 and 1900. But the benefits from this decline were not equally distributed. Rate making in the early days was largely a matter of bargaining; and in territories where railroads had merged or made pooling agreements, power lay with them rather than with farmers and other small business men. In the period of consolidation and expansion between Civil and World Wars more than 200,000 miles of track were laid down over the United States. During the process, railroad companies time and again went through bankruptcies and receiverships (unhappily this still goes on). Thousands of small investors periodically saw their savings swept away; other thousands, including the Vanderbilts, Drews, and Goulds of our history, made some easy money. For the legitimate costs, as well as for those due to fraud and inefficiency, the public who used the roads eventually paid. Why the farmers' share of the burden pressed hard on them will be seen shortly.

Financing was one of the greatest difficulties in a farmer's business, especially in the South. After the Civil War confederate finance was in ruins. The South was in debt. Not only that: more money was needed for seed, for fertilizer, for living expenses till income could be restored; most of all, for labor, since the huge investment in slaves had been wiped out. True, many of the bewildered Negroes could do no better than to keep on working for the master and take what sustenance he gave. But with recovery, however slow, "freedom" began to assert itself. To the extent that plantation owners lacked payroll money, sharecropping was the result. Cotton producers generally were and remained in the grip of their creditors. A city merchant would lend a farmer money, sell him his supplies, and act as selling agent for his crop. As the strategic power of the merchant was great, his charges were high. Often the merchants themselves were driven by the high cost of the bank credit that they in turn depended on. Ultimately, much of the responsibility for the money troubles of the South lay with their close-fisted northern conquerors.

To a smaller but serious degree farmers in all regions were at a disadvantage because of their credit needs. The higher land values rose, the more frequently farmers had to borrow to get a start. At this point land speculation did its harm. Railroads, lumber companies, and other large landholders (many of whom got their holdings by fraudulent violations of the Homestead Acts) often created artificial land booms. Here was another easy-money game; and it left farmers to struggle for years with unwarranted mortgage debts at high interest rates. Theirs being a seasonal business, farmers often needed short-term loans, too. They found borrowing difficult and interest rates high (15% to 20% was not unusual) —partly because theirs was a risky business; partly because they borrowed in small amounts; partly because they were far from the centers where money was most available, and so borrowed on unequal terms compared to city enterprisers.

How great a hardship were high interest rates and freight charges? The answer must be pondered in terms of ability to pay. Farm prosperity, as has been said, depended not merely on the amount of production but equally on prices. The fourth and crucial difficulty of farmers was the low amount of their real incomes.

There was a fundamental difference in the way prices of farm products and those of other goods were determined. Tariffs bolstered prices in many American industries, while the price of the great cash crops— notably wheat and cotton—was set in a free world market. The dice were also loaded in the case of nonexport products. Prices in general tended to rise when demand grew, if the supply did not increase proportionately, but to fall when supply increased, if the demand failed to rise in pro-

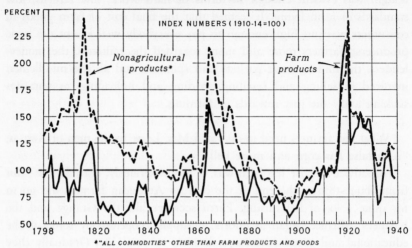

WHOLESALE PRICES OF FARM AND NONAGRICULTURAL
PRODUCTS, 1798-1939

*"ALL COMMODITIES" OTHER THAN FARM PRODUCTS AND FOODS

U. S. Department of Agriculture—Bureau of Agricultural Economics

portion. When a manufacturer of farm implements, for example, found that he could not sell all his pitchforks at the announced price, he could do one of two things. If he alone controlled the whole supply of pitchforks, or belonged to a combination of companies working together in that direction, he might hold up the price and make only as many pitchforks as would sell. Smaller income would be partly offset by reduced expense for labor and materials. Otherwise, he would have to lower the price. In case it were forced below the cost of manufacture, he would have to stop making pitchforks.

For a farmer, however, the situation was different. Prices could not be controlled, for no farm product was monopolized. Quite the opposite. Each product was grown by thousands of individuals scattered through the country, or at least through several states, who worked not only in isolation but under unpredictable weather conditions. So production could not be effectively adjusted, either. Nothing stayed the fall of prices when demand shrank on account of lower purchasing power among consumers or when Mother Nature raised a bumper crop. Not until the cost of moving it to market exceeded the price offered would a farmer leave his produce to rot in the fields. Most farmers did not know how much it cost them to grow a bushel of this or a pound of that. Their accounts were too often mere records of cash payments, ignoring such items as work done by the whole family, father, wife and children.

But the disparity between prices of what farmers sold and what they bought was evident enough in terms of hard work, low returns, low standards of farm living. It seemed that the final cost of farm goods to consumers was just high enough to pay everybody well except the basic producers. Farmers more and more regarded the railroads, the money-lenders, the millers, meat packers and spinners, and all the middlemen involved in selling and reselling, loading and unloading, as parasites sucking away the just rewards of farming.

"What you farmers need to do," said Mrs. Lease to the men of Kansas, "is to raise less corn and more hell!"

This advice to raise less corn was, if meant seriously, not taken so; but from about 1870 to the end of the century American farmers did go in for quite a lot of hell-raising. Farm societies like the Grange and the Farmers' Alliance began as efforts to supply cooperatively some of the educational and social advantages lacking in rural life. Gradually they extended their activities into the economic field, then—under the Green-back, Populist, and (in the Bryan campaign of 1896) Democratic parties —into state and national politics. They formed cooperatives for purchasing supplies, marketing farm products, owning grain elevators, providing credit and insurance. Politically they agitated for regulation of the railroads—even for government ownership of them and of communications; for income taxes, antitrust legislation, monetary inflation, cheaper farm credit, rural free delivery of mail, and the creation of parcel-post service.

The results, if meager, were certainly not negligible. The head of the nation's Bureau of Agriculture was made a cabinet officer, his department enlarged to begin much-needed research and educational work. In 1887 the Interstate Commerce Commission was organized to prevent unfair rate-fixing by railroads; however, it was not given considerable powers until later. An income-tax law was passed but was soon declared unconstitutional. Rural free delivery of mail was begun in 1896 (parcel post not till 1913). Nothing was accomplished in the way of improved farm-credit machinery. Several states enacted antitrust laws, and in 1890 Congress passed the Sherman Act. Thus an important groundwork, at least, was prepared.

But as things turned out, the angry farmer in American politics became something like the "woman killed with kindness." Under Roosevelt and Taft in the first decade of the new century, and especially under Wilson, railroads and big businesses were regulated more vigorously than before. Wilson's tariff revisions were meant to help, among others, the farmers. He also made the first real attempt to provide better agricultural credit facilities. Whether such reforms would alone have served to divide and divert the farmers' indignation, no one can tell. But less purposeful economic factors were working with kinder effects at the same time. Credit difficulties were eased by a more plentiful supply of money, due less to legislation than to increases in the world's gold supply. Prices for farm products went up, both absolutely and relatively to other prices. Occasional short crops abroad were partial causes, but the expanding domestic market was more important. As population grew, urban sections gained faster than rural: thus agriculture had relatively more mouths to feed. Technological advances seemed a happy sign, too. With better seed and fertilizer, better knowledge, and new inventions in farm machinery, land in some sections and labor almost everywhere became more and more productive. Rural America was flourishing. Houses and barns got a coat of paint, roads were improved, children went oftener to school.

As farmers pushed westward, gradually changing from pioneers into producers for a market, regional specialties became distinct everywhere as they had always been in the South. When plows broke the vast western plains, shunting the cattle into ever smaller enclosures and preparing the earth for golden wheat crops, farmers in the East turned from cash grain farming to supply vegetables, poultry and milk for the seaboard metropolises. Truck farming and dairying areas developed, too, in other regions where great cities clustered: around the Great Lakes and on the Pacific coast. An intensively used corn-and-hog belt grew up in the fertile prairie east of the Great Plains. In the South cotton moved westward to gain fresh soils and a climate less favorable for weevils, and broad-leaved tobacco plants filled some of the gaps in the Carolinas and near by.

The Department of Agriculture, rising to its new importance, kept finding new ways of serving the nation. Its Yearbook of 1913 contained this proud tale with happy ending. The action takes place partly along the border of Tennessee and Georgia, partly in government experiment stations. In Tennessee, copper is being smelted. Fumes rising from the chimneys create a waste land for miles around, killing every growing thing; they blow over into Georgia and blight its valuable forests. The State of Georgia brings suit to enjoin these Tennessee companies from continuing operations. Long and expensive trials are in prospect. Meanwhile, some government scientists have been analyzing the fumes. Others have been working on fertilizer formulas. It becomes clear that these fumes actually do destroy the trees. Smelters must be forced to condense the fumes rather than let them blow. But this can be to their advantage! From the condensed fumes sulphuric acid can be recovered, a necessity in the making of fertilizer. Now the Tennessee copper companies, interested in profits if not in safeguarding land resources and the human lives dependent on them, install condensers. Soon they are making 100 to 300 tons of sulphuric acid a day. Quantity production of the acid reduces the price of fertilizer. Thus a devastating waste product becomes usable, to the benefit of the smelters, the forests, and the farmers!

Well might the Department be proud. But it had its worries, too. In years of poor crop yields, a hue and cry about a national food deficit began to be heard. Here spoke the voice of industry, convinced that on ever more abundant crops depended low cost of living; on this, in turn, depended low labor costs, which would enable American industrial goods to undersell others in the markets of the world. It was actually true that agricultural production, though expanding, was not keeping up with population growth. Exports, while rising prices kept their total value high, dwindled in volume from the peak year 1898 on. As agriculture slowly lost its preeminence in foreign trade, its importance in the whole national economy began to be overshadowed by industry. Farming had engaged about half of the nation's gainfully occupied workers in 1870, but less than a third were farmers in 1910.

Government added its energies to the drive for bigger and better farm yields. Yet specialists realized that to reduce living costs by more abundant crop production was by no means a simple problem solvable merely by improving plant species and animal breeds, scientifically combating pests and disease, reclaiming swamp lands, and developing irrigation projects in the arid but fertile Southwest. Notwithstanding the call for bigger crops, some staples were already periodically overproduced. The Department of Agriculture began serious attempts to help farmers fit production to demand, by circulating quicker and more complete market information and crop reports and by advising them how to diversify farm operations. It saw, too, that the whole productive structure, from individual farms to the economic organization of all rural life, had serious weaknesses.

We have unmistakably reached the period when we must think and plan [the Secretary wrote in 1913]. Recklessness and waste have been incident to our breathless conquest of a nation, and we have had our

AMERICA BECOMES
AN INDUSTRIAL NATION

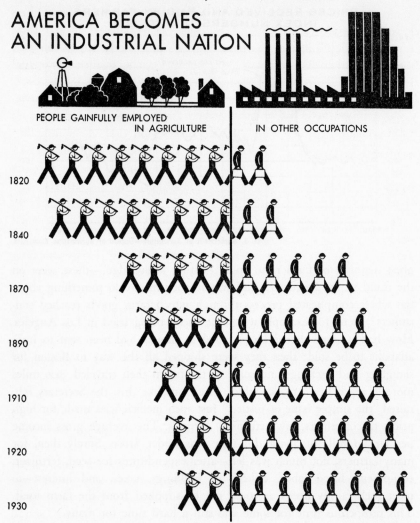

Each man represents 10 per cent all people gainfully employed

From Hacker, Modley and Taylor, "The United States: A Graphic History,"
Modern Age Books, Inc.

minds too exclusively directed to the establishment of industrial supremacy in the keen race . . . with foreign nations. We have been so bent on building up great industrial centers by every natural and artificial device that we have had little thought for the very foundations of our culture.

"Increased tenancy, absentee ownership, soils still depleted and exploited, inadequate business methods, the relative failure to induce the

PRICES RECEIVED AND PAID BY FARMERS,
INDEX NUMBERS, 1910 TO 1938

U. S. Department of Agriculture—Bureau of Agricultural Economics

great majority of farmers to apply existing knowledge"—these were on the mind of the Secretary. And was it not time to do something about the whole complicated process through which farm goods reached consumers? Here, for example was some bacon being fried in Los Angeles. How had it come there? Hogs raised in Illinois had been sent to Indianapolis to be sold; then they were shipped all the way to Boston for slaughter and packing; and some of the bacon then traveled 3000 miles more to reach Los Angeles tables. Situations like this, the Secretary felt, raised "the simple issue of justice." Just such inefficiencies made for high prices to consumers, low returns to farmers. The average gross income per farm family at about this time was under $1000. Surely then, for many farmers, not much was left—after expenditures for seed, fertilizer, equipment, hired labor, upkeep of buildings, taxes, and interest—to meet such family needs as could not be supplied from the farm itself. This prosperous time for some was still a hard time for many.

THE WORLD-WAR BOOM AND ITS AFTERMATH

Suddenly all budding efforts to make sense out of America's sprawling farm business were interrupted. War broke out in Europe. After a time of confusion in all markets, from which the cotton South suffered most, it appeared that Europe's tragedy was to make America's fortune. Avid bidders abroad bespoke all that could be sent—food, textiles, minerals, machinery. Prices soared: as usual, some more than others. And farm prices rose most! Hopes for the future rose accordingly: a huge boom in farm-land values was under way.

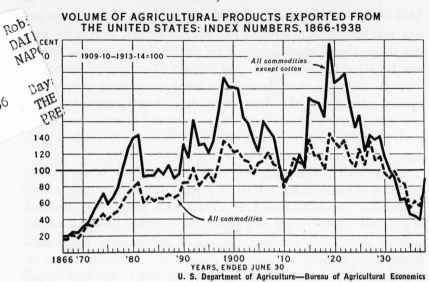

VOLUME OF AGRICULTURAL PRODUCTS EXPORTED FROM
THE UNITED STATES: INDEX NUMBERS, 1866-1938

1909·10–1913·14=100

All commodities
except cotton

All commodities

YEARS, ENDED JUNE 30
U. S. Department of Agriculture—Bureau of Agricultural Economics

Terrific impetus was given to the already powerful urge for bigger
farm crops. No worries now about overproduction of this or that
product. Everything that could be raised could be sold. However, Mother
Nature still indulged her caprices. After a billion-bushel wheat crop in
1915, the yield was hardly more than 630 million in 1916, even less the
following year.

This soon became the worry of the whole nation. For in April, 1917,
America decided to save the world for democracy. Our man power, our
armed might, our industrial machinery, our good earth—all were thrown
behind the war drive of the Allies. National control of food production
and distribution was set up. Lest patriotism and already high prices
should not spur production sufficiently, even higher prices were set in the
case of important commodities. The government contracted to buy at
$2.20 a bushel all the wheat that could be grown. Wheatless and beefless
Mondays were instituted, by which sacrifice American families could
release more supplies for the fighters "over there." In every farm center
government posters cried "Food will win the war!" Not an acre of farm
land must lie unused.

Fifty million acres went out of production in central and western
Europe during the war. The United States expanded its crop acreage by
nearly forty million. It was our poorer land that now had to be put to
use. In the oldest, most thoroughly settled areas this meant pushing upward from fertile valleys, tearing the cover from thin-soiled hillsides.

After a season or two of scant crops the second yield, erosion, came year after year automatically. Erosion, too, was the ultimate crop in the semi-arid plains. There, where already in the prewar drive to increase exports new battalions of homesteaders had taken up the doomed struggle to make small sections of dry land yield a living, yet another wave of farm families enlisted. Did they know what their chances were—that nearly half of all the homesteaders before them had failed to make their entries good? Probably not. They knew merely that land was free, wheat prices high, the country at war and in need of crops.

Another kind of pioneering went on in the dry plains. Where so many thousands of homesteaders had failed, perhaps a steel army could prevail. Landholders who had accumulated, or were now able to buy, thousands of acres also invested in the new giant farm machines: powerful tractors, multiple plows, great combines that reaped and threshed broad bands as they moved along. All over the country, in fact, farmers were encouraged by the promise of larger incomes not only to buy land if available but to build new barns and modernize their equipment. Yet with all these efforts, crop production in 1917–19 failed to exceed that of the bumper year 1915. Extra work, both human and mechanical, could not bring rain to dry lands or change other natural forces on which yields ultimately depended. Ironically, the greatest crops of all came to harvest in 1920, with Europe already replanting her shell-torn acres.

The war boom over, prices collapsed. Farm prices had risen most; now they fell lowest. Again the disparity, as for years before the war, handicapped farmers. Gross farm income went from 17 billion dollars in 1919 to 9 billion in 1921, a drop of nearly 50%. Total national income fell by about 15%: from the 1920 peak of 74 billion to 63 billion in 1921. This the whole country felt. "Back to normalcy!" was its weary slogan. And soon business revived. That the war had left an anything-but-normal world, Americans began cheerfully to overlook.

But the situation for farmers, for the second time within a few years, was turned completely upside down. Before 1914 exports had been dwindling. Efforts to adjust and diversify production were getting a start when war demands swept everything else out of mind. Hardly had farming geared itself to this abnormal export market when not only the war impetus but also the traditional motive of American indebtedness to Europe was suddenly wiped out. In 1914 the United States had been a debtor nation owing a balance of 3 billion dollars. The war made us creditors to an overwhelming amount, our investments abroad exceeding

U. S. TOTAL IMPORTS AND EXPORTS AND AGRICULTURAL EXPORTS, 1923-38

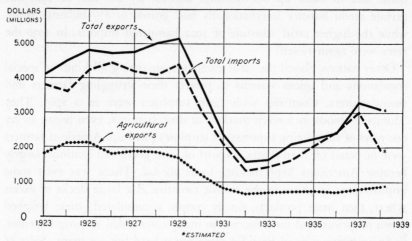

*ESTIMATED

U. S. Department of Agriculture—Bureau of Agricultural Economics

In 1907–11 the value of agricultural exports averaged 974 million dollars annually. The war boom raised the average to 2856 million dollars yearly, 1917–21. The chart shows the postwar decline.

foreign claims here by 6 billion dollars in 1922, not counting the official war debt of 10 billion. The European nations to whom America had always exported farm products, of course, emerged deeply in debt. A sharp decline of export demand was therefore inevitable. Not only would these countries resume prewar production as fast as possible; but lacking foreign exchange with which to pay for all kinds of needed imports, any who were able would produce farm goods for export. In whatever markets remained, American farmers would meet intensified competition. Canada, Argentina, and Australia had also expanded their agriculture in response to the war boom.

The United States faced these changes like the proverbial ostrich. Farm production of export commodities went on at wartime levels, driven, apparently, by momentum alone. Nor did our industrialists and financiers make much adjustment to the reversal of international debts. Europeans could pay off only by exporting gold to this country (of which they had little), or by selling securities (of which they had few, having sold most of them to pay for war purchases), or by exporting merchandise. The United States, if it wanted debts reduced, would have to allow imports of goods and capital to exceed exports. But its whole economy was geared to run in the opposite direction! Its industries were ambitious to supply America and the whole world besides. Profits accumulating from these industries continued to overflow investment opportunities at home and to build up our holdings abroad. By the end of 1929 our private credit balance internationally had grown to 8½ billions. Meanwhile the higher tariff schedule of 1922 hampered imports. In 1930 the rates were again raised!

Other nations played the tariff game, too, inventing all kinds of special regulations and quota systems to protect their struggling farmers and manufacturers. Countries with farm surpluses were in a spot. They "dumped" goods in foreign markets at distress prices, even began to try out ways of subsidizing exports; yet surpluses piled up. American farmers were no better off than others. Exports of farm goods did continue, largely because Americans kept making loans abroad. There was even some improvement in prices in the middle twenties. But large stocks of excess wheat, then meat products, finally cotton, accumulated; these weighed down on prices, and farm income in many cases failed to cover expenses.

Again it was a good time for some but a hard life for many. Sales of farm machinery, having started to boom during the war, continued. Farmers on good land who could take advantage of improved technology made money. Prosperity in the cities led to profitable expansion in poultry, dairy, and truck-crop farming—enterprises comparatively immune from foreign price influences. Farmers who could obtain capital for expanding along these lines made money. But mounting long-term debts and increasing tenancy showed that others were traveling a downward path. Some western grain farmers had gone heavily in debt for land and equipment at high wartime prices, while in the South soil depletion and weevil infestation made for high operating costs and low yields. In these export farming areas the failure of income to meet expenses forced conversion of short-term borrowings into mortgage debts. If returns still failed to cover interest charges on these larger debts, taxes based on boomtime land values, and other expenses, what then? Foreclosure. More than 450,000 farmers lost their farms in the postwar decade. The number of tenant farmers increased by 200,000. Regional differences show up in the tenancy figures. Between 1920 and 1930 there was a decrease in the New England states; in New York, New Jersey, Pennsylvania; and in the Pacific states, Washington, Oregon, and California. The East North Central district around the Great Lakes showed small change. But in the Great Plains and Mountain regions west of the Mississippi, and throughout the South, tenancy increased seriously.

With a downward turn of industrial activity in the summer of 1929, which became a steep plunge after October's stock-market crash, the bottom also dropped out from under whatever prosperity farmers had

WHEAT EXPORTS AND

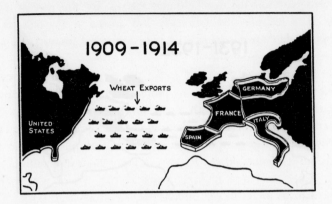

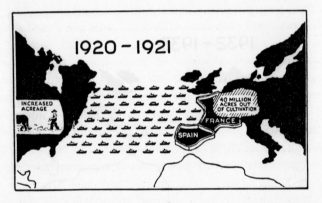

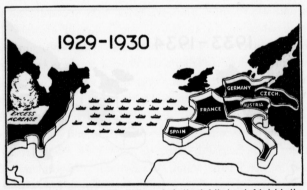

U. S. Department of Agriculture—Agricultural Adjustment Administration

TARIFF WALLS

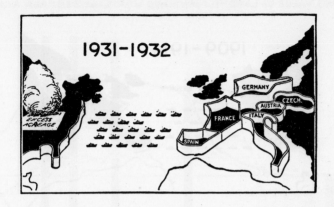

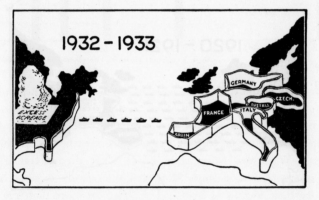

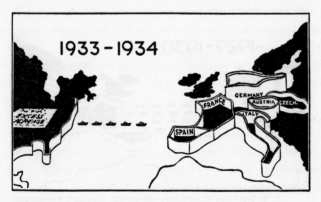

TAXES, VALUE OF LAND, RETURNS, AND MORTGAGE DEBT PER ACRE
OF FARM REAL ESTATE

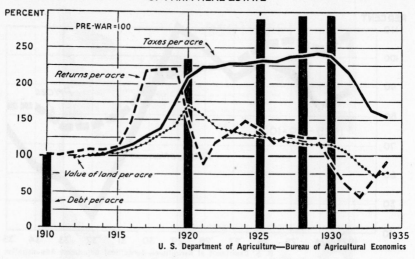

U. S. Department of Agriculture—Bureau of Agricultural Economics

retrieved. They found themselves sinking down a deep dark passage, like
Alice in the rabbit's hole—only there was no free marmalade. If the
collapse of industrial prices was sharp, that of farm prices was sharper.
The already weak export demand practically vanished: depression was
world-wide. What was worse, demand at home shrank, too. That frequently imagined visitor from Mars would certainly wonder how the
demand for basic sources of food and clothing for more than 120 million
people could change appreciably in the space of a few months. But in
our economy demand represents not simply what people want but what
they can and are willing to pay for. As one wheel after another in the
complex industrial machine obscurely stopped, workers were laid off,
and those whose work was still required had to take reduced pay. Less
and less money flowed out to the nation's families in the form of wages.
Buying had to be curtailed, even to the point where people went hungry
and cold. Some of those industrial wheels had stopped in the first place
because of the relatively low income, low purchasing power, of agricultural communities. Now as city families had less to spend, farm income
shrank further, then more wheels stopped turning. A vicious circle if
there ever was one! Or rather, a vicious spiral; for its direction was from
bad to worse.

The underworld in which American farmers landed had none of the
amusements of Alice's wonderland, but all of its strangeness. Long-time
troubles had grown to frightening proportions. President Hoover and

PRODUCTION AND PRICES OF MANUFACTURED PRODUCTS

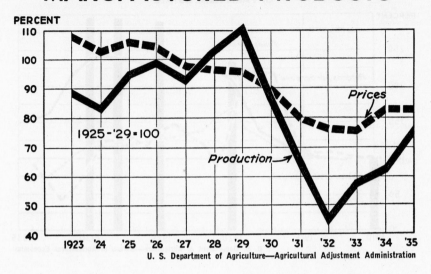

PERCENT

1925-'29=100

Prices

Production

1923 '24 '25 '26 '27 '28 '29 '30 '31 '32 '33 '34 '35

U. S. Department of Agriculture—Agricultural Adjustment Administration

PRODUCTION AND PRICES OF AGRICULTURAL PRODUCTS

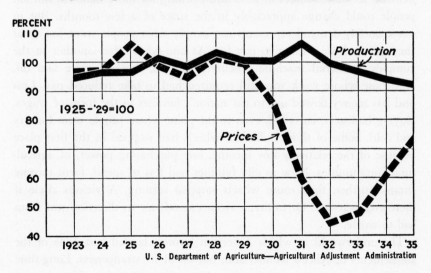

PERCENT

1925-'29=100

Production

Prices

1923 '24 '25 '26 '27 '28 '29 '30 '31 '32 '33 '34 '35

U. S. Department of Agriculture—Agricultural Adjustment Administration

the lawmakers looked around for some convenient mushroom whose magic powers would shrink the awful surpluses of farm goods, some bit of cake that would turn the trend of prices upward, a little bottle of something to start credit money flowing into impoverished farm sections, especially those devastated by 1929's severe drought. They provided special public-works projects in drought areas, set up emergency-loan funds, and concocted the Agricultural Marketing Act of 1929. Its aims were many and wide, but in practice two stood out. These were to improve the prices of farm produce: first, by strengthening the bargaining power of farmers through encouragement of cooperative marketing associations; second, by urging farmers to curtail production and setting up government machinery to get rid of the surpluses once they were produced. With credit help many important cooperatives got a start. For the second purpose a Federal Farm Board was authorized to buy up surplus wheat and cotton, to be held off the market in storage so that prices would be pegged. The Board made sizable purchases, at one time holding 250 million bushels of wheat and 3½ million bales of cotton. Prices were temporarily bolstered. Meanwhile persuasion failed to make farmers cut production. How could it succeed, against the harder persuasion of necessity? Fixed charges—interest and taxes—and family needs went on, whether farm goods could be sold or not. The miracle of simultaneous good yields and good prices could always be hoped for; but if one farmer were to cut production while his neighbors planted freely, he was sure to lose out. It soon appeared that nothing could be done with the surpluses except eventually to put them back on a still oversupplied market. Prices weakened. In 1932 the Farm Board declined to spend any more public money in a project that obviously must fail without production control. With the Board's liquidation, prices sank lower than ever. The bottom of the rabbit hole had not, after all, been reached. Down, down—all through 1932 and the early months of 1933.

THE NEW DEAL IN AGRICULTURE

When President Roosevelt and the new Congress came to Washington, a national bank panic was the most dramatic problem to be met. The situation in agriculture was at least as desperate, and far more difficult to help. These two kinds of trouble, in fact, were related. As farm income fell, so did the valuation put on farm land and improvements: a hard blow to the banks and insurance companies whose assets included farm mortgages. Country banks closed by hundreds.

What was happening on the farms? Incredible things. Returns were

PRICES RECEIVED BY FARMERS AND BANK SUSPENSIONS, 1923 TO 1934

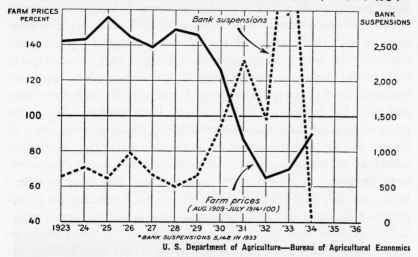

U. S. Department of Agriculture—Bureau of Agricultural Economics

so low that occasionally peaches, grapes, even hay or corn, when sent away to market could not command a price equal to shipping costs. Farmers were billed for the privilege of giving away their goods! So it came to this: in some places produce rotted in the fields, while city children starved.

Gross farm income, after recovering to 12 billion dollars in 1929, was only a little above 5 billion in 1932. This shrunken amount had to be divided among a larger farm population. Troubles had been mitigated during the 1920's by a constant exodus of farm people to the cities, where growing industries called for workers. But now as wheels stopped turning, thousands of industrial castoffs were thrown back onto farms, where the land—they hoped—would at least yield a bare subsistence.

Long-time troubles suddenly grown to emergency size: this was even more the case in 1933 than it had been in the three years before. Cheerful evasion was no longer possible. America had to face facts.

But where were the facts to face? As government officials rolled up their sleeves, the first problem they met was the lack of usable information. Much was available, of course, but often unformed; and there were serious gaps. The difficulties of local relief offices, suddenly commanded to know how many people were in need and how desperately, had their counterpart in every undertaking. The National Resources Committee, a board created in 1934 for the purpose of studying and advising the gov-

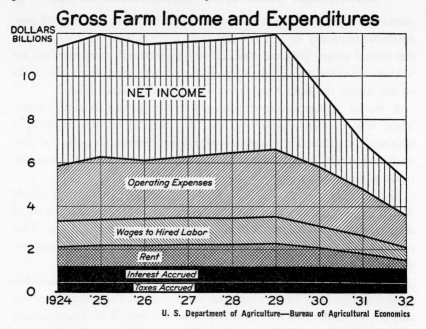

Gross Farm Income and Expenditures

DOLLARS
BILLIONS

NET INCOME

Operating Expenses

Wages to Hired Labor

Rent

Interest Accrued

Taxes Accrued

1924 '25 '26 '27 '28 '29 '30 '31 '32

U. S. Department of Agriculture—Bureau of Agricultural Economics

ernment about the country's use of natural resources, promptly attacked
the problem of land utilization. They found that, despite the far-flung
investigations of the Census, the Geology Survey, the Agriculture Department, fundamental facts were lacking. There was no complete classification of American land according to what was being done with it and
what it was fit for. Counties and states could offer estimates, but a major
job of research was called for. Armies without uniforms have been put
to work on such jobs, of which there are thousands. Day by day and
month by month they have been building a picture of America—its land,
its people, its ways of working and living.

The more facts were put together the plainer it became that the farm
problem was more than a farm problem. To be sure, this was old news—
recorded in the Agriculture Yearbook of 1913 and probably elsewhere
and earlier. But the New Deal constitutes the most comprehensive attempt by a peacetime government to make a *coordinated* attack on national social and economic problems. The State Department's efforts to
break down tariff walls by reciprocal trade agreements are part of the
farm program, since farm goods enter both import and export trade.
New Deal efforts to strengthen workers' bargaining power and income
are part of the farm program, for only in this way can the domestic

market for farm goods be revived. Of course, the many activities of government frequently do not dovetail. But projects like the TVA, where the federal power program and regional agricultural improvements are worked out coordinately, certainly show progress away from old habits of not letting the right hand know what the left hand doeth.

A second important aspect emerged as the picture became clearer. There was a present emergency, and there were difficulties requiring a long-time program. The two kinds of problem sometimes called for contradictory action. And sometimes temporary emergencies disappointingly failed to be temporary!

This was the case with relief and with farm surpluses. Farm people shared in the need for, and in the workings of, all the various forms of direct and work relief with which Americans are by now familiar. This program goes on, and will have to be continued until long-term improvements can be made to happen less slowly.

Facing the immediate problem of destructive surpluses and intolerable price disparity, New Dealers acted on the disbanded Farm Board's advice and at once undertook nation-wide production control of wheat, cotton, corn, hogs, and several other products. The Agricultural Adjustment Act was passed in May, 1933—after spring planting had been done and spring litters born. Consequently a drastic step seemed necessary: farmers were paid to plow up 10 million acres of cotton (about a fourth of what had been planted) and to slaughter several million baby pigs and pregnant sows. Probably more tears were shed over the slaughtered piglets than over the desperate plight of several million farm families. An odd reaction—in a country with commercial habits, where an undeclared moratorium on housebuilding is accepted calmly while families live nine or ten to a room! The waste of farm produce was tragic. So is every failure to make or distribute needed goods and services. Our whole economy is shot through with such failures. Protest will be to the good when intelligence, courage and persistence make it active.

But as to the AAA and its continuations. Details of the program had to be varied so much and so often that it is hard to generalize, but to call it "production control" undoubtedly claims too much. It was acreage that was regulated. This left the results still subject to Mother Nature's whims, and in the crucial 1930's her moods went from hot to cold and from wet to dry most confoundingly.

Effectiveness also varied according to the extent to which farmers cooperated with the government. Lawmakers and administrators believed that this experiment in concerted action by millions of farmers ought to be worked out democratically, even though this would delay results. For example, a majority of tobacco farmers voted for 1939 marketing control, but the prescribed two-thirds vote was lacking. Later at the auctions an oversized crop brought such low returns that sales had to be discontinued in many markets to prevent even lower prices. Should one wish that regulation had been forced? Whole communities suffered —directly, on account of the problems of relief, and in many indirect ways. Or should one simply be content if hard experience prompts a vote for future control? Notwithstanding this sad example, whoever cares to investigate how the whole program has evolved will find that, considering the urgency of the problem and the long isolation of farmers, Americans have reason to applaud both official encouragement of farmers' initiative and the progress made by farmers themselves in cooperative action.

Effectiveness likewise varied with shifts in the methods of compensating farmers for reducing acreage. Originally the AAA offered benefit payments based on the difference between production or acreage as regulated and as of some past period. Controversy raged around the plan for financing these benefits. Economists had noticed that when retail food or textile prices fell the price to farmers fell accordingly, while the aggregate margin of processors (textile mills, meat packers, flour millers, etc.) and of distributors (railroads, commission brokers, retail dealers) shrank hardly at all. The AAA provided for a direct shift of some of the burden. Benefit money for farmers was to come from taxes applied to processing companies. Protest by one of these companies resulted, $2\frac{1}{2}$ years after the program began, in a broad condemnation of the AAA by the Supreme Court. The federal government lacked constitutional power to regulate farm production; so said the Court. Congress promptly replaced the AAA by the 1936 Soil Conservation and Domestic Allotment Act, under which acreage was to be controlled indirectly by taking sick land out of production for restorative treatment. Benefit payments were offered to those who would practice contour plowing, terracing, fertilizing, replacement of robber crops by soil-building legumes or pasture cover. Drought in 1936 turned this program into one of relief rather than of curtailment. More recently, with kinder weather, oversized crops—especially of corn—indicate that this forced yoking of acreage control and soil conservation hampers both programs.

Of sick land there was, unfortunately, plenty. One of the earliest acts of the New Deal was to set up an expert Soil Conservation Service and to put at its disposal some thousands of young men from the Civilian Conservation Corps. Their achievement in the first six years has been

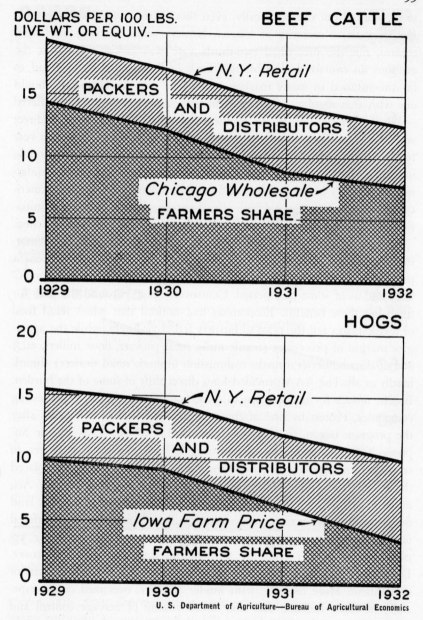

DOLLARS PER 100 LBS.
LIVE WT. OR EQUIV.

BEEF CATTLE

N. Y. Retail

PACKERS AND DISTRIBUTORS

Chicago Wholesale

FARMERS SHARE

15

10

5

0

1929   1930   1931   1932

HOGS

20

N. Y. Retail

PACKERS AND DISTRIBUTORS

15

10

Iowa Farm Price

FARMERS SHARE

5

0

1929   1930   1931   1932

U. S. Department of Agriculture—Bureau of Agricultural Economics

a thrilling one. Sand dunes threatening to blow onto good farm land have been anchored, tree shelters have been raised up against the eroding winds, life-giving rains have been caught and held by terraces and contoured furrows, gullies eating into hillsides so hugely that barns seemed

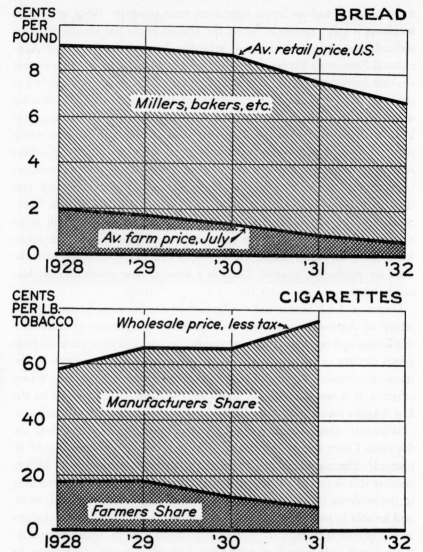

fated to tumble into them have been healed over. Much has been done; much remains, as the following chapter will show.

Production control, variable though its methods were, and subject though it was to weather factors, did make progress in adjusting supply to demand. In many cases surpluses were prevented or were kept from increasing. But not altogether. The worst surplus of all, cotton, has increased. Wheat stocks remain large. Lately corn has become a "problem crop." And occasionally there are surpluses of almost anything—butter, milk, potatoes, various fruits, vegetables, meat products. What to do with surpluses is still a question. So far the United States has shrunk from an indiscriminate program of export subsidies. Instead the Bureau of Agricultural Economics has been sending its men abroad to study the economy of other countries in order to attach meaning to that favorite phrase "a fair share of the world market." Constant research is carried on to develop new uses; for example, cotton fabric can now be used as reinforcement in bituminous road surfacing. But more hope is placed in the new stamp plan for distributing excess foodstuffs to families on relief and others with low incomes. Early operations of the Federal Surplus Commodities Corporation consisted of buying surpluses and distributing them free through various welfare agencies. Retail grocers objected to this "competition." The new plan, therefore, uses regular retail outlets. Still in an experimental stage, it may turn out to be a permanently workable device for making surpluses usable. Of course, it can never do away with the need for production control. There is a limit to how much of a product can be used.

Under an AAA section not condemned by the Supreme Court, the Secretary of Agriculture has power in certain emergencies to enter into marketing agreements regulating quantity, grade, and even price, of farm goods coming to market. This power is hampered in some cases by the unconstitutionality of federal control over intrastate transactions. Where effective, it is not primarily an attack on the inefficiencies typified by the Los Angeles bacon story but is rather a prop supporting crop curtailment.

Whatever acreage control can be accomplished without offending the Supreme Court has to be planned flexibly. How many acres should be planted? The answer is one thing if the national income is 70 billion, another if it is 100. Government experts must shift their advice according to the evidence on two questions. (1) What will the nation need, want, and be able to pay for? This kind of guesswork must deal with changes in diet preferences, with the rate of population growth, with business recovery—still only part fact, part hope. (2) How much is likely to be produced from a given acreage allotment? This kind of guesswork must deal with knowledge about climate and soils, with trends in technical efficiency. If the use of fertilizer is increasing, if species of plants with higher life potentiality have been found, if water pumps have been installed here and there to help straighten out the moisture cycle, greater output per acre is to be expected. No one can doubt that this guesswork is a government responsibility, something no farmer can do for himself.

No farmer. Our account of the New Deal so far almost sounds as if there were no farmers, as if the farm program bothered only with figures on a page! Nothing could be less true. New Dealers have looked long and hard at the 31,800,000 people who live on 6,800,000 farms covering more than half of the country's land area.

Some live happily, some miserably; some with hope, others without. Until the WPA began its studies in rural regions, the nation had not known how many of the unfortunate were literally without prospect of a better life. In the hilly Appalachian–Ozark region, where lumbering and mining industries have despoiled the land and disappeared; in the northern strips of Great Lakes states, where ax and saw have also slain the chief source of life; and in the dry western plains, where cattle, sheep, plows, wind, and rain have together made a desert—in these places live thousands of stranded Americans. They are what remain of our pioneers. They live to themselves, away from the bustle of commercial America, producing families of the good old size—six or eight children, born without medical help, raised with very little schooling. They keep alive the folk songs and balladry born centuries ago in England, and flavored with a sense of American blue ridges or the vast expanse of American plains. Themselves they keep more or less alive in crowded leaky cabins, living on turnip greens, potatoes, salt pork, corn, and perhaps a little milk. This is the life on ruined land. Why don't the people move on? The old, perhaps, would rather not try. The young have run away, some of them, and come back—defeated by the closed doors of city shops.

A rehabilitation program has been begun. For some, if relief tides them over a few months or years, the land can be restored and better methods taught so as to permit cooperative "subsistence" farming—production equal to community food needs. If supplementary industries can be set up, decent living may be possible. Several government projects of this sort are under way, but financing many more would be an enormous problem. Plenty of money lies idle in our banks. But this kind of program requires careful planning. It could not rescue thousands of stranded pioneers overnight, even if our investors thought it worth while. Many farm families can never make a living where they are. For these there is the beginning of a resettlement program—only the beginning. Again deliberate plans and some trial-and-error will be necessary.

The cotton-and-tobacco South is another area where a too large rural populace asks more life than the soil can give. There, too, only new industries can bring real hope. In the 1920's increasing tenancy was the sign of trouble. More recently we have been seeing the next step downward: the desperate exodus of migrant farm families pushed off the land by the

SHARECROPPER'S HOME

In one cotton-growing county of Alabama over half of the families live in one- and two-room cabins. One man said, "My house is so rotten you can jest take up the boards in your hands and cromple 'em up. Everything done swunk about it."

Agricultural Adjustment Administration and Bureau of Agricultural Chemistry and
Engineering—From "Consumers' Guide"

FARM MECHANIZATION

About 2 acres a day with the walking plow; about 160 acres a day with these
tractors and harrow plows, two shifts of men operating the machines 24
hours a day.

MIGRANTS

Two families from Missouri looking for work in the pea fields of California.

SHARECROPPER'S DAUGHTER

new tractors: the tragic history of the Joad family multiplied by thousands. We are only beginning to find out how many thousands there are. What to do about them remains to be worked out. A few camps have been built for the homeless. California public schools are making first efforts to meet the migrant children's educational needs. Agencies have been set up to provide emergency credit, even to help some tenant farmers to purchase their farms and improve their methods so as to keep the migrant stream from swelling. But the help offered has hardly begun to answer the need.

That agricultural adjustment to date has chiefly benefited the "top third" of the farm population is now recognized more by the administrators themselves than by the voting public. Will the American people get behind an even more courageous program of rehabilitation and resettlement? The need for it, as we shall see, is not likely to diminish. Indeed, it is bound to become more and more urgent.

The Future of Farming

The unhappy condition of so many farm families should not blot out the real advances of the last few years. The ascent from the rabbit hole has begun. Gross farm income increased nearly one billion dollars annually from 1934 through 1936 and was over 9½ billion by 1937. Aside from its struggle with all the emergencies, the New Deal program has made contributions of lasting effect in further encouraging farm cooperatives and in improving the permanent facilities for farm credit. Much sick land has been healed, farmers have learned more about their business, government has learned more about its job, the American people have been seeing their country in new ways—not only by auto and trailer but through magazines, books, movies, radio programs—educational materials of unprecedented quality and timeliness. The government itself has contributed two fine movies, *The River* and *The Plow That Broke the Plains.* Surely there should be more of these, and surely more people ought to see them. We need to wake up and learn not only how bad things are but how wonderful they can be.

Farmers and farm laborers are still an underpaid group. They constitute more than a fourth of our gainfully occupied workers. Yet only a tenth of the national income goes to them and their families! The depression for farmers is not yet over.

Is the farm program on the right track? Some say no. The bugaboo of regimentation is raised less often than at first; the most frequent criticism is that government policies conflict and cancel each other. Why pay some farmers to restrict production, while spending other public money bringing ruined land back into use and maintaining laboratories whose findings will constantly increase productivity? ask the critics. But this is a contradiction presented by all the long course of our history, not cooked up by a few public servants. Can a farm program be made of armchair logic? Must it not, rather, be shaped by the varying and sometimes conflicting needs of all the people involved?

The trouble with farming seems to be that there are too many farmers, too much land being farmed, too much produce being grown. This is true in one sense if we accept present ways of doing things, in a different sense if we want to improve on them. Under our present habits, if business should boom and more people could eat what they like, we might conceivably need to expand acreage in some crops. In any case, control of acreage is necessary: to shrink or to expand, according to what people can buy. Whether we take deliberate steps to expand purchasing power or not, the very least we are called upon to do is to give the federal government clear power to lead the farmers in adjusting their plantings. The welfare of some 30 million people directly dependent on farming demands this. If there is really no constitutional basis at present, now is the time to "promote the general welfare" by an amendment. As to Mother Nature: though man cannot yet command the wind and the rain, he can apply insurance methods. The "ever normal granary" plan for storing staples in bumper years and drawing on the surplus in short years would probably be workable if acreage control were clearly authorized—instead of being, as now, an appendage of the soil-conservation program precariously supported by marketing agreements. However well acreage control worked, there would still be "extra" farmers—migrants and other unfortunates—who would have to be kept alive through public help until the hoped-for industrial recovery should call them.

But can we really get by with such a minimum program for making the cyclical jolts of economic life humanly bearable for farm people? Perhaps we could—if mankind could be cured of constantly inventing better ways of getting work done. This seems, however, to be a habit that even depressions cannot squelch. In recent crisis years a better and cheaper tractor has been put on the market. Agrobiologists have kept on finding out how to make plants grow fuller, animals grow fatter. Phrases like "too many farmers" and "too many acres" take on new and startling meaning when we look down the future promised by such improvements. An expert agronomist estimated in 1934 that if the most efficient farming methods now practiced by a few were put in use all

FARM MODERNIZATION IN THE MISSISSIPPI VALLEY

HAVE | HAVE NOT

ELECTRICITY

WATER PIPED INTO HOUSE

RADIOS

TELEPHONES

CARS

EACH SYMBOL REPRESENTS TEN PER CENT OF ALL FARMS EQUIPPED WITH ELECTRICITY, WATER, RADIOS, TELEPHONES, CARS
From the Report of the Mississippi Valley Committee, 1934

over the country (to say nothing of putting new discoveries to work), we could let 5 out of every 6 acres now tilled for staple crops lie fallow, do without 3 out of every 4 of the farmers growing these crops, and still duplicate present output! This is the kind of technological pressure that is driving our less efficient farmers into tenancy and homelessness. It will lead to further land misuse of the kind that breeds clogged reservoirs, floods, and dust storms, unless the soil-conservation program keeps pace. Doubtless before the tractor has finished its dislocating work, some other invention (a mechanical cotton picker is already on the market) will have set more social changes in motion. Shall technical advance continue to be a matter of recurring human tragedies and successive programs of emergency relief? Or shall we go about matching technical progress with social inventiveness, working together in new ways to build a better America? We, the people, can have what we want. But not for the wishing! Democracy demands brainwork as well as good will from all of us. Or rather, it demands action springing from both. Only as more citizens explore, both feelingly and intelligently, the processes of modern life—and act on their convictions!—can we improve our society.

Another aspect of the task needs emphasis: one already implied by the phrase "what people can buy." It has long been our habit to look at things from the production end of the cornucopia. We incline to measure success in terms of how much is being produced and whether at a profit or at a loss. But the shock of the depression has thrown at least a brief spotlight on the other end of the economic process: on consumption, on standards of living. We have been told that even in the "prosperous" year 1929 two of every five American families had annual incomes under $1500—at a time when $2500 was required to provide healthful living for the average family.

Surely the quality of living is the important thing. Not that a full stomach alone promises the good life! But if undernourishment is widespread, the very groundwork of abundance is lacking. The brief flash must be made a stronger light that will illuminate every sign of failure in this richest country of the world. The New Deal has already magnified the light considerably. It has seen a connection between underfed, ill-clad city families and struggling farmers. Its program is our most courageous attempt so far at acting on the nation's economic life as a whole. To think of this approach as an emergency one, to be abandoned as soon as the depression eases, will not do. The next steps must be ahead, not backwards.

Between the farmers (who want to produce more) and the consuming public (so many of whom would like to eat more) lies a complex distributive system. It does not work very well. In a way, the wonder is that it works at all! The job of getting foodstuffs for some 350 million meals a day from several million farms to the kitchen doors of all the houses, hotels and restaurants, is an overwhelming one. Many businesses and many people make a living doing this job. They transport farm goods in trucks and trains, load and unload, process, store, grade, weigh, buy and sell. The trouble is, again, that there are too many people, too much equipment, and too little planning involved in all this. Social engineering lags far behind mechanical invention. As has been pointed out in the Los Angeles bacon story, the results are low prices to farmers, high costs to consumers. The problem is put on plain view in streets where three or four groceries are competing for business that one could handle. Consumers individually may think this kind of competition a blessing, for it often leads to price cuts. Yet who but the consuming public eventually pays for these duplications of equipment and work? And such duplications exist all the way from farm to kitchen.

But what do we suggest should become of the too many farmers and too many grocery stores? And, it might be added, of the too many garment makers, too many laundries, and so on and on. We reiterate: this is a national problem and can be dealt with most effectively by the nation itself through the federal government. From this broad point of view, possibilities open up. That is, while there are too many farm hands and too many grocery counters, millions of families lack adequate housing and a hundred other things that man power and equipment are needed to produce.

The American people have needs still unmet; they have resources—human and material—that want using; they have constitutional power to create social means for turning these needs into opportunities. We have indicated the urgent next steps most directly concerning agriculture. These are not enough: the farm problem is more than a farm problem. Our fuller outline of a national program for the future can only be drawn after we have seen two of the great industrial resources, coal and oil. But first, a brief look down the long ages when soil was in the making. For geology has a special light to shed on our use of American soil—the greatest of earth's gifts.

Chapter III—SOIL: THE SOURCE OF LIFE ON LAND

Case History Number One

Soil in the Making

America's Use of Soil

Geologic Inheritances of the Natural Regions
New England
The Western Mississippi Drainage Region
The Great Plains
The Cotton Lands
California

Three Man-made Diseases of the Soil
Wind and Water Erosion
Depletion
Leaching

Who Will Cure and Care for the Soil? New Trends

Chapter III—SOIL: THE SOURCE OF LIFE ON LAND

Case History Number One

Soil in the Making

THE LAYMAN THINKS of soil as inanimate, as inferior to living things. He shows his disdain by such common expressions as "mere dirt," "dirty stories," "he treated me like dirt under his feet," "clod," a "soiled reputation." Dirt and soil have acquired derogatory associations.

The agronomist thinks of the soil as a truly living thing. He shows his respect and enthusiasm for a healthy living soil much as a forester does for a fine tree or a horse fancier for Man-of-War. More than that, he thinks of soil and its care as basic in civilization.

The geologist, too, has great respect for soil. Soil represents a long history in the behavior of the earth. Moreover, the early stages in the making of soil made life possible on the land, though life began in the sea without the aid of soil. The preparation for soil began before there was any life at all on dry land. And living things in their later complexities, and in the phase of life that we call death, added and are still adding new elements to soil that give it its functional activity.

The basis of soil is disintegrated, broken-up rock. The original rock was cold or frozen magma, the original earth stuff from which have come all elements on the earth in solid or liquid or gaseous state. The history of the behavior of the magmas is geology. It is a history of constant change, fascinating but complicated (if that is not a contradiction of terms to any of our readers!) and only a trained geologist can read the history told in the rocks. Even the experts interpret the remote history in different ways—the early, early days where geology joins hands with astronomy and the origin of our world has to be read, or rather reconstructed, through revelations of the telescope. But the basic facts of mineral substance subjected to slow but constant change can be glimpsed by a layman; and with even a superficial understanding of the processes by which the earth changes, the long-ago world which made our natural resources becomes real.

The making of soil involves several kinds of past behavior of the earth, as, indeed, does the making of all natural resources. Air, sunlight, water, soil, rocks, clay, sand, vegetation, animals, coal, oil, natural gas, ores—such is the list of our chief natural resources. They are all inheritances of the past made in the dim days before human masters existed to lay claim to them. All have taken geologic eras to reach their present state and, if dissipated, will take geologic eras to be formed again. Each of the natural resources is traced backwards from its present condition by a long case history, a case history that guides the techniques and work processes of the present-day masters of our natural resources.

Fortunately, in the case history of soil we do not need to concern ourselves with the beginnings of the earth, for astronomers differ as to the way the original hot earth stuff got gathered into a whirling ball. Nor need we go back to what the geologists call the Azoic or Lifeless Era, about which cautious geologists will say nothing is really known. We can begin after the ball has become somewhat cooled on the surface so that the molten lava has frozen and become what we laymen call rock. Gases and masses of water have been released. All water has come from the original earth stuff. The water that, as steam, comes up with the hot magma (lava) in eruptions of volcanoes is even now adding to the surface water. How the land and water was distributed in these early, early days no one knows. But geologists do know that as far back as they can read geologic history different parts of the land have been rising and falling; so that the water, which gathers, of course, in the hollows or low places, has covered different parts of the earth at different times. How has this strange movement of the earth's crust come about?

The answer to this is tied up with an important trait of earth behavior. The interior of the earth is growing cooler; the total volume is growing smaller. But the crust is frozen into rock that cannot shrink. Something has to happen. What happens is a giant crumpling. For rock is not nearly so rigid as the layman thinks. When a quarry has cut into a solid hillside, granite will sag so quickly that it may catch and jam the mechanism put into the cut. Everywhere we see twisted and folded rock. The crust crumples into wrinkles like the wrinkles of an apple's skin when it gets smaller through drying. The crumpling may be only a single local bubble like the Black Hills of Dakota. It may be an uplift over a large area causing extrusion of lower igneous (fire) rock. Or the crust may fold in huge waves, as in the Folded Alleghenies, where the first wrinkle is supposed to have been some 40,000 feet high. These wrinkles are mountains. Mountain building has taken place since the crust began to cool and is still taking place. Each mountain range has a particular history of its own. Here all we have to be aware of is this tendency of the earth to crumple. When it crumples, it develops cracks or semicracks. If it then slips in a giant fault, it makes a fault block like the Sierra Nevada. And up through these weakened places the hot magma rushes. So most mountains have at some time had volcanoes. Mountain building, which is this movement of the earth's crust, has taken place in different parts of the world at different times. Geologic eras, of which there are six, are named from the state of organic evolution present. They are bounded by great changes both in the physical aspect of the earth and in its life. Such major times of earth shrinkage are called "revolutions." Eras are composed of a group of periods, and periods are usually named from these times of mountain building.

No sooner has this change of the surface, this mountain building, been effected than another change begins. The surface has been pushed up: change number one. The surface now begins to be worn down: change number two. Before the earliest stages in soil making, rain had long been a surface phenomenon. At first the earth's surface was relatively hot—cool compared with the interior hot magma, but hot compared with the present surface. Hot acid water lapped the rocks. Steam rose; cooled in the upper atmosphere, forming clouds; and fell again. The earliest rains never reached the earth but turned to steam as they approached the hot surface. The eternal water cycle, which is still going on. Evaporation and condensation. Up and down. The familiar weather phenomena of clouds (water vapor), rain and snow. When the first warm rock surfaces appeared, warm rain forever rose and fell on them. It continued to fall on the cooling rock. And as it fell, it began to disintegrate the rock. Bit by bit, little by little, it began to separate the crystals of various minerals in the molten magma. Wind, too, blew over the early rocks. And as it blew on the surface rocks, it, too, began to disintegrate them and bit by bit helped to separate the crystals. Erosion had begun. Soil was in the making.

When the surface grew cool enough to permit the freezing of water, another great erosive factor was added. For water, unlike most things, expands when it freezes. It fell into cracks of rocks in the cooler mountaintops; and when it froze, split off big, jagged, coarse boulders. Boulders were rolled by wave and river action into rounded boulders, then into a coarse gravel which became finer and finer, until at last the crystals contained in the original hot magmas were separated. And the crystals, compounds of the various elements, being of different weight, tended to fall in layers of similar kinds when they were blown or washed out of the place where they originally formed a part of a rock mass. So the earth, largely in its seas, received from the disintegrated rock layers of sand or layers of clay, these two kinds forming the greater part of the earth's rocks. And the sand or quartz crystals, being many-sided with many angles which get worn off into spheres, could not pack close together. So water can easily seep through the interstices between the sand crystals; whereas the crystals in clay are excessively thin and scaly, so that they pack into a dense mass through which water drains slowly and with difficulty. As these layers of disintegrated rock themselves got covered by more layers of more disintegrated rocks, they solidified through heat and pressure and mineralizing solutions. Thus over vast areas on the earth's crust was built a kind of rock layer-cake: different rock crystals deposited in horizontal sheets. Thus were the mountaintops lowered and the places between the mountains raised. Thus were formed our enormous deposits of sedimentary rock.

All this disintegration of rock made a redistribution of the surface weights. Slowly the earth responded by another change. Deep below the surface, some forty miles or so, the hot semiplastic magmas flowed to create a new balance and on the earth's crust came new upheavals or subsidences. New mountains—sometimes made of the sedimentary rocks themselves pushed high above their original position; sometimes made of the original igneous rock, the hot magma, pushing up and through the layer cake. In the new disposition of surface rock, erosion set in anew and the sedimentary rocks themselves became boulders, gravel or finer silt. Great bodies of water formed in the hollows. Great rivers ran from the high land down to the seas. All this process of constant change, rock being pushed up, rock being worn down, crystals being separated and laid down in vast layer cakes, went on for millions of years when soil was in the early stages of making. And some time during these dim days of the Archeozoic (Earliest Life) Era, came life.

First life, from the nature of the case, meant an organism capable of making its own food from inorganic stuff. For obviously that was the only food available on the earth. This was about 1,600,000,000 years ago, an age which is calculated by the time it takes radium to break down into lead according to the physicist's "radioactive clock." The single-cell organisms, probably marine algae and bacteria, which first appeared are capable of finding food from the inorganic mineral substances. They live and feed this way to this day. Their dead bodies accumulating, falling to the bottom of the acid Archeozoic seas, formed a new substance mixed in with the disintegrated crystals of rock.

Sea plants developed and furnished food for sea animals. Animal life in the sea developed from primitive Proterozoic invertebrates to the Paleozoic (Ancient Life) mollusks and trilobites, to fish and corals, to lungfish and scorpions and to amphibians who were capable of sustaining existence both in water and on land. At this time, too, came the first land plants.

These first land plants prepared the atmosphere for animal use, for until this time there probably was no free oxygen in the air. They were capable of taking carbon dioxide from the atmosphere, turning the carbon into their own growth and throwing the oxygen back into the air. The primitive land plants did this. Present-day land plants do this (with the exception of plants that are not green, like mushrooms).

They were also capable of taking raw materials from the soil. Different plants take different things out for their growth, so that soil needs to be restored according to the elements extracted by the plants that have lived on it. Natural fertilizing takes place when plants (or animals) die and decay. The nitrogen they have taken out of the soil is restored to it. This is one phase of "the nitrogen cycle." When the plants are removed, as in man-planted crops, an artificial fertilizer has to be substituted. Otherwise the soil gets "exhausted." It no longer contains the elements necessary for the growth of the plant.

As plants increased on the earth's surface, they threw off more and more free oxygen into the air. Then came land animals, beginning with the amphibians who were at home both in water and on land. Land animals cannot live without oxygen in the air. They could not develop until land plants gave them free oxygen to breathe. Practically all are still dependent on plants for their food. Inorganic mineral stuff to plants, plants to animals. Such has been the history of life since it developed on land. Thus land animals came late in geologic history.

Soil was, through the period of primitive plants, becoming more and more a living thing. A modern soil chemist means exactly what he says when he speaks of a "living soil." For there is real organic activity taking place in the soil. He expresses the various physical happenings in the soil by analogies to the physical happenings or make-up in our own bodies. The original pulverized rock becomes merely the skeleton of the soil and is, by itself, not much use to the highly evolved modern plants. The real functioning activities take place in the soil colloids, which act as organisms. What we ordinarily call decay is caused by the growth and action of bacteria, minute organisms, and is a process of oxidation. The colloids fill in the gaps of the inorganic rock particles and serve to cement them together. These colloids absorb and regulate the food supply in the soil, withdrawing from active solution mineral and organic substances which would otherwise be washed out. Soil scientists speak of the tendons and muscles of the soil, meaning this power of the colloids to hold the rock fragments together. They speak of the soil's digestive system, meaning these bacterial activities within the colloids which prepare food for plant assimilation and take care of waste material thrown off by the plants. The soil digests the organic debris, breaking it down by a process finally forming *humus* that approaches the hydrocarbon stage, with most of the oxygen eliminated from the organic matter. Humus is the natural sewage disposal of material, a form that is harmless to the plant and generally beneficial to the physical condition of the soil.

The soil breathes. Its respiratory system is called aeration. It sometimes breathes to a depth of fifty feet or more. This breathing of fresh air brings about oxidation, assists digestion and elimination of the gaseous products of the soil.

The soil has a circulatory system in the movement of moisture. When any of these functional activities are checked, we get a sick soil and eventually we get a dead soil in which only the inorganic skeleton remains. Depleted soil—that is, soil that has been leached by an abnormal amount of water carrying off soluble compounds, or soil that has had some essential colloidal activity removed from it by too constant growing of one type of plant—is sick soil. Sick soil may be cured by the restoring of organic substance which, through decay, starts the bacteria to work again. Dead soil can be brought to life again only through the age-long process of building humus, a process which the world accomplished though it took millions of years.

Soil furnishes the home for most plant life. Thus it is the ultimate home of land-animal life as well, for animals (other than the unicellular) have no power to make their own food out of mineral substances, though, of course, they require minerals such as water and salt in addition to organic matter. But every higher animal eats plants directly, or indirectly by eating other animals who have themselves eaten plants. So the history of soil is very closely tied up with the evolution of living things as well as with the evolution of topographical forms such as mountains and valleys. The skeleton of soil comes from disintegrated inorganic rock, but its colloids come from the bacteria that live in the interstices of the rock particles and are the means through which it performs its complicated function almost like a living creature itself. Thus soil became the home of the ever-developing plants whose dead bodies gave new and richer material for the colloids. And animals in turn took on new habits as new plants appeared. Trees, for instance, are earlier than grasses. Grasses were not fully evolved until after mammals, poor treebound creatures, had developed. With the appearance of grass, these small, hesitant, new mammals descended from the trees and grazing began upon the earth. Some animals whose bones appear in ancient rocks have entirely disappeared. Why this happened is often a matter of conjecture. It is not known what disaster overtook the primitive horses of North America. Their bones are found in many places, but they disappeared before they could develop into the modern horse.

Soil has thus been produced by a variety of earth behaviors. Taken together they present a drama of building up and tearing down—a drama that continued for incalculable millions of years before the earth furnished a home for even the simplest life—a drama that has continued at least sixteen hundred million years during which life developed from microscopic algae to man—a drama that is still in process and, so far as we know, will stretch into an indefinite future. During this incessant drama of change, of water and gas pushing their way up from the hot interior, of upheaval and subsidence, of forming of mountains and wearing them down, of taking out nitrogen and returning it to the soil, of taking up water vapor into the atmosphere and dropping it back again to the earth, from this great geologic and biologic drama, the earth produced within itself the various rocks, the mineral ores—iron, copper, gold, silver and many others—it produced all kinds of coal—anthracite and bituminous and the half-coals, lignite and peat—it produced oil and natural gas; and on its surface it produced water, atmosphere and rock, then soil; and with the coming of land plants it produced free oxygen, the element necessary for land animals. Thus the earth produced the natural resources that men now use for their needs and pleasures.

For man, himself a land animal, the greatest of these natural resources is undoubtedly soil. For soil was and is and probably will always be the ultimate larder for the living things most valuable to him, from the microscopic bacteria which find their home in the soil colloids to plants and animals which give him his chief foods. Its care includes far more than the mechanical mixing of its parts as in simple plowing. To keep healthy it needs food, air, moisture. Such brutal slaughter of the soil as produced the Dust Bowl, such starving and draining of the soil as produced the depleted or exhausted lands of the cotton and tobacco culture, such careless neglect of its surface as produced the eroded lands of most of our agricultural areas not too flat to erode, come to seem like the brutal killing of animate things. Soil is not mere dirt. It is a finely adjusted complicated thing, functioning only with care suited to its physique. When it is so adjusted, it furnishes men with their food, shelter and raiment. When it is maltreated, it grows sick or dies. And men simply go without the products of a healthy soil.

AMERICA'S USE OF SOIL

The United States is still using one of the natural products of her soil—trees. No pioneer could ever have believed that we should some day fear a lumber shortage in this country. Yet here is the present situation.

A glance at the map shows the overwhelming reduction of our forest reserves. Originally we had from 800 to 850 million acres of virgin forests. There are now less than 100 million acres of virgin growth of saw-timber size. The rest of our 457 million acres of forest not in farms contains trees available for fuel, pulp and other uses, and includes about 83 million cut-over or burned-over acres that are being restocked poorly or not at all.

Good forestry demands cutting only trees of a given size and replanting currently to keep the forest alive. But our lumber industry, privately owned, has usually been conducted like a mining enterprise—"take what you can and move on"—with little thought for renewing the forests. Some great fortunes were made in lumber in the early days. But on the whole, the industry is now "sick": in 1935 the losses of companies having deficits exceeded the profits of other companies. Until the NRA code it always paid extremely low wages.

In 1925–29 we used up about twice as much timber of all sizes as was replaced by new growth. We used five times as much saw timber as was replaced. Already we are having to import half of our pulpwood supply.

There are other results of forest "mining" even more important than the loss of the raw material. Forests are regulators of stream flow: that is, they moderate the runoff of water during the annual floodtime, thus decreasing the danger of bad floods, and they hold some of the moisture for a following drought period. The moisture is held both in the forest duff—the decaying organic material on the forest floor, which acts like a sponge—and deep below the surface in the ground water.

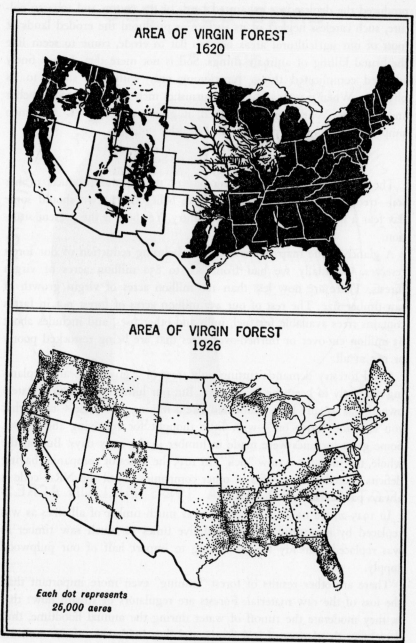

AREA OF VIRGIN FOREST
1620

AREA OF VIRGIN FOREST
1926

Each dot represents
25,000 acres

LAND USE 1930

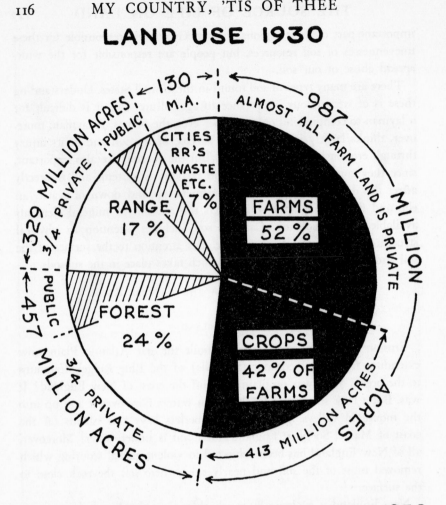

TOTAL LAND AREA 1903 MILLION ACRES

Some of the moisture returns to the atmosphere by evaporation. Some is absorbed by the roots, carried upward into the stem and foliage, and finally returns to the atmosphere by a process known as transpiration. We have no definite knowledge how much is given back by transpiration, but it has been estimated to be about 25% of the total annual rainfall. When the forest is cut, of course this 25% is added to the runoff and helps to produce floods. Moreover, it changes the humidity of the air.

America's chief use of her soil is, however, for agriculture. The striking unevenness of soil resources in the great natural regions accounts for an important part of these regions' history. Geology is responsible for these unevennesses of soil resources, but people are responsible for the widespread abuse of our soil.

There are many types of soil found in the United States. Understanding these is of tremendous importance to agriculture. But it is difficult for a layman to comprehend or remember even the names. A layman, moreover, thinks largely in terms of the surface of the soil and of its injury through erosion by wind and water. But the subsoils are also important, since they control the circulatory and respiratory systems and indirectly affect the digestive system. The movement up and down of water, an ebb and flow through the soil, affects the amount of mineral elements available for surface use. Care of soil includes attention to physical structure and chemical agents. It includes attention to the surface of the soil and to the organic functioning which takes place in the subsoils.

GEOLOGIC INHERITANCES OF THE NATURAL REGIONS

NEW ENGLAND

Erosion of ancient mountaintops built the flat Atlantic Plain now extending from the Piedmont (foothills) of the Blue Ridge Mountains to the ocean. Why was no plain built off the coast of New England? It was. But a later subsidence let the ocean waters flow over it and up into the mountain valleys, giving the numberless bays and islands off the coast of Maine. So New England's best soil is under water! Moreover, all of New England has been subjected to violent glacial scouring which removed most of the soil and nearly everywhere left the rock close to the surface.

New England is geologically much older than the Appalachian range. It consists of violently folded and bent igneous rocks with preserved pockets of various sedimentary rocks. This gives New England her quarries of granite (metamorphosed igneous rock), of marble (metamorphosed lime), and slate (metamorphosed clay). The great faults in the Triassic Period and subsequent fills have given rich soils in the Connecticut Valley. With this exception and that of Aroostook County in Maine, New England is not good agricultural land except for hay and dairying. With the opening of the great agricultural lands of the West, New England farms began to be abandoned. They are now returning naturally to forests and to summer homes for people of the crowded coast cities. New England's soil was never thick, and erosion has never been a serious problem. (See map, page 14.)

EROSION CONDITIONS
IN 8 GREAT PLAINS STATES

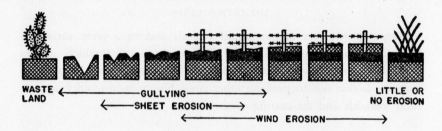

WASTE LAND ←————————GULLYING————————→ LITTLE OR NO EROSION

←————SHEET EROSION————→

←————————WIND EROSION————————→

EACH BLOCK REPRESENTS 50 MILLION ACRES
From the Report of the Great Plains Drought Area Committee, 1936

THE WESTERN MISSISSIPPI DRAINAGE REGION

The great flat slope from Rockies to Mississippi River was made by great marine deposits and from eroded tops of ancient mountains. The soil is varied. On the whole it increases in richness and in depth as it approaches the Mississippi River since, naturally, the finer particles were carried farther by the great plains' rivers. Richest and deepest are those of the Delta, still largely unused because of the expense of drainage and of building levees. The Mississippi River carries a vast amount of top-soil, at the rate of about thirty-three carloads per minute, which it deposits as silt, thereby filling its own bed. Probably 400 million tons of soil material are washed annually into the Gulf of Mexico. This has necessitated building 1500 miles of artificial banks—levees. Left to itself, the river would change its course and make a new mouth. The rich wind-blown soil, known as loess, consists of a veneer lying on top of coastal-plain sands or other deposits and erodes very easily. From the Ohio to the Gulf a band of loess soil has been viciously eroded.

THE GREAT PLAINS

Closest to the river in the moister regions grew the long prairie grass. To the west, as the regions grew drier the grass grew shorter. This drier region is called the Great Plains. On top of these plains, still farther west and close to the foot of the Rockies, lie the outwash deposits from the mountains known as the High Plains. (See map, page 8.) The soil of the High Plains is readily eroded, and the whole region receives less than 20 inches of yearly rainfall. This region is suited to grazing. Overgrazing and the unwise plowing of the High Plains gave us the Dust Bowl. Both water and wind erosion have been great since the sod was plowed under and the few trees along the banks of the river were cut.

THE COTTON LANDS

Cotton grows over many natural regions and in a great variety of soils. (See maps, pages 27 and 14.) The serious erosion which appears everywhere except on the flat Atlantic Plain and on the Mississippi Bottoms is due not to geologic inheritance but to man—faulty agricultural methods and the cutting of the forests.

CALIFORNIA

No better soil exists than that in the small valleys in California's coastal range and in the colossal inland valleys of the San Joaquin and Sacramento rivers, known together as the Great Valley (not to be confused with the Great Valley of the Folded Alleghenies). The Great Valley is dry—semidesert. But a great reservoir of ground water lies under it which can be tapped by artesian wells for irrigation. Anything, practically, will grow there. The crops have shifted from wheat in the days of early settlement to truck, fruit and rice. Because of its flatness, erosion is slight. Orange groves grow on the foothills of the Sierras and in the more southern San Gabriel Valley. Here erosion is severe. For the rivers are seasonal—some disappearing entirely in the dry seasons and without banks to hold the flood waters which follow the seasonal rains. The frequent hillside fires burn off the chaparral covering and increase the floods and the destruction of lowlands.

Three Man-made Diseases of the Soil

Can a sick soil be cured? That is like asking if a sick person can be cured. It depends upon what disease he has and how sick he is. We have three great man-made diseases of the soil—erosion, depletion and leaching. Some of our soil (about 100 million acres) is sick unto death. This is an out-and-out loss of our natural wealth. Some of our soil (about 125 million acres) is seriously sick, and 100 million more acres are threatened and will be gone beyond recovery if action is not taken soon. It is for this soil that we need planning. What is the cure?

WIND AND WATER EROSION

Erosion means the disappearance of topsoil by action of wind or water. How can we stop the soil from blowing off the High Plains? By restoring the sod which held the soil before it was plowed under. This involves a rain-conservation program through contour plowing and through plowing up earthen ridges with water gaps in them where rain may accumulate and be distributed as needed. Furthermore, the areas to be returned to grazing lands must be thrown out of use until the grass roots can get a foothold. Such a program the government is now undertaking, both indirectly by educating the farmers to change their farming techniques and directly on the damaged land that has reverted to the Public Domain now that it has been made into the Dust Bowl. (See erosion map, page 14.) It is estimated that already many millions of gallons of rains have been preserved for use in the Dust Bowl which otherwise, as sheer waste, would have run into the Missouri, the Mississippi and on to the Gulf. Is it worth the cost? Probably, considering the fact that the soil blows onto better farm lands and ruins them as well.

There is another proposed cure for wind erosion. Check the wind. With this cure in mind, the Plains Shelter Belt Project was proposed. This plan involved planting trees in strips running north and south, from Texas to the Dakotas, the width of the belts and their distance apart depending upon local soil and climate conditions. Planting was begun, but the project was opposed and did not pass Congress. A less ambitious substitute measure called the Cooperative Farm Forestry Act was passed, however, early in 1937. Now the farmer who wishes to cooperate has his land examined by government foresters who determine what trees and shrubs to use and plan the most effective shelter-belt system. The government furnishes the trees and foresters who give current advice and supervision. The farmer prepares the land, furnishes fencing material, land and labor. Already, within six states from Texas to the Dakotas, 2600 miles of shelter-belt strips have been planted with nearly 45 million trees on 6500 farms. An average of 66% of these trees have flourished, though 1936 was a year of severe drought. Many are 20 to 24 feet high. In these shelter-belt regions the wind is checked locally. It is hoped that this frequent checking of the wind will prevent its reaching the violence that is common when it has an unbroken sweep of some thousand miles.

Both these methods of planting windbreaks and resodding through preserving the rain are hospital care of damaged soil. Just as doctors now recognize that their job includes preventive medicine—attention to *keeping bodies healthy,* as well as curing sick people—so agriculturists recognize that a part of their job, and perhaps the more important part, is to *keep soil healthy.* That, obviously, means using the soil of any region

EXTENT OF EROSION IN THE UNITED STATES

1492

SOIL PRESERVED   WASTE

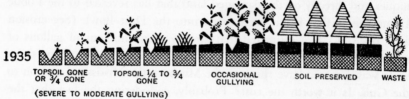

1935

TOPSOIL GONE   TOPSOIL ¼ TO ¾   OCCASIONAL   SOIL PRESERVED   WASTE
OR ¾ GONE   GONE   GULLYING

(SEVERE TO MODERATE GULLYING)

U. S. Department of Agriculture—Soil Conservation Service

Each block represents 135 million acres.

only in ways that will not produce sickness. Part of the wind erosion in the Dust Bowl was caused, as we know, by faulty farming techniques. But the worst parts were caused by planting wheat on land that should have been kept for grazing. Some bad wind erosion has been brought about by overgrazing. So planning for wind erosion includes both a restoration of abused soil and *regulation of the use* of grazing lands.

The disease of *water erosion* appears naturally on slopes—the steeper the slopes, the more likely that the disease will be galloping consumption! (See erosion map, page 14.) Water erosion has two stages —sheet erosion and gully erosion. Sheet erosion can be checked by checking the innumerable small rivulets that cut into the plowed fields after each rain and carry topsoil off with them. The same trick that saves the water in dry lands and prevents wind erosion will save the soil in wet lands from water erosion. It is the now familiar contour plowing instead of plowing up and down the hillside. In contour plowing, the furrow itself constitutes a small terrace and checks the runoff of water; in up-and-down-hill plowing, the furrow constitutes a trough for runoff. There is on the market a new terrace plow that leaves the plowed hillside in sizable terraces. In severe erosion, strips of unplowed land must alternate with plowed. The natural vegetation—sod or otherwise—will check the runoff. Contour plowing and strip plowing not only prevent erosion but hold the much-needed moisture for the crops. Both techniques are coming into wider use.

GRASS AND WOODS CHECK EROSION LOSSES

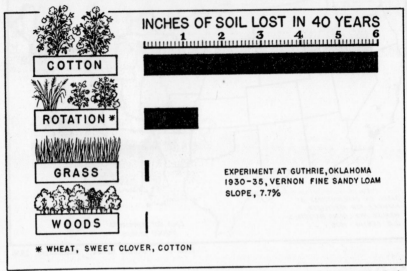

EXPERIMENT AT GUTHRIE, OKLAHOMA
1930-35, VERNON FINE SANDY LOAM
SLOPE, 7.7%

* WHEAT, SWEET CLOVER, COTTON

U. S. Department of Agriculture—Soil Conservation Service

If sheet erosion is unchecked, it will develop into gully erosion. Each rain enlarges the gully by simply crumbling the banks regardless of crops or buildings. Small gully erosion can be checked by throwing brush into the gullies or by building a simple wooden dam. The soil which is washed down accumulates at each brush pile or dam and gradually fills up the gully. Severe gully erosion requires the same treatment but on an engineering scale.

Here, again, we have a situation which demands both cure of damaged soil and care of healthy soil to keep it from getting damaged. So planning again involves hospital cure of badly eroded land and preventive care in the use of the soil. Some hillsides are too steep to be plowed without risking erosion. All hillside farms should be plowed on contour lines.

Many hillsides now plowed for crops should be replanted with trees. All America has watched the CCC boys at this task. Tree planting is necessary both to check erosion and as flood control. Obviously, the disease of floods is closely connected with the disease of water erosion.

DEPLETION

Depletion comes from taking plant food out of soil without restoring it. If this is continued, soil loses the functioning activities of the colloids.

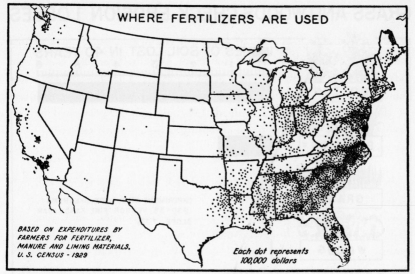

WHERE FERTILIZERS ARE USED

BASED ON EXPENDITURES BY FARMERS FOR FERTILIZER, MANURE AND LIMING MATERIALS. U. S. CENSUS - 1929

Each dot represents 100,000 dollars

From the "Fertilizer Review," March–April, 1938

The single crop is public enemy number one in this line. By the very nature of the case it takes out, year after year after year, the same materials. What has made matters even worse is that two of the great single crops, cotton and tobacco, are "robber crops" extracting an excessive amount of plant food from the soil. How can depleted land be restored? Obviously by putting back what the crops have taken out. This is the principle of fertilizers. Under natural conditions (unmodified by man) fertilizing takes place continuously through decaying vegetation and decaying bodies of animals. But crops are removed from the land, and with them goes the food they took from the soil for their own growth.

In the great depleted areas of the South where both cotton and tobacco are grown, the need of fertilizers is overwhelming. A glance at the map shows this. A costly man-made disease, depleted soil!

There is another method of restoring depleted land—the well-known historic method of rotation of crops or of letting the land lie fallow once in so often and plowing under the natural growth. Plants take different things out of the soil. They restore different things to the soil. So that if potatoes or legumes are planted in a soil depleted by cotton, the soil actually gains the food needed for cotton.

Once again we have the hospital-cure and the preventive-care aspects. Planning for depleted soil again means taking measures to restore the soil and regulation of the use of the soil so that it doesn't get depleted.

LEACHING

When there is a heavy runoff from soil, the water carries away in solution many chemicals necessary for plant growth. Leaching is not synonymous with erosion but often accompanies it. The soil colloids whose functions keep the soil alive can be washed away with excessive drainage. A thoroughly leached soil is dead. Leaching can be prevented by controlling the drainage and by maintaining a high humus content.

WHO WILL CURE AND CARE FOR THE SOIL? NEW TRENDS

It is all very well to outline cures for sick soil or care which will keep it healthy. But who will attend to it? Through the 1920's knowledge of the problem was growing; and government agencies, both state and federal, together with agricultural colleges, were enlarging their programs of experimentation and education. With a series of severe droughts which brought about crop failures and dust storms, and violent floods beginning in 1929 and continuing through the 1930's, the need for a drastic program of hospital care became plain.

Who could undertake such a program? The farmers? They were the ones who used the soil. But history shows with tragic certainty that in the United States they have used the soil in ways which have brought this wholesale sickness. Farmers were in a bad way—that we certainly knew by this time. Unaided, could they be expected to undertake a big program of cure of the soil when they couldn't even make ends meet without this expense? It was idle to expect them to. Such a program demanded two things that most farmers simply did not have. First, capital; second, technological skill. These two bases for a healthy modern culture under our present economy are conspicuously lacking in the South, where the need for soil planning is ominously clear. But there was no damaged soil in the United States which, by the nature of the case, was worked by affluent farmers. No. If soil was to be cured, the government had to provide both diagnosis and advice, and finance the hospital program. The emergency called for direct outlays, not necessarily for purchase of land, but to pay for activities like the erosion-control work by the CCC, the flood-control benefits of which directly concerned many more people than the farmers on whose land the improvements were made.

So the New Deal program of soil conservation was put into operation. Already results are showing, as witness the prospective crops in the Dust Bowl region. Cure of the soil has begun. The same arguments hold for restoration of soil that has been damaged by excessive cutting of trees.

GULLY EROSION

Typical tenant house in a badly eroded area of South Carolina. The land is going fast. It will soon take the house with it.

OVERGRAZED COW COUNTRY

It takes about 70 acres to support one cow in the High Plains even under natural conditions. Overgrazing has depleted natural forage until feeding scenes like this are common.

GRASS HOLDING THE SOIL

In this sand-hill area of Nebraska a concentration of livestock killed out the vegetation. The soil has gone with the wind, except where tufts of grass were left to hold it.

CONSERVATION METHODS

Strip cropping on contour in hilly country, North Carolina. This method holds more of the rain and keeps the soil from running away. The crops are rotated to conserve plant foods in the soil.

When the trees are gone, the lumberman goes too. His interest is not in the soil but in forests. We shall have to look to government regulation or planting to insure care and cure of forests and flood control. At the same time that the government started these hospital activities, it enlarged its educational program looking towards better care of the soil. Emphatically the government is on the job.

But it is an overwhelming job which the government has undertaken. Even the hospital measures cannot be completed without years more of effort, we are told by Dr. Bennett, head of the Soil Conservation Service. For help he looks to a continuation of the CCC, "a highly efficient type of labor," for a "twenty- to thirty-year program" engineered by soil-conservation experts. This is in order to save the soil which is not already too far gone. One hundred million acres, he estimates, have passed beyond hospital cure, dead from the disease of erosion.

Is this program of cure and care worth the price? The answer really involves our idea of waste. We talk much about waste: but just what do we mean by it? Waste has been defined in connection with a different natural resource as a loss, the remedy for which would not be more costly than the loss itself. Loss to whom? Here it is to the Nation. Determining the cost of anything is no easy matter, as any business man knows. It is particularly hard in such great enterprises for a *nation* to figure costs and gains. It must deal with more of the imponderables that can hardly be expressed in dollars and cents. It must take into account all the resources, and all the people involved. It must sometimes weigh a gain in mechanical efficiency against a loss in social welfare.

What kinds of gain and loss are involved in our soil-conservation program? Dr. Bennett, according to a report in the *New York Times,* April, 1939, recently calculated the loss to farmers alone:

Estimating the annual direct cost of soil erosion to farmers alone, not counting damage to reservoirs, stream channels, irrigation ditches, highways and railways, at $400,000,000, Dr. Bennett said that the damage of the past fifty years could be placed at $20,000,000,000 and that the next fifty years would cost just as much if the present rate of erosion was permitted to continue.

We are losing every day, as a result of erosion, the equivalent of 200 forty-acre farms.

The nation must balance the cost of the program against what it saves: losses involved in farming poor land, losses on better land due to dust storms, losses due to clogging river beds and reservoirs, losses due to floods.

These are the main factors connected with what the Soil Conservation Service is doing. But there are other important activities of technicians both in and outside of government service which are also conservational, though not generally thought of as such. Real conservation of the soil seeks not merely to prevent the needless destruction of life-giving substances: it works in positive ways to recover more of their potential productivity. For example, agronomists have found that the potential yield per acre for corn of the type now in use is 225 bushels. The present *average* yield in practice is hardly more than 25 bushels. The *best* yields practically demonstrated are quite a different matter. The agronomists have learned what moisture conditions are required for higher yields, and they have worked out a formula for the amount of fertilizer which will produce economically almost the full potential. The results possible through using such knowledge are illustrated by the accomplishments of some Indiana farmers. Records kept by the Indiana Corn Growers Association showed a maximum yield *in 1914* of about 110 bushels. In 1932 the maximum was 165.

Such gains technology makes possible. What loss must the nation balance against them? History has shown: production is already crowding over demand; as the more efficient farmers increase their production, more and more other farmers will be driven off the land—or if there is nowhere else to go, will be driven into the kind of living that goes on now in subsistence areas like the Appalachian and Ozark hill lands, which yield their few crops most sparingly. The soil and plant life technicians alone cannot make such people flourish or prevent their numbers from increasing. As we have seen, the more abundant life which modern technology promises waits upon an effectively coordinated program to conserve—to make the best use of—*all* of the nation's resources: natural, technological, human. It waits, in short, upon our national courage and intelligence as planners.

At Washington there are new trends in the thinking along these lines. The Department of Agriculture, the Department of the Interior which controls our parks, the Forestry Bureau, have all come to think of the *natural* physical *resources* under their control—the stage set for our American drama—as being *national resources*. They have started national planning, both the hospital cure of abused soil and preventive care by regulating the use of soil.

Their programs are based on thorough and scientific research, an essential part of all sound planning. Farmers cannot undertake such research: the government can. The government, in addition to the activities already discussed, is buying up marginal or submarginal lands which are unfit for agriculture and turning them into reserves. We now have large parks, both the Federal and State, which serve the double purpose of conservation and recreation areas. And recently we have had a National Planning Board, appointed in 1934 and now called the National Resources Committee. This Committee conducts research, publishes reports containing their factual findings and their recommendations. Moreover, forty-six states have instituted Planning Boards with like purposes. These Planning Boards are advisory only. But they indicate a widespread concern for the nation's natural resources. Surely they will make for a program which shall both restore and conserve our damaged soil, which shall stop waste in the greatest of our national resources. And surely we need such a program.

WHAT A LAND!

What a land!
What a land!
The endless trees
The endless grass
The endless boundless fertile soil
Free to those who dared to toil.
Old Europe gasped
Old Europe grasped
And young America was born.

The pioneers were hardy folk
They bowed their necks beneath the yoke
They held the gun
They held the plow
They tended pigs
And milked the cow
They cut the trees and built them homes
They cut the trees and planted corn
They worshiped God and took his land
When first America was born.

The pioneers were ruthless folk
(Sound of ax and smell of smoke!)
They mined the forests in their haste
They plowed the plains and laid them waste:
With gallant toil, they bled the soil.
They left it bleeding
Little heeding
As young America swept west.

What a land
What a land
Is left us by the pioneers!
For petty gains they plowed the plains,
The ancient gracious soil is dead.
They cut the trees; we build levees
To hold The River in his bed.
Yet we who live in after years
Do homage to our pioneers.
They left for us a grand tradition
Frontier days no longer known.
They left for us a nation's mission
Now America is grown.

We still adore
The land they claimed:
Can we restore
The land they maimed?
Replant the trees
Resod the grass
Restore the ancient fertile soil?
A careful, gallant, mighty task
For those who still shall dare to toil:
A thinking, planning Nation's task
To give a nation back its soil,
That those who come in after years
May say again with pioneers
What a land!
What a land!

L.S.M.

Chapter IV—UNDERGROUND WEALTH AND AN UNDERPAID INDUSTRY

We Look at the Coal Fields and Their People

In the Shadow of the Culm Heaps. Anthracite Bootleggers

More Culm Heaps. Legal Mining, Anthracite

In the Shadow of the War Brides. Bituminous

Chapter IV—UNDERGROUND WEALTH AND AN UNDERPAID INDUSTRY

We Look at the Coal Fields and Their People

In the Shadow of the Culm Heaps. Anthracite Bootleggers

WE REACHED THE CREST just before sundown and looked from our Ford window down into a strange valley known as a coal basin. Mountains, man-made mountains. Dark pyramids two, three, four hundred feet high, with white snow running in stylized streaks from tip to bottom. Huge breakers, gaunt and black, close to the mine entries. And, huddled in the bottom of the bowl, a drab town, drab from its covering of soot, drab from its lack of trees, drab as only an industrial mining town can be even when enlivened, as this one was, by the bulbous domes of Greek churches with their distorted double crosses. Yet the whole scene held a wild beauty from its very completeness and consistency, like a modernistic poster. We, who were used to the green hills of New England, to the endless waving grass of the prairies, to the gaudy grotesque rocks of the southwest desert, to the orchards and purple mountains of California, had never seen anything like this basin in the central anthracite coal fields of Pennsylvania. We had not been prepared for it by our up and down journey over the Folded Appalachians. We thought we knew Pennsylvania. But below us lay an unknown incredible world. Was it real? Did real people live there? What manner of folk had made those giant culm piles? What were men like who spent their days underground or in the violent noise of the monstrous breakers? What did women care about who hung their wash in the shadow of a culm heap? What did children play? And *where* did they play? Slag, cinders, drabness intensified by a sunset sky that glinted on the high windows of the breakers and turned to pink the streaks of snow on the incredible man-made cones.

Even as we watched, the lights came out one by one in the huddled houses. Homes. These were homes. It was suppertime. Families were gathering. Why had we been so emotional about breakers and culm heaps? They were only the stage set. The drama was a human drama. Men, women and children lived down there in Mahanoy City. The sky faded and the lights in the homes brightened as our little Ford made its way down the steep grade into the heart of the region of illegal or "bootleg" coal.

There had been signs of bootlegging along the route before our plunge down into the coal basin. All the way from New York we had met or passed a more or less steady procession of coal trucks, largely nameless, loaded going to the city and coming back empty. Then, too, in the smaller valleys we had seen an occasional fox hole in the side of the hill with one or two men at work and sometimes a truck getting loaded. And, of course, we had come armed with many facts gleaned from newspapers and reports; "4,000,000 tons of stolen coal are being sold annually," we had read in the righteously indignant leaflet of the Anthracite Institute. (A figure reduced to 2,400,000 by the Anthracite Coal Industry Commission.) "Poor preparation and short weight are only natural by-products of an industry that starts with theft and ends with deception." With the expected conclusion, "The moral lesson in all the foregoing is—Buy through Your Local Retail Coal Dealer."

The situation seemed clear. No wonder the owners had asked Governor Earle for military protection of their property. But in the *New York Times* of November 18, 1936, we read the headlines:

GOVERNOR EARLE ASSERTS SOCIALIZATION MAY END THE BOOTLEG COAL WAR

Federal Government will have to take over anthracite mines unless owners reopen enough pits to give jobs to the diggers.

Apparently the Governor thought it more than a case of simple "theft and deception." Again the *New York Times,* December 27, 1936, came out with big headlines, "Bottleg Coal Anarchy Baffles Pennsylvania," and reported that "Governor Earle Inspects a Problem":

So strongly organized are the outlaw miners that local politicos hold them in awe, sheriffs and peace officers refuse to act against them and the courts are powerless to give to the corporate owners of the property the protection to which they are entitled by law. This fact was dinned into the ears of Governor George H. Earle on his survey of the region this week by bootleggers, clergymen and business men of the locality, all of whom warned him that a resort to force would bring civil war to the community.

And on March 3, 1937, the *Times* headlines read: "State Board to Control Coal Is Discussed. Earle Administration Sees Commission as Remedy

for Bottlegging." In 1938 a recommendation from the Governor that the
federal government take over the anthracite coal fields, which lie entirely within the State of Pennsylvania. Then the final report of an expert
investigating commission, outlining a vigorous program under state
authority.

Yes, we had followed the newspapers. Even so, we were not prepared
for either the sights or the psychology of the region. We came to know
the drab town so well that its initial sense of unreality entirely disappeared. And we soon found that men, women and children in the shadow
of the culm heaps were fundamentally like those in green hills or in the
sun of flat prairies, in their love and pride of the place they called home.
A main street, flanked by small stores—grocery stores, hardware, men's
clothing, women's clothing with wares much like New York's, insurance, five-and-ten-cent stores—restaurants, a movie house, churches, and
four overpoweringly large banks dominating smaller buildings as medieval cathedrals did of yore.

The people inside the stores presented a singularly united response
to our questions. "Approve of bootlegging? Sure. It's saved the community. Why wouldn't we approve?" This with variations from grocer,
haberdasher, dentist, priest—and, yes, from bank presidents. The economic relationships of these dwellers in this little town emerged starkly.
And behind these relationships loomed the one overwhelming economic
fact—the whole community was dependent on the coal industry. "It's
the miners' money that keeps me and every store on the street going,"
explained the grocer in his back store office. Last year he had been the
head of the business men's organization, and he knew what he was talking about. "It's the most valuable land per square acre on God's earth,"
said the present head of the business men, leaning on the counter in his
men's furnishing store and looking with admiring eyes through the
open store door to the ever-present skyline of culm mountains. "Why
should it lie idle while the town goes on relief?" "I'm afraid it seems
like socialism or communism or something terrible," sighed the white-
coated dentist who was head of the Board of Education in a neighboring
town, "but I can't believe we should close our schools as well as our
mines." The same story, one after another. A common need had made
a common psychology. So when we sat in the dignified directors' room
at the bank, we were no longer surprised when the president explained:
"Yes, I approve of bootlegging coal, until an adjustment can be made
somehow and the mines be opened. We'd have no depositors if bootlegging stopped. Yes, we all know bootlegging is illegal. But perhaps there's

a higher right than the right of property and that is the right to live."
And the mahogany wainscoting did not crack or the marble pillars rock
at such a presidential utterance!

Here was a new social phenomenon. Local labor and capital on the same
side: miracle number one. And that side an illegal use of other people's
property for the good of the community: miracle number two. Could it
be that here was the first emergence of a new social pattern in America?
Superficially, this town and all the neighboring towns of this anthracite
coal field appeared to be evolving a social philosophy which placed community needs above the rights of the rugged individual.

Then we went with the bootleggers to their diggings. Vigorous, excited,
voluble officials and members of the Union of Independent Miners, some
old miners, some new recruits, largely neighborhood boys, all full of their
inventions, proud of their prowess, admiring their adventure. Hundreds
of holes had been sunk alarmingly close together in an area just outside
the town. Their preposterously small shafts lined with wood, with
nailed-on strips for ladders, went down from 50 to 200 feet. We peered
down. At the bottom, one or sometimes two men worked getting out the
coal and loading it into a garbage pail which was hauled to the surface
by a rope attached to the rear axle of a snorting old Ford anchored near
the mouth.

Close by each bootlegger's shaft was some kind of breaker, for anthracite must be broken into assorted sizes and washed for the market. No
two breakers were alike. Each inventor eagerly explained his own. Some
cracked the hard coal with a hammer, some in ice-cream freezers; then
they sorted it through graded sieves, washed it with a hose, and sold it
on the spot direct to truck drivers from Philadelphia or New York. We
who were used to experimental schools felt we were back with eleven-
year-olds! But we were haunted with memories of our earlier visit to
the near-by 200-foot-high breaker of a great company mine with its elaborate machinery and its violent noise; with memories of great elevators
with safety devices that had borne us to the lower levels where we wandered for miles underground through tunnels breezy with fresh pumped
air; with memories of coal cars running on tracks deep underground,
rising on the elevators and moving into the breakers.

So we had visited "the monster"? we were asked, which was the
indignant nickname by which everyone referred to this huge combination breaker which now did the work of eight old breakers, thereby
throwing out of work thousands of men. The old story of resistance to
mechanical improvements by those who suffer through the period of

adjustment. And yet within five minutes we were being told with exulta-
tion of an invention of one of the men for a handmade breaker. "We
used to need five men to work it and now we can manage with three!"
Thus, apparently, began the later and larger breakers run not by the
bootleggers who got the coal out of the ground but by a special group
who bought the bootleg coal, sold it to the truckers and so made their
middleman profits.

These bootleggers were full of the excitement of righteous indignation as well as of adventure. They took us to see the big companies' latest
development in the basin—"stripping" instead of digging. And it was a
ruthlessly efficient process. First great quantities of dynamite had been
buried in a long line running parallel and close to the cliff which
marked the edge of the coal basin and the beginning of the plateau.
When this dynamite was exploded the surface ground heaved and
cracked. So did the surface roads which happened to run across the line
of explosion. So did the near-by houses—company houses, to be sure, but
homes of human beings. One particular old lady, who had been forcibly
removed from the house at the time of the explosion but had returned
immediately, was now sufficiently recovered from her nervous shock to
enjoy our attention. She pressed souvenirs upon us—splinters of cracked
walls and even bric-a-brac that had been jostled from its shelf.

Close by yawned the final stage of the stripping process. After this
initial breaking up of the ground an incredibly huge steam shovel designed to move in hops like a dinosaur had dug up the surface soil to
the depth of 100 to 200 feet. Then a smaller steam shovel scooped up
the exposed coal. These deep ravines flanked by mountainous piles of
dirt had approached a small schoolhouse situated on a "barrier" (the
strip of coal left between holdings so that gas or water from one cannot penetrate to the other), devouring the playground and even the approach to the front door. The children played in the deep gorges that
had suddenly surrounded their school. But the bootleggers shuddered at
the mine owners' ruthless waste and indecent disregard of children's
rights.

A new social philosophy? Scarcely. Just a new set of individuals temporarily on top: those who had been the underdogs enjoying a brief exciting triumph—for bootlegging coal is an exciting adventure, requiring
courage, ingenuity and hard work. These men were functioning in a
pioneer pattern and with the pioneer psychology of little thought for the
future. Their own diggings were endangering future development, probably putting large areas permanently out of use. Their uncontrolled work-

ings had undermined roads. (We had not understood the collapsed roads we had passed with the ominous sign "Closed. Detour.") They called themselves a union. And so they were. But their illegal activities were jeopardizing the wages and work conditions in the larger union—the United Mine Workers—which they themselves had helped to establish. They had their own rules in their workings. They maintained that they were scrupulous about not using coal which the companies who owned the land had got to the surface or had begun to remove below. Apparently work was to be respected. But the coal itself in its native state they felt the community had a claim to, and they naïvely represented the community and the community accepted them as their representatives.

"The land was stolen in the beginning," they indignantly declared. Point number 1. "The people who make money out of the coal don't live here." Point number 2. "If the mine owners would spread the work among the men and the mines, they could keep the community going." Point number 3. "The companies claim they are losing money. Well, they would still be making money if they hadn't watered the stock." Point number 4. "They won't lease the land to us, so we have to bootleg or go on relief." Point number 5. "They pay extravagant salaries to the officials." Point number 6. "They don't try to create a market." Point number 7.

Boiled down, the community argument voiced by bootleggers and citizens alike seemed to be:

The anthracite region is a one-industry region. The community thrives or dies with this industry. The land is not good for much else, nor for factories except as cheap women workers are available (the wives and daughters of the miners). Therefore the community, for self-preservation, has a right to demand that the mines give their men a means of earning a livelihood either through employment by the legitimate owners, through government regulation or through bootlegging.

This main contention contains a philosophy. It may be the philosophy of economic self-interest which we have encountered before. It may be the philosophy inherited from the famous document of our ancestors that declared

these truths to be self-evident, that all men are created equal, that they are endowed by their Creator with certain unalienable Rights, that among these are Life, Liberty, and the pursuit of Happiness. That to secure these rights, Governments are instituted among Men, deriving their just powers from the consent of the governed. That whenever any

Form of Government becomes destructive of these ends, it is the Right of the People to alter or to abolish it, and to institute new Government, laying its foundation on such principles and organizing its powers in such form, as to them shall seem most likely to effect their Safety and Happiness.

At any rate, philosophy is not a thing that can be proved or disproved by facts. Some of the corollaries to this main contention are, however, subject to factual scrutiny. These communities maintain, for instance, that the industry is sick. No one can doubt this. Bootlegging itself is a symptom of sickness. But that is a different matter from specific diagnosis of the ill as the result of mismanagement of the industry (high official salaries, neglect of market, relation to railroads, watered stock). Diagnosis can come only after careful weighing of all the evidence. Here is a "why" we jotted down for later consideration.

These communities maintain that government can make some adjustment with the big companies which would be cheaper than putting whole communities on relief. Is this practical? The reader will find some basis for judging when he comes to pages 166 and 167.

But the main contention involves more than factual considerations. Indeed, it raises the whole question of the treatment of a great natural resource as unregulated private property. It raises the question of our American standards of living. It raises the question of government responsibility towards property and towards human lives. It raises the question of "Who owns the earth?" and of what "ownership" really means in our present American culture. Here again is the same question which our visit to the farm lands raised, expressed dramatically and perhaps more obviously because, unlike the farmers, the anthracite communities have become articulate. For answer to these questions we cannot conveniently refer the reader to a page in this or any other book. We shall give our own answers in the final chapter. Still, the answer lies for each reader in his own weighing of values and his attitude towards government responsibility.

MORE CULM HEAPS. LEGAL MINING, ANTHRACITE

These questions we took with us as we headed for the northern anthracite fields. We knew we should not find bootleg coal there, not because of higher principles but partly because the coal in these fields is too deeply buried for bootleg mining techniques and partly because these communities were too far from New York and Philadelphia to make trucking illegal coal pay. Again we wound up and down over more folded Appalachians across a stretch of barren flattish plateau denuded of trees and devoid of habitation. The plateau ended abruptly. Below us lay the long Wyoming Valley, a long narrow finger projecting into the plateau whose opposite level rim showed only a few miles across from us. There, suddenly, were the now familiar man-made conical mountains dug from the underground world which honeycombed the entire valley as far as the eye could reach. Just below us sprawled the city of Wilkes-Barre, spreading from skyscraper center to shanty suburbs. Everything, even at a distance, spoke of anthracite; and everything, we soon found, on nearer view spoke of a sick industry. We stopped to visit a small rural school on the rim of the plateau. Forty shy friendly children in charge of a young friendly teacher. "The children should go down to Wilkes-Barre for school," she told us, "as their fathers do for work. But we're afraid to send the school bus over Burning Mountain."

"Burning Mountain?"

"Yes, it's been burning about twenty years, I guess, at any rate as long as I can remember. They used to try to put it out. Now they just let it burn. I suppose it may cave in some day. I don't know."

And so we started down Burning Mountain. From cracks on every side rose clouds of steam and smoke. A dramatic man-made volcano. How much coal had burned up in this twenty-year-old fire? Could they ever burn coal in place and use the heat to make power? We wondered. And still we descended. More steam and smoke, acres—no, miles—of subterranean fires.

At the foot we came to the wretched houses of Georgetown with one rickety Community House manned by a courageous staff. We had not seen such slums in the bootleg region. And Georgetown proved typical of the outlying regions of this sprawling city ringed around with closed mines and with schools not yet closed but without salaries for their teachers. We never got over the sense that things had simply stopped, never got over a feeling that fear dominated these people, not merely the vast group on relief (21.9% in the whole anthracite region in 1935) but also those still with jobs (100,000 men in the whole anthracite region). We found that newcomers to Wilkes-Barre felt oppressed by this atmosphere of fear which dominated professional as well as industrial groups and seemed like a shadow cast by the few great coal companies who controlled the community in a life-and-death fashion. One of the companies took us through a show mine. Engineering efficiency which made the bootlegger contraptions seem grim jokes. Mechanical efficiency, yes, in a community desperate but cowed. The old line-up of hatreds between workers and mine owners splitting the community into social inefficiency.

The outlines of the picture grew sharper. Again a region of a single basic industry with supplemental silk mills and tobacco factories moving into the community of cheap women labor. Again a sick industry—closed or partly running mines. A monopolistic control of a natural resource by seven or eight companies who were still linked with the railroads in intangible ways, though open linking had been declared illegal. But here the resemblance to the southern fields stopped. Hopelessness instead of protest. Relief instead of bootlegging. Despair instead of impudent buoyancy. The union men were reticent about the bootleggers. We thought they sympathized, feeling that it might be their turn next, and yet resented an activity which jeopardized the hard-won union gains which gave good wages to the few employed. Bootlegging seemed more than ever a symptom of sickness, not a cure. How did one cure a sick industry? And whose patient should it be? The state's? The federal government's? Once more our questions trailed the need of a social philosophy.

In the Shadow of the War Brides. Bituminous

Was monopolistic control to blame? Would the anthracite industry have been better off if competition had functioned? Suddenly I was back in Scott's Run in the stranded mining towns of West Virginia. Here in the bituminous coal region monopoly had *not* been the pattern. What had competition done for the industry and for the mining communities where it had functioned? I have not been to Scott's Run for several years—not physically. Spiritually I go there often—perhaps I always shall. It is a little valley used some twenty years ago by Morgantown fishermen. The little brook, the Run, wandered down a green valley to the Monongahela. When I first saw Scott's Run some seven years ago, the brook had become the community sewer, flanked by privies which emptied direct into its waters. Children with boils on their legs played in it and then returned to their other playgrounds, the slag mountains which filled the narrow valley on either side. The privies have now been moved, though not yet does each boast of a door nor each family possess one to itself. Houses, if such they can be called, though many were not designed for household uses but only for shacks in which the miners could change their clothes, line the muddy street on the side not occupied by the railroad tracks and wander up the steep slopes. The uppermost are usually occupied by Negroes since they are the least desirable, being furthest from the pumps, the source of all water. The relief agency had supplied the most energetic households with newspapers and paste, so that a few houses have inside walls covered with newspaper, a slender stoppage of the cracks. Potato-sacking doors are not unknown. Saloons, an occasional church, a white school by the street and a Negro school high on the slope, an occasional company store, an occasional mine-company office, complete the habitations. For a brief time a nursery school for colored and white children, founded under the stimulus of the Federal Emergency Relief Administration, opened its doors, its dining room and its playground to the spindle-legged children and its sewing machines to their mothers. (When the state took charge of nursery schools, the colored babies were excluded by law.) Small garden patches clung to the steep hillside—the necessary requisite for obtaining relief and the original inspiration of resettlement plans to move these people to land where farms and gardens were possible. Indeed, such a plan was successfully carried out near by at Reedsville, where about a hundred families of once unemployed miners of Scott's Run now live on five-acre lots, farming or working in a small factory, their children attending a fine modern school and their wives learning many household arts such as home canning of vegetables—a thriving cooperative community, with Uncle Sam as a gradually disappearing landlord.

If in the surroundings of Wilkes-Barre one felt fear, at Scott's Run one felt apathy. Only a few grimy miners emerged daily from a few of the mine pits. Most mines were closed, probably permanently. Many were small—"war brides," they are called, opened to meet Europe's temporary demand for coal during the war and closed when the war market stopped. For it is easy to open a mine in the bituminous region. Unlike anthracite coal, which has been twisted and hardened by the folding of the mountains, bituminous coal lies in level sheets the edges of which are everywhere visible in the eroded valleys. It takes little capital and few men to dig into the side of the hill and hack out the soft coal. The farmers have their little fox holes for private supply. The "fly-by-nights" and the "snow birds"—small mines which open when prices are good and close when they are poor—abound in the soft-coal fields. And as it was easy to open the war-bride mines when the demand for coal was great, so, if the investment had not been large, it was easy to abandon them when the demand ceased. And as it was easy with the promise of good wages to tempt the neighboring farmers from their poor farms or to bring

IN THE SHADOW OF THE CULM HEAPS:
MAHANOY CITY

These man-made mountains in the anthracite region are the refuse that piles up around the coal breakers.

ILLEGAL MINING FOR ANTHRACITE

Homemade conveyor apparatus at a bootlegger's mine.

LEGAL MINING FOR ANTHRACITE

Coal breaker at a large railroad-owned mine.

A COMPANY TOWN IN WEST VIRGINIA

in Negroes or cheap foreign labor, so it was easy to abandon them even as the mines were abandoned.

Closed mines mean scarred hills and waste of capital. They also mean scarred lives and waste of people. Free competition? Perhaps it had kept the price of coal down for consumers, but it certainly had not prevented the soft-coal industry from deathly illness felt by both workers and owners. And by the communities, too, throughout these coal mines. In this land of rivers, pure drinking water is rare enough to be announced by a sign. One learns to watch for these signs "Pure Water" or often "Dangerous Water" as one enters a West Virginia town. Some of the larger mines were still running. Here the towns presented fairly comfortable company houses turned out on a standardized pattern, a well-equipped company store at which the miners had to buy or risk their jobs, even clinics and libraries and other signs of benevolent paternalism. Some of these mines were impressively well equipped. We were never allowed to see those that weren't. But even in these communities there was unemployment, and the relief rolls were crowded. And in the hill towns we found one Negro community with many out of work and the conditions of Scott's Run duplicated. Mellon owned this particular mine. At the time that Mr. Mellon was claiming income-tax exemption, these Negroes, employed only part of the year, were having their poll taxes deducted from their wages so as not to risk evasion. An irrelevant fact, perhaps, but dramatic. Rockefeller, Mellon, Morgan and other millionaires own mines in these stranded areas. Ironically, both abandoned mines and abandoned communities are left for West Virginia to cope with, though the wealth taken out of the West Virginia hills has enriched the mine owners of Pennsylvania and New York.

Here we have something in common with the anthracite coal industry and something with which we have become familiar in the farm lands. It goes by the big name of absentee ownership. Has this common method of owning the earth something to do with the sickness of these differing coal industries? Another "why" to be tackled later.

Far off to the west, where the Rockies abruptly rise from the plains, is another coal mine where another conception of ownership has been put into business practice. Josephine Roche, in her inherited mines, has tried an experiment in sharing her mines with the workers. Not only do the miners have a voice in determining their living and working conditions; they share in the profits earned by the mines. It seems to have worked, this experiment, not only in giving the workers a decent dignified work life, but in making money. "Buy Josephine coal" is a slogan in many a Colorado home.

So we have the picture. A beautiful land—anthracite in three basins of northern Pennsylvania, bituminous on the Allegheny Plateau stretching from Pennsylvania to Alabama and west under the prairies, appearing again where the western mountains begin, and valleys and plateaus —all scarred by man-made mountains of refuse and unsightly breakers or tipples which the people are so used to that they forget their ugliness. Gorgeous plateau rivers and little runs turned orange with polluted mine water, poisonous to fish, though small boys seem to swim therein and survive. Other rivers flowing sluggish and black with hard-coal dust. A sick industry, where unemployment started long before the depression and is lasting after other industries are reviving. Lost markets—lost to substitute fuels, or through mismanagement or through a type of organization inappropriate to present-day culture; an industry in the red. A powerful union among the anthracite miners and northern bituminous miners, making headway among the miners of the South; semimonopoly in anthracite (seven or eight big companies), and free competition in bituminous (8000 mine owners), and one little experiment in shared ownership in Colorado. Work so dangerous that miners can get insurance only at exorbitant rates. Stranded communities with 200,000 miners and their families looking to the government for relief; some small groups removed to resettlement projects. Fear, low standard of living, sickness, high death rate, children without shoes and so without schooling. Houses unsanitary for pigs holding two or three families. Company towns with the questionable benefits of paternalism. Coal—the basic resource of our industrial culture—plenty of it, good quality both hard and soft. A sorry picture—sorry to the eye and sorry to the heart. An unprofitable picture to workers and capital alike. A staggering responsibility for the country, for the government. How did we get this way? How was the coal industry developed? Who were the men who set the pattern? In what state of social thinking was our country when they flourished? We have had past glimpses of our country's development seen through the eyes of farmers. And the farmers caught glimpses of coal as its development affected their own problems. Set the clock back again, and this time revisit the coal fields themselves.

Chapter V—HARD AND SOFT COAL. HARD AND SOFT PEOPLE

History Lives in Present Coal

Before America Wanted Coal

The Industrial Pattern Develops

In the Hard-coal Lands
    Railroads Become Mine Owners
    Trouble in the Market; Trouble in the Field
    The Great Strike, 1902
    From the 1920's to the Present

Hard and Soft Coal: Two Industries or One?

The Smoke of Soft Coal Covers America
    The Actors in an Overdeveloped Industry: Railroads, Operators, Miners
    "Down the Canyon": Ludlow, 1913
    The World War and After
    The New Deal in Coal
    What Remains to Be Done?

Chapter V—HARD AND SOFT COAL. HARD AND SOFT PEOPLE

History Lives in Present Coal

Before America Wanted Coal

WILDERNESS RIVERS. Small canoes paddled by red-skinned guides slipping down wilderness rivers. Keen hunters' eyes searching the endless forest for wilderness animals, for places for trading posts where the pelts could be brought. Keen Jesuit eyes searching for heathen souls, for places where the holy cross, symbol of the Church, could be raised. Baptisms in the wilderness rivers. Rejoicings over the dead papoose who died in the faith, baptized in the wilderness river. Strange companions, these shrewd hunters and zealous-eyed monks, first white men to look upon a new country, charting the wilderness, writing in their diaries, pushing on and on down the great Ohio searching for wealth for man and souls for God. An entry in 1679 in the diary of one Father Hennepin, explorer-missionary, whose fanatic's eye scanned the river bank where a dark band showed among the variegated bands. "Traces of coal on the banks of the Illinois River."

Thus the eyes of explorers first saw the soft coal of America. Casually, indifferently, the world of Europe heard their reports. The struggling seaboard settlers heard of them too, but with equal indifference. Not yet had these homeseeking farmers any use for coal. Not yet, in any case, did they want to look behind the mountains. And it was behind the mountains, under the Allegheny Plateau and under the thousand-mile stretch of the Central Lowland drained by the Mississippi that the great soft-coal beds of America lay, waiting their day of use.

The homeseekers from the settlement of Pennsylvania were beginning to push in from the coast. From Philadelphia they had trekked south down the Great Valley which lay behind the Blue Ridge Mountains, a valley to rejoice these farmer hearts. From Philadelphia, too, they had pushed north up the Pennsylvania rivers to the less gracious valleys which ran like deep fingers into a wild and desolate plateau, valleys which held the only hard-coal deposits in America. A better land for trappers and hunters than for farmer folk. It was from these lonely men, Necco Allen and others, that the government of Pennsylvania first got reports of "black stone" which, they said, when heated long enough in their outdoor fires, burned with a slow steady glow. The government sent for specimens, handled the strange glistening lumps and marveled piously at the ways of God in a strange land. Then in 1748 these thrifty Pennsylvania Dutchmen voted the large sum of $2500 for buying "the Wilderness of St. Anthony," a tract of land thirty-five miles wide and one hundred and twenty-five miles long where stone coal was found.

The rumors spread. They reached distant Rhode Island and troubled the mind of a blacksmith, one Obadiah Gore. He would find out. Stone that would burn? Better than the tedious charcoal. And off went Obadiah in 1769 to the little settlement of Wilkes-Barre, whose citizens smiled incredulously as he gathered these useless black stones for his experiment. But they smiled again with a different smile when they saw the black stones glowing in his smithy as his bellows wheezed and sighed and sent a draught of air up and through the stones. "We can burn the whole valley," they thought. But that time had not yet come. Still, now and again, they gathered the strange substance. When the great rebellion came and the colonies united to cut the silver thread which bound them to their mother England, these valley folk burned their stone to fashion arms for their soldier-farmers. With the heat from the black stones they even forged nails, precious in a world of wooden pegs. But as yet the world had little need of their hard shiny black coal.

Then after the Revolution came more and more homeseekers trekking west. Some of these processions, first on trails and then on turnpikes, crossed the soft-coal lands of the Allegheny Plateau on the way to Pittsburgh. This plateau city, long a trading post, was by the end of the eighteenth century a great embarking point for the undeveloped West. (See map, page 46.) Across the plateau on either side of the slender turnpikes, Braddock's and Forbes' roads, the buffaloes still wandered; and along the trails left by their cleft hoofs, the Indians still stole. For the white homeseekers did not want the great plateaus. Not yet. These farmers and lumbermen still passed the plateaus by, leaving them to the Indians for hunting grounds. Only a few stopped, forming a thin line of settlements clustered around protecting forts.

North of the plateau went the leveler route to the west. The procession of homeseekers that, after the Revolution, headed north up the

Hudson and then west up the valley of the Mohawk found better farming lands than did the processions that crossed the Allegheny Plateau. Many homeseekers stopped in the fertile Mohawk Valley, where once the Indians of the Five Nations had blocked the way; others went farther west to the Lakes and stopped around Lake Erie and Lake Ontario. Both thin lines of settlements, through northern valley or over the plateau, were largely made up of farmers. For the young United States was still primarily an agricultural nation. And what cities there were, were essentially commercial: trading, not industrial centers.

There were exceptions, however. In poor agricultural regions like New England, mill towns grew up, run by the power of waterfalls. But coal was also used. Since 1709 some soft coal had been made into coke and used for the smelting and manufacture of iron. Yet in 1850 there were only four furnaces burning coke. The peak in soft-coal production for coke did not come until some sixty years later, by which time coke had assumed a major role.

Hard coal, too, was used for smelting as early as 1812. But its use was unimportant until 1840. Most of the iron was still smelted by charcoal. The trees of the New World seemed endless. So the forests turned into charcoal for the 558 furnaces, 396 forges and bloomeries and the 210 rolling mills which are listed in 1858. Then came the Civil War. And with the triumph of the North came industries, and with industries coal came into its own.

THE INDUSTRIAL PATTERN DEVELOPS

For some twenty years before the North faced the South in its bitter four-year war, a new breed of Americans had been dreaming a new dream for themselves and for their country. It was a dream that had started America's smoking chimneys and turning wheels; a dream that was to breed the great American railroad men, industrialists and bankers, that was to lay the foundation of the fabulous fortunes of Gould, Hill and Vanderbilt; of Armour, Andrew Carnegie and John D. Rockefeller; of J. P. Morgan and Andrew Mellon; a dream that was to open up the coal fields, then the oil fields, the iron and copper mines; a dream that was to build the railroads and help to settle the West; a dream that was to bring a new economic pattern to our country. Beginnings of this pattern appeared in the 1830's; from the 1850's on, it grew with mushroom rapidity.

Andrew Carnegie, John D. Rockefeller, John Pierpont Morgan, Armour and Gould were of age to enlist in the Civil War. They did not. They

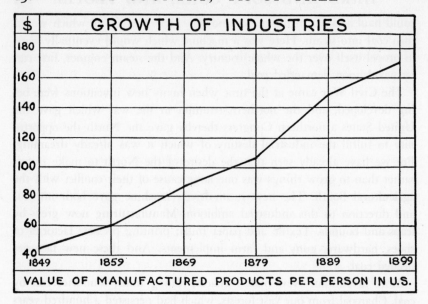

were of age to be drafted when conscription came. They were, but they paid substitutes to fight in their places. Not that they were pacifists who felt that war was a social crime and were willing to suffer imprisonment rather than kill their fellow men. No. They were the same men who in their later years profited greatly by other wars. During the years of their young manhood, years which racked and nearly wrecked their country, these future barons of industry were already laying foundations of business, of trade, of an industrial culture to be added to agricultural United States. Some ten years later their dreams came to fulfillment.

In Europe, particularly in England, a new machine pattern had been developing. Manufacturing centers with smoking chimneys and workers tending machines in factories were growing fast. The great Industrial Revolution was launched which was to transform all Western culture. It reached us later than Europe. But when it came it developed with characteristic American speed. To our early agricultural culture, we added an industrial culture. The early mills were run by water power. Then, in the 1850's, came coal. It soon became a basic commodity. The eyes of America now turned to the coal fields. For the Industrial Revolution was in a real sense the Mineral Revolution.

Now in many lines came new inventions, speeding up the new machine culture. Above all, the *steam engine*. Here was a new tool which could haul and lift in the mines and out. Here was a tool which would turn coal into steam. Here was a machine which would eventually learn to propel itself over the whole country. And the steam engines, first run by wood, soon demanded coal.

The Civil War came at the time when many new inventions were being developed, and the northern triumph in the war which gave the United States a northern Congress thereby gave the North the opportunity to fulfill the industrial destiny of which it was already dreaming. For we have already seen that the desire of the North to make things rather than to grow things was one large cause of their conflict with the agricultural South. The new steam-driven machine gave both impetus and direction to this industrial ambition. Manufacturing now grew by leaps and bounds. Textile and paper mills; printing presses; factories of shoes, hardware, guns and farm implements. And these new factories needed coal.

More inventions. New blast furnaces, rolling mills, foundries run by coal. Charcoal from our vast forests, which had persisted a hundred years after it had ceased to be a fuel in England, gradually gave way to coke. Coal and iron. Coal close to iron, close to the river roads which could carry these bulky loads. The coal lands now held a new opportunity for the pioneering spirit. The industrial pioneers responded.

To which of the coal lands did they turn first? Which did they know? They had long known both the coal and iron of the Allegheny Plateau, where the old routes led to Pittsburgh; and the plateau cities along this route had been the home of iron works since about 1800. But more, much more coal was needed now. And as yet they could only guess how far under the vast and inaccessible Allegheny Plateaus the bituminous fields stretched. So now they turned to the wild narrow valleys of the anthracite basins. From these closest fields this strange new hard coal could be piled on barges and floated down the rivers to the iron of eastern Pennsylvania. Thus most of the earliest iron works, and later the great chimneys of the first steel rolling mills, foundries, and blast furnaces, rose in the eastern Appalachians of Pennsylvania; and the Lehigh, the Susquehanna, the Delaware rivers became filled with rafts as the culm heaps began to grow in the hard-coal fields.

The machine pattern was spreading. The demand for manufactured goods grew apace. The pioneer self-sustaining pattern waned; and people of America looked to factory-made clothes, household and farm equipment, tools of all kinds, clocks, locks, and gadgets to supply their needs.

Based on maps by A. K. Lobeck in "Airways of America" and "Atlas of American Geology"

(1) The Northern Basin is the Wyoming Valley, containing the cities of Scranton (north) and Wilkes-Barre (south). The more complicated fields to the south are sometimes spoken of as (2) the Middle Basin (the northern lobe containing Hazelton, the western lobe or Shamokin Basin containing Shamokin) and (3) the Southern or Pottsville Basin, which contains Pottsville. The towns are marked by letters. The anthracite basins lie at the northern tip of the Folded Mountain Region where the Allegheny Front (the edge of the Allegheny Plateau) breaks into complicated irregularities. West of them is the northern tip of the Great Valley. Their total area is less than 500 square miles, but they contain all of the anthracite in the United States. Note how the older portions of the rivers cut through the mountains in water gaps, whereas the younger portions run down the valleys.

Increased demand, increased factories; increased factories, increased demand. And this all meant more coal for the steam-driven engines of the factories. To the bituminous land, then, to get the needed coal.

Men now pushed back into the deep-ravined plateau, under which lie the twenty-nine horizontal layers of soft coal. North, up the Allegheny River; south up the Monongahela, up the Youghiogheny, still farther south to the Kanawha and the Tennessee; until the hills of the wide plateau were dotted with heaps, diggings of pioneer miners, and the wilderness rivers of the plateau with their many forks and banded ravines held a stream of floating rafts piled with cargoes of soft coal. In from the Great Valley came more people; in to the head of navigation at Cumberland, Maryland, where the valleys and the ridges cease and the plateau begins. Coal in wagons lurched over the hilly roads to the docks of Cumberland, was piled on rafts and floated down the Potomac. Canals were built to shorten these river roads or to let the rafts down the too steep grade. Coal from the faraway unsettled places was finding its way to market—to factories and to homes.

The line of new smoking chimneys followed the old routes to the west across the Great Valley, over the plateau to Pittsburgh, and along the easy grade of the Mohawk Valley road to the west and around the Great Lakes. (See map, page 46.) Over the young cities of Pittsburgh and Chicago hung a sun-concealing screen of smoke, and dainty ladies threw aside their grimy white gloves after a few hours' wear. America's pattern of smoking chimneys and turning wheels was launched.

Coal must be brought to the new factories. Food must be brought to the new industrial towns. Wagons on wilderness roads, rafts on wilderness rivers were too slow. The business North got busy. The eyes of the world and those of young America's new industrial pioneers turned to the development of another of the recent revolutionary inventions. The steam engine had become a locomotive. The era of railroads began, railroads which not only were to open up the new country but were to deepen the new pattern of business organization. Without railroads, the country was really only a group of regions loosely tied together by a common faraway government. With railroads, a nation emerged. A colossal task, this building of America's railroads, accomplished with incredible speed—from 30,000 miles of tracks in 1860 to 164,000 in 1890! As early as 1869, the golden spike was driven in the last rail near Ogden, which united the East and West. The tracks had spanned the continent.

The noisy little steam engines left a trail of smoke and soot from wide-spreading smokestacks as gleaming tracks pushed westward and criss-crossed the more settled East. We know how they brought western farm crops east, and eastern manufactured goods west. They also opened up the coal lands. They pushed up the valleys of the same rivers on which the coal barges floated—the Lehigh, Lackawanna, Susquehanna—into the narrow valleys of the hard coal. They pushed across the Allegheny Plateau following more raft-laden rivers, the Allegheny, Monongahela, Kanawha, Tennessee. They pushed across the prairie land where coal lay under farms, across to the great mountains where again soft coal lay close under the ground. Train wheels were turning in the new country.

Coal cars were moving to factories, power houses; to cities and villages to east, north, west and south.

But railroads are costly to build. No single man had enough money. It needed business pioneering to get capital to stretch tracks over the vast reaches of young United States. The railroad men responded. They utilized a kind of organization that worked with the money of many people, corporations with bonds and stocks sold to people who had money to invest. So another kind of absentee owner developed—the stockholder. But the railroad pioneers wished to keep control of the corporations in their own hands, or at least in the hands of the few. Yet they had constant need for raising additional capital in large quantities. To meet this situation, the railroad corporations developed new powers of control of the rights of their stockholders, both of those already holding stock and of prospective buyers. Not merely was the technical conduct of the business to be under managerial control but the rights of the stockholders as well. At first the railroads sold stock chiefly in the localities to be served by them. These did not furnish enough money to finance their costly undertakings. Banks and capitalists in foreign countries began buying bonds of the United States railroads. Thus, though the stock and bond holders really owned the railroads, they never saw them and usually knew nothing about the way they were run. Theirs was a pen connection with the industry. Over the United States and England these stockholders signed their names to checks and received their bonds or stock certificates. And far away in the companies' city offices, officers signed dividend checks for their absentee owners. The era of pen scratching had begun.

Thus through manipulation of the neat business device for using the money of many people and still keeping the power in the hands of the few, railroad builders crisscrossed the vast regions of America with rails. These "Builders of a Nation" were shrewd business men. They were shrewd enough to get the government at Washington to help them, and Washington was shrewd enough to offer big baits to induce railroad building. It was when the tracks were stretching westward that the railroads got those colossal land grants—20, 30, 40 miles on either side of the shining new tracks. And the railroad barons became land speculators. Later, in the 1870's, came new figures on the railroad scene. Men like Gould and Fiske who wrecked railroads in order to make money through the panics they induced on the stock exchange. In railroad history they added the name of "Robber Barons" to the proud name of "Builders of a Nation."

In the Hard-coal Lands

In the hard-coal lands the railroads played a very special role; indeed, they became the leading lady in the anthracite drama. For they became not merely *carriers* but *owners* of the coal lands. It is a little area where anthracite is found, less than 500 square miles. It was strategically placed both for the great cities of New York and Philadelphia and for the fast-growing steel works for which, until about 1875, hard coal provided the best fuel. In the new industrial era, anthracite was therefore of overwhelming importance. The ownership of the anthracite basins meant wealth. Who would get possession?

Many small operators had found their way to the anthracite basins and had gradually bought up the land. It was the part of the railroads to carry out the coal of those hundreds of small operators. Or was it? Why, thought the railroads, be content with such a small role? Why not be operators themselves and carry out their own coal? Control these small coal basins and you controlled this whole important industry. But how get possession?

RAILROADS BECOME MINE OWNERS

Franklin B. Gowan, one-time District Attorney of Schuylkill County, by 1870 president of the Philadephia & Reading Railroad, had the answer. His railroad served a circular area around the anthracite fields with a radius of about one hundred miles. The area was owned by hundreds of small operators. Gowan's stockholders were largely British investors. They approved the plan which the ambitious and eloquent Gowan proposed; and Gowan went into action, at first in the northern anthracite fields.

His plan was simple. He used the power of the turning wheels which hauled the coal. He raised freight rates. Who was there to prevent? And he withheld coal cars. Who was there to prevent? The small operators were caught. They could not get their coal to market—or if they did, they were forced to pay freight charges which took away their profit. So they sold their coal lands to the Philadelphia & Reading Coal & Iron Company. By the latter part of 1871 this company owned about 70,000 acres of coal lands, and within the course of a few years it acquired 30,000 additional acres. Its holdings were then approximately one-third of the coal lands of the whole anthracite basin. These holdings of the Philadelphia & Reading Railroad are now the chief field of the bootleggers' workings (65%).

Yes, Gowan had the answer as to how to gain possession of the hard-coal lands. By his answer and that of the other railroads that followed the same plan, the small operators practically disappeared. And with their disappearance, free competition in the anthracite fields disappeared. Semimonopoly became and remained the region's economic pattern.

But all was not well with the Philadelphia & Reading in spite of its success in driving out the small operators. In the first place, it had rivals—particularly the Pennsylvania and the Lehigh Valley railroads, which were playing this same game of buying up the coal lands. Up went the price of land. In order to keep these rivals out, the Philadelphia & Reading bought more and more land at high prices, some with good coal reserves, some with poor or none. The money for these land purchases was raised by mortgaging the railroad. And on good and bad land alike, the company had to pay interest and taxes. The clever plan had over-reached itself.

In the second place, the despised soft coal was stealing the market from hard coal.

TROUBLE IN THE MARKET; TROUBLE IN THE FIELD

About 1875 coke, whose use had long been known, was becoming popular. Coke, made from bituminous coal. Uneasiness spread through the hard-coal fields, where now the culm heaps and breakers covered northern, central and southern fields. Coke, made from dirty lumps of soft coal, could now make a hotter fire than clean hard anthracite itself, and did not impede the blast in the new larger and taller furnaces. New-fangled ovens shaped like beehives were built in long rows by the plateau rivers. Each sent out a curl of smoke from the top of its beehive, with now and then a spurt of flame. And soon sprang up the plateau coke towns of Pennsylvania—Connelsville, Johnstown, McKeesport—all feeding to Pittsburgh, meeting place of the northern plateau rivers where the great Ohio begins. Coke for the iron dug from the new mines around Lake Superior. Coke for iron furnaces. Coke for the rolling mills, where for years men had shoveled the gleaming hard coal into the fires. Anthracite had lost its chief market. Would it find another? Would it again become a growing industry? Not for fifteen years. Not until still another invention came, a new kind of furnace for city homes, which could burn anthracite broken into small fragments. Then stove, egg or chestnut coal was fed from overhead bins into waiting wagons and pulled by sturdy horses, three abreast, to houses all over the cities, dumped down chutes clattering into basements and finally shoveled into the new furnaces of city homes. Still later, in the 1890's, came another invention. Even smaller sizes of anthracite could now be blown into furnaces to make steam. Then culm banks were picked over, washeries installed; and the great heaps, discarded as refuse from the breakers of years ago, were once more sifted through graded sieves, washed, loaded into cars, transported to the factories and actually sold. Sold as rice or buckwheat. But it was fifteen years or so after coke became a threat that these new markets were found for the clean hard coal.

Still more troubles plagued the anthracite industry, troubles that lay not in the business offices of the railroad-mine operators, not in the market, but in the coal fields themselves. These were bloody and violent days when Gowan and his successors ruled. For the resourceful Gowan gradually developed a special mode of life for the workers and their families in order to keep dividends flowing to his British and American stockholders.

The situation as it finally evolved was simple. The company controlled everything in the towns. Railways, mines, of course; but also telegraph lines, iron works, houses, stores, schools, police. What could a miner earn? The company looked at its balance sheet and kept wages low. How many hours? The company paid dividends, 10%, 15%, 20% and kept hours long. Where could he live? In a company house with rent subtracted from his wages, in a crowded town with open country all around kept empty for future mine workings. Where could his wife buy her groceries, her clothes? At a company store, with prices kept high for additional company profit. Could a man control his working conditions in the mine? Could a sick child get a doctor's service? Only if the company said so. And the company's mind was fixed on keeping the returns to absentee investors high, not on the lives of workers and their families. Low wages. Many accidents. Inadequate or no insurance. Low standard of living. Misery. Such was the company-town pattern.

Why didn't the men get other work? There was none, and is none, in an isolated one-industry community. Why didn't they fight? They did. Men banded together in secret lodges and brotherhoods. But company spies entered even there. They tried strikes. But the company had armed Iron and Coal Police to shoot them down. The violence of those days, saloon fights, murdered men in mines, strikes, hanged miners, brought few gains to the workers. Yes, they fought; but often enough it was with each other. For even among themselves there was little unity. Who were they, these miners and their families? And how had they come to the hard-coal basins? For answers we must again look to the railroads. The railroads had brought the workers to the fields.

More inventions. Wheels were turning on the sea as well as on land. That long procession of ships that for two centuries had headed west towards the land of promise had changed from sails to engines which pounded as the wheels turned in their small holds. On the wave-washed decks and smothered in the steerage quarters, people were headed for the hard-coal lands. First had come the Welsh and English, trained miners seeking their old trade in new fields in the towns of the Quakers and Dutch of Pennsylvania. Then, in 1847, the potato crop failed in Ireland and the decks were filled with Mikes and Paddies and merry gray-eyed Irish girls and curly-headed babies. They, too, had heard of the promise of the coal lands from the railroads that paid their fares to their new jobs. Such were the men who banded into lodges and brotherhoods, who fought the railroads in the bloody days of Gowan.

Later came workers from Austria, Hungary, Poland, Russia and Italy. In the late 1880's more and more of the crowded steerage folk spoke strange guttural Slavic tongues, and the men were stocky and strong, and the ample women smiled at their many children. All Europe seemed crowding the ships, crowding the trains, heading for the hard-coal lands. Bulbous domes of the Greek churches began to appear in Wilkes-Barre, Scranton, Shenandoah, Hazelton, Pottsville, Shamokin, Mauch Chunk, Mahanoy City, and the host of small towns throughout the anthracite basins. Polish quarters; Russian quarters; Austrian, Hungarian, Italian quarters—where no word of English was spoken. A long line of Slavs went to the mine pits. Fewer and fewer of the early Pennsylvania Dutch. The Welshmen and English became superintendents; the Irish turned political. More and more the careful Slavs held the pick and ax.

Soon there were too many workers for the jobs. Too many languages and habits for common understanding. Miners sit on their doorsteps more than half the working day. Wives count the earnings of their husbands: $22 a month; $500 a year. Wives count the needed shoes for the five, six, eight, ten children, the needed bread for the hungry little stomachs; count the accidents to their neighbors and wonder when their time will come. Wives and disabled men wonder again why insurance companies will not insure miners and why a leg is worth so little and a son only $200 in the reckoning of the companies. Send the children to get a job; that is the only answer. Pretend that Johnny is over fourteen so that he can tend the door inside the mine. He'll bring us 67½ cents a day. He can be spared from home for his ten-hour day. Pretend that Willy is over twelve, so that he can pick slate outside the mines in the breakers. He'll bring 27 cents or, if he's very quick, 39 cents a day. He, too, can be spared for his ten-hour job. There they sit, thousands of boys picking impurities from the coal as it passes by on the belt. They are doing their bit to help the pens to scratch a higher dividend that year.

One day a new model of car rolls into the mine entry. "These cars must be made of live oak," says one miner as he measures it with his eye. For the car grows in size from year to year. But it has to be filled for the same wage. Another day the men must load the car six inches above the rail "to cover the impurities we have to pick out of the coal," they are told. Another day they are told to load nine inches above the rail. At this mine the men are paid by the carload. At another mine they are paid by the ton. But the ton grows even as the car grows at the other mines. In the market a ton is still 2240 pounds, but at the mine it is 3190 pounds. But jobs are scarce. A docking boss inspects each car. "Take off 4%, 5%, 6% for impurities," he rules. The miners get together, talk, complain and go back to work. Jobs are scarce. The men stagger home after their ten hours underground. The engineers and firemen stay twelve hours. Then comes Sunday, the historic day of rest. "It's my twenty-four-hour shift," say half the men. Glad to have work; for jobs are scarce and company-store prices are high. In two weeks comes pay day. They take their en-velopes. Empty! They have paid for the company doctor's fee, for rent of the company house, for food at the company store, for company-bought powder, for tools. For their work most have drawn a "white horse," as they call an empty envelope. But jobs are scarce, and the pens have to sign dividends for the stockholders.

The motley group that the railroads had brought to the hard-coal lands did not melt immediately into brotherhood in this section of the "melting pot of the world." Nationality factions, religious factions, job factions. Factions which were encouraged by operators, who feared collective pro-test. Yet this group had common grievances and a common interest in protecting their jobs. And to them as early as 1842 came an idea, still little developed in America, an idea that was to become a major issue in the rapidly developing fight between the railroad operators and the workers. The idea was a union. The first feeble attempt of the anthracite miners to improve their wages and living conditions through organization—the first coal strike in 1842 near Shenandoah—was a failure. But the idea per-sisted and revived, and suffered again and again under the attacks of company pens and company police. After the destruction of the Miners' and Laborers' Benevolent Association in 1875 it lay dormant for nearly twenty years.

Also in the northern bituminous fields of Illinois, Indiana, Ohio and Pennsylvania the idea of organization had been gathering desperate men into groups demanding this and that change from the operators. There, as in the early attempt in the anthracite basins, the operators refused. Now in 1897 a strike was declared in the soft-coal lands. Only 10,000 members of the seven-year-old United Mine Workers. The men were out twelve weeks. They won. They won their demands. More precious and more startling, they *won recognition of the union.* The miners had established the right to come together into an organization of their own choosing and with their own leaders.

Then in 1899 came John Mitchell, young, cultivated, handsome, the new president of the United Mine Workers, destined to be loved and reviled through his brief ten years of office. He came to the anthracite basins sent by the successful young union of the northern bituminous fields to get members in the hard-coal fields. Soft- and hard-coal miners were sometimes rivals in trade. For a strike in the bituminous field could be broken if homes or factories turned to the use of anthracite when there was a shortage of soft coal. Did they not have a common fight to wage? Should they not join in a common union?

Why not? Why not? The union had succeeded in its first strike in the soft-coal fields, why not in the hard-coal basins? It was hot July when the convention of the United Mine Workers met in the shadow of the growing culm piles of Hazelton. They represented only 8000 members distributed among 144,000 anthracite workers. Jobs were still scarce and white horses still common. Some unsuccessful attempts to meet the operators. Then strike was declared on September 17. The anthracite men went out; the bituminous miners sent them money. Eight thousand members of the United Mine Workers in the hard-coal fields. But 129,600 men and boys quit work within two weeks: 90% of all the workers. Perhaps . . . perhaps . . .

A hundred and twenty thousand voters, thought Senator Mark Hanna as he sat at the headquarters of the National Republican Committee: 120,000 voters, and the election approaching. Something must be done about this strike. And there are many loyal Republicans among the operators who must wish to see McKinley elected. Something must be done about this strike.

On October 3 the men crowding the company store read a notice announcing 10% increase in wages. For how long? they asked. The notice did not state. What about the other demands? The notice said nothing. They voted to continue the strike.

A hundred and twenty thousand voters, thought Chairman Hanna. Something must be done about this strike. On October 17 the men read another notice: 10% increase in wages; reduction in price of powder, which the men had to buy at the company store. The union was making progress, though not yet recognized. The men went back to work on October 20. But they knew that this was a truce, not a victory.

Not until 1916 did the union in the hard-coal fields win recognition. Before that came many fights. In 1902 came the Great Strike which shook all America.

THE GREAT STRIKE, 1902

The arena for the fight seemed to be the isolated anthracite basins of northern Pennsylvania. Here was the coal and here were the miners, and here were the communities whose very existence depended on the mines according to the familiar pattern of a one-industry region. Here, in the actual fields, were the fighters on one side: the workers—largely Welsh, English, Irish and Slavs—the men who mined the coal, whose wages constituted the major cost of the mining operations and the basic support of the whole community; the men who had been brought to this country by the railroad owners of the mines and shipped straight through to the anthracite fields, they or their fathers. Supporting them by funds were the miners in the bituminous fields.

On the other side were the railroads that had shrewdly bought up much of the anthracite fields and were now the great operators as well as the exclusive carriers. Directly this side controlled wages, hours and conditions of work for the miners on the other side; thus indirectly controlled the health and well-being of nearly every man, woman and child in the coal basins.

But the list of the dramatis personae is not yet complete. For back of the railroads, back of many big industries in the United States, was appearing a new and strategic group—the big bankers. This new actor who had entered the drama in the anthracite fields when Gowan collapsed and the Philadelphia & Reading went into receivership cast a shadow over the whole struggle in the anthracite fields from 1885 on. The fight was fought in the arena of Wall Street as truly as in the arena of the mine pits.

1885. The great man sat at his desk. One knew that he was a great man not so much by what he did as by the attitude of others towards him. For this heavy face with its ponderous nose was already well known and feared in the world of finance and railroads. On the desk lay the documents relating to the Philadelphia & Reading Railroad which had recently gone into bankruptcy. Leases and deeds of purchases. Contracts in perpetuity. That was satisfactory to the great man. Capital must be protected if it were to run the risks of expansion. Ledgers and reports, dividend payments, taxes, deeds of sale. And a document providing for a reorganization of the railroad, creating a voting trust of five members which was to run for five years and take over the voting powers of the stockholders. From Wall Street outside his bank came the clatter of wheels and horses' hoofs. From inside, the shuffling of papers, sharp short questions, prompt answers. Finally, the scratching of a pen. J. Pierpont Morgan, banker, financier, inheritor of wealth, dweller in New York City, chief member of the voting trust, had gained control of the Philadelphia & Reading Railroad and of a vast domain in the anthracite coal fields. Thus for the hard-coal lands began a new era of pen scratching. Those pens of Wall Street which are surely mightier than the sword and which played such an important role in the great strike of 1902.

Companies against workers. Wall Street against isolated anthracite towns. The stage was set. In 1902 strike was declared, after arbitration had been refused by the operators. The big operators were prepared. And with them stood the railroads (when they were not the same), refusing to carry coal for independent companies. Stockades and barbed-wire fences had been thrown around many collieries, vast places built for storing coal were filled. Three thousand Coal and Iron Police and a thousand secret operatives were on hand. Guns, flashlight cameras. Yes, the operators were prepared. The miners were prepared, too. They flooded some of the mines. No scab should work there! They organized a boycott against all who supported the operators, a boycott which penetrated the mills, schools and stores, and which brought into being an indignant Citizens' Alliance at Wilkes-Barre.

Gowan had been gone from the office of the president of the Philadelphia & Reading for seventeen years. His post was now held by President Baer, friend of President Truesdale of the Delaware, Lackawanna & Western and of the mighty J. P. Morgan, just returned from Europe. A safe man. A sound man, this President Baer, who could read his Bible as well as his balance sheets. Had he not told the reporters who had asked him if peace were near: "The great peacemakers, the members of the Civic Federation, will try to make peace. Blessed are the peacemakers for they are the children of God." And though these children of God had not yet brought about peace, President Baer's faith was unshaken. In the *New York Times* appeared his reply to W. F. Clark, a Wilkes-Barre photographer who wrote him begging him "as a Christian" to make some slight concession to the strikers and "thus earn the blessing of God and the thanks of the nation":

I see you are evidently biased in your religious views in favor of the right of the working man to control a business in which he has no other interest than to secure fair wages for the work he does. I beg of you not to be discouraged. The rights and interests of the laboring man will be protected and cared for, not by the labor agitators, but by the Christian men to whom God in His infinite wisdom has given control of the property interests of the country. Pray earnestly that the right may triumph, always remembering that the Lord God Omnipotent still reigns and that His reign is one of law and order, and not of violence and crime.

Strange that these pious words should incense the striking miners! A sound man, thought the operators, the pen wielders, and the Iron and Coal Police.

It was Sunday, October 12, 1902. The pens had stopped scratching to observe God's Holy Day. Their owners in New York City had donned Prince Albert coats and gleaming top hats, and with their full-skirted wives and daughters had walked down Fifth Avenue to the Marble Collegiate Church. Secure and sedate, they sat in their accustomed and high-priced pews in the sanctified dim light of the stained-glass windows. Then came the voice of their pastor, the Reverend Dr. David James Burrell. The struggle of the coal fields had reached even the pulpit:

The time has come to say frankly that they [the labor unions] are not fighting for the rights of labor, for the freedom of the workingmen. There are many men in the ranks of the union today who are unable to do it. They are the cowards of the situation. They are afraid to cut loose and declare their rights. They are not indeed led as mercenaries to "crimson glory and undying fame"—they are merely slaves who cannot call their souls their own. They fighting for the rights of labor? No! a thousand times no! They are, in fact, arrayed against the fundamental rights of honest toil . . . the seventeen thousand independents today are working behind barricades maintaining the right guaranteed in the preamble to the Declaration of Independence, the right to life, liberty, and the pursuit of happiness. I sing the praises of that heroic 17,000 who stand today as brave vindicators of the rights of labor.

The congregation filed down the aisle as the tremulous organ notes rolled out the closing paean. Top hats were lifted, long skirts were gathered up in gloved hands. "Pleasant day. Good sermon." "Yes. A sound man is Dr. Burrell." "Yes, a sound man. Pleasant day." Thus the Church sanctioned the support of scab labor thirty-six years ago.

There was turmoil in the White House—more than the usual turmoil that reigned wherever President Theodore Roosevelt trod with vigorous step. His mail brought more and more protests and appeals from a public that dreaded an eastern winter without coal. The collieries must be opened. And even the "17,000 heroes" behind the company barricades, whose praises Dr. Burrell had sung, could not run the mines. The President sent for J. P. Morgan and his partner Robert S. Bacon. He talked with John Mitchell. His teeth flashed. His mind flashed. His big stick flashed. And, finally, a Commission of Arbitration was accepted by both sides. Ten percent increase in pay, a reduction in the working day from ten to nine hours. But no recognition for the union. Was it a victory? Had John Mitchell betrayed his men? Had J. P. Morgan lost a point? The public who bought the coal did not know.

FROM THE 1920's TO THE PRESENT

The public got used to strikes in the hard-coal fields, usually brief except in 1922 when the soft-coal miners joined in a strike which lasted five and a half months. The public got used to reading of new wage agreements: 1906, 1909, 1912; 1916, when the anthracite workers finally won recognition of the union; 1917, two this year; 1918, the boom years of the war; 1920, 1922, 1925. They read in 1923 that the Supreme Court had declared that the railroads and the mine operators must be separated. But they read also in 1925 the report of the U. S. Coal Commission (appointed by the President following the great strike of 1922 to investigate the coal industry) which said:

The fundamental evil of the anthracite industry is that of monopoly—the treatment of limited natural resources as if they were like other private property. Reliance on competition without supervision has resulted in a permanent level of high prices, above which extortionate increases were made whenever a suspension of mining or other disturbances gave rise to the phenomenon of premium coal . . . there is a rising flood of costs and of prices which does not recede with the fall in the prices of commodities in general and which does not yield to such measures, entirely justifiable and desirable for other reasons, as the separation of mining from the railroads.

The public got used to high prices for anthracite, too, and comparatively well-off consumers began to buy in bags. The high prices made
them notice the new advertisements. Soft coal was cheaper. So through
the twenties into the thirties in the cities of New York and Boston they
got used to more smoke, to dirty curtains and grimy children. For the
second time in its history anthracite was losing its market to soft coal.
The public got used to being told that the eight great anthracite companies were in the red. How could that be, when prices were so high?
They even got used to the idea of oil furnaces. Papers and magazines
were full of alluring remarks. "Cheaper, cleaner fuel." No need to shovel
coal any more.

So the anthracite market declined, and for a number of reasons. In the
first place, the industry was mismanaged; it made no effort to develop
by-products, and it was out of contact with its market. Secure in the
belief that they had a monopoly of an indispensable product, the companies made no effort to *sell*. Why should they? The public had always
bought. Secondly, railroad freight rates had always been higher for coal
than for other commodities. When coal companies were under the management of railroads, they deliberately kept the margin of profits at the
producing end small to give support to the operators' statements that
they couldn't afford higher wages—and set the freight rates high. When
railroads and coal companies separated, the practice of high freight rates
continued. This alienated the consumer and lost them tonnage. And
thirdly, anthracite followed the common practice of monopolies and
modern industries of adjusting production to what the market will take
at a given time. But this policy didn't work in the case of anthracite, because anthracite's chief competitors, soft coal and oil, were not controlled
that way. The soft-coal industry was demoralized and prices were extremely low at this period, and the oil industry had adjusted its prices to
capture the domestic market. And so anthracite production fell from
90 million tons in 1920 to 50 million in 1932, at about which figure
it has remained ever since. This shrinkage in output was accompanied by severe and protracted unemployment which has been still further increased by mechanizing the mines. Fifty thousand men who
formerly worked in and around the anthracite mines are now unemployed.

When, about 1932, the papers began to talk about bootleg coal, the
public realized that here was something new in their democracy. And
once more anthracite, now coupled with "relief," became the subject of
dinner conversations, of magazine oratory, of public concern and of

Washington consideration in the way of relief appropriations. But there Washington stopped. Anthracite is a Pennsylvania problem. It was Pennsylvania troops that the coal operators in 1936 were asking for, to give protection to their mine property. And Governor Earle knew that it would be Pennsylvania money that would go to support the bootleggers and their families if their illegal earnings were stopped. So in 1937 he appointed an Anthracite Commission.

The four men who composed this Commission at first brought in three tentative reports with differing recommendations—a depressing testimony to the complicated evidence they had to consider and the difficulty of arriving at a solution in a situation which involves both critical business judgment and social interests. However, in March, 1938 they brought in a unanimous Report and Final Recommendations, the opening paragraph of which reads as follows:

> The commission still holds . . . that the ultimate solution of the anthracite problem may and should be either Federal or State ownership and operation of the industry, preferably the former. On the occasion of the meeting called by Governor Earle at the Governor's Mansion in Harrisburg on January 18, 1938, it was thought that this solution of the anthracite problem was at the point of realization as it appeared that the Federal Government might favorably consider a plan for acquiring Pennsylvania anthracite deposits and making leases to the anthracite producing companies. The Governor, the representatives of the United Mine Workers, and the operators (in their personal capacities), and the Commission unanimously endorsed this proposal, for it was realized that such conditions could be incorporated in Federal leases as to insure the rehabilitation and profitable expansion of the anthracite industry. Later, however—and much to our disappointment—it was found that the Federal authorities had finally decided not to recommend the creation of a national anthracite reserve, but to leave the anthracite problem entirely to the constructive action of the authorities of the State of Pennsylvania.

So if the industry is to be helped out of its present condition through any government ownership or regulation, it will have to be through the state in which 98% of the anthracite fields of the United States lie. To quote further:

> The Commission believes that the acquisition of excess anthracite reserves by the Commonwealth of Pennsylvania is impracticable at the present time but we are convinced that the people of Pennsylvania will, in the future, overwhelmingly sanction such a proposal when it can be drawn so as to protect fully the sources of taxation for anthracite communities.

(Pennsylvania has no income tax. Ninety percent of the schools and most of the civic services are supported by the real-estate taxes paid by the large coal companies, who pay taxes on their huge reserves though these may not be developed for many years. Since some of the companies have succeeded in getting their taxes reduced, there has been no available salary for many teachers. In some cases salaries have been paid for a year from relief funds which are regarded as a debt on the community, to be repaid later.) Further, the Commission believes that "purchase of anthracite lands" would be "extremely profitable to the State." The Commission therefore recommends

that future acquisition of the anthracite lands be studied by a permanent coal commission when it is established [such a commission to act as] a regulatory body as to prices and production [and—through its planning and investigation division—] to collect data bearing upon the increased consumption and production of anthracite, and if necessary, after public hearings, to impose new policies upon the industry by executive order.

Something will have to be done. Anthracite is still one of Pennsylvania's and the nation's most prized national resources. Approximately one-sixth of Pennsylvania's people are in the anthracite regions. The industry, which employed roughly 152,000 in 1929, employed only some 99,500 in 1936; and these employed miners did not average much over three and a half days of work a week. Annual earnings of those employed averaged around $1600 in 1929, shrank to about $1400 in 1932, with a still further decline in 1936. Bootlegging was a response to this fall in annual earnings and to unemployment. The anthracite industries must be revived and rehabilitated by constructive business changes rather than by a mere repression of bootlegging. The Commission has embodied its recommendations in a "Tentative Outline of Provisions of the Proposed Anthracite Industry Act." Whether or not these recommendations will ever be made effective through law, depends upon public opinion—and politics. In the anthracite towns, we found some hopeful of the modest cooperative ventures of groups of miners. Others looked for help to the rise of more small independents. But no one on the spot seemed to feel that these new activities could do more than mitigate the worst for a few. We still must look to the state for any measures adequate to cope with the size and seriousness of the present crisis.

Once more we are back to the present which we found when our little Ford went on its adventure to the anthracite fields. Many things happened also in the soft-coal fields while the railroads became the owners of the anthracite basins, while the anthracite miners were fighting their fight, while the anthracite mine owners were losing their market and while the country passed into a machine culture and changed from an almost exclusively agricultural nation to an industrial one, then passed through the war boom and the following terrible depression. The most important of these happenings in the bituminous fields have already been told up to and through the great anthracite strike of 1902 to which miners from the soft-coal fields gave financial support. By 1916 their joint action had forced recognition of the union in the anthracite basins, where the union waxed strong but the jobs failed.

One industry in many ways: two industries in others. Back, then, to the early days of bituminous mining to see what problems this branch of the industry and its miners faced.

Hard and Soft Coal: Two Industries or One?

One in the common economic and social history of the United States. Pioneering; development of industries; opening up of country by railroads; business administration; absentee landlords. These developing American patterns were a background against which all coal industry must be seen.

One in a common union of workers.

One in a common threat of substitute fuels—oil and electricity—though sometimes stealing each other's markets as when coke (soft coal) began to replace anthracite about 1875.

One in their dependence on railroads, though the railroads have functioned in very different patterns in hard- and soft-coal regions. Railroads never went into the commercial mining of soft coal as they did of hard coal.

One in a shrinking market. Both anthracite and bituminous production reached their peak during the World War and declined afterwards, especially after 1926.

One in their history of strikes, of booms, of present misery.

But hard and soft coal are two industries in many ways.

Two in their very products, which means, of course, in their market. Anthracite is sold, now, largely to small domestic consumers. Bituminous, to big industries, railroads and also to domestic consumers.

Two in their processes of mining, soft coal lying in horizontal layers, easy of access and easily mined; anthracite lying in distorted seams and difficult to mine. This has led to many small operators of soft coal in contrast to the monopolies of the few large anthracite operators. And many small operators have meant cutthroat competition, overdevelopment, and disorganization.

Two in the spread of their deposits. Anthracite is local—all in Pennsylvania; bituminous spreads over a thousand miles in the Appalachian fields and stretches west under the farms of the prairies and appears again 1500 miles away in Colorado. This makes it more difficult for a union to work, to organize miners in scattered sections. It means also that the bituminous operators function under the influence of widely different regional standards of living which are reflected in wages and work conditions. This again means that they put their products on the market at wide variations in price, whereas anthracite companies have what amounts to price agreements. The wide spread of bituminous deposits leads to differential freight rates for northern and southern operators.

THE SMOKE OF SOFT COAL COVERS AMERICA

To most people "coal" simply means soft coal. For the tonnage of bituminous coal which goes up in smoke and dims the American skies is far greater than the tonnage of anthracite. (In 1937, 425 million tons of soft coal were consumed as compared with 50 million tons of anthracite.) If the United States should suddenly be deprived of soft coal, most of our streets, our offices and our houses would be plunged into darkness; most of the wheels of our railroads would cease to turn; most of our factories would shut down. Probably no other single industry touches as many Americans, directly or indirectly, as the bituminous coal industry. It employs 470,000 miners. And for the whole country, 130 million people; it supplies half of all the power used. In both figurative and literal sense we live, breathe and have our being in soft-coal fumes.

How, then, has this vital industry been run? Under what kind of business pattern did it develop?

Unlike the anthracite industry, which has been and still is monopolistic, with sharp competition among the few big owners but with negligibly few small operators, the bituminous coal industry has been a highly competitive enterprise with many small scattered operators, each endeavoring to conquer the other's markets.

What physical forces brought this about? What human forces set the pattern of competition in the soft-coal lands? The natural environment and history provide the answers and give us the stage set for the present.

We already know that the great industrial activity so familiar to us now was released with the ending of the Civil War. Manufacturing grew with incredible speed. Henry Bessemer and the Siemens brothers by their new processes had started the world on steel, and the spectacular output of the blast furnaces from the 1870's on would have been impossible without a cheap and abundant fuel—coke. Coke, made from soft coal. Soft coal to make steel rails for new railroads. Soft coal to run the engines over the new rails.

Enterprising individuals sought the soft-coal lands. Bargain hunters. Speculators. Engineers sent by city investors to spot out the best fields. In the Allegheny Plateau they found thousands of scattered farmers tilling the soil above an unsuspected black treasure, making a modest living from their small rectangular holdings. Land was cheap as long as its use was for agriculture. But with the growing demand for coal and the discovery that it underlay these poor farms, land acquired a new value. The coal under the ground belonged to the owner of the surface. So said our common law, handed down from Anglo–Saxon days and brought over by the English colonists—unlike the laws of other European countries, where the minerals in the ground belong to the state. Here in America a coal seam might have many owners. Each farmer had the right to dig out the coal under his property. And he could lease or sell the coal rights while he continued to farm the surface.

One day no less a personage than Senator Johnson N. Camden strolled into the Clarksburg-Fairmont territory in West Virginia, shotgun in hand. He was hunting squirrels, so he said. And hunt he did for two weeks, stopping to talk with the neighborhood farmers. By the time he arrived in Fairmont, he had acquired large holdings on both sides of the West Fork River. And he gave his now useless shotgun to Governor Fleming's son. He had bought at thirteen dollars an acre from the local farmers, who had come to believe, after talking with the Senator, that the coal would not be developed for "ages." So runs the tale in the Upper Monongahela Valley.

Not all these bargain hunters made such good bargains. Some bought at fabulous prices land that proved later to have no coal. For neither the lay of the deposits nor the vast extent of them was known in those days. Only as the railroads extended their tracks across the Appalachian plateaus, then across the prairie lands to the west did the extent of the soft-coal deposits become known. Not concentrated pockets in one state as the anthracite fields, but scattered through twenty-nine states. They stretched some 800 to 900 miles under the poor soil of the Allegheny

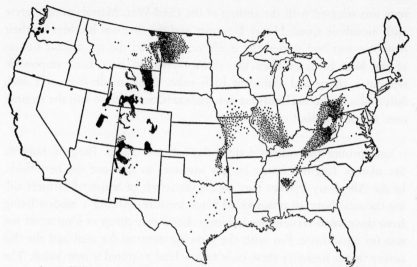

One dot (•), the equivalent of 1 billion tons medium rank bituminous (heat value 12,500 B.t.u's)
From "The Case of Bituminous Coal" by Walton H. Hamilton and Helen R. Wright,
based on figures of the U. S. Geological Survey

BITUMINOUS AND LIGNITE RESOURCES IN TERMS OF HEAT UNITS

plateaus from Pennsylvania to Alabama. Even greater deposits lay under Indiana, Illinois, Iowa, Missouri, Kansas, Oklahoma and Texas. And on the edge of the Rockies and in the inland mountain plateaus the coal appeared again.

The first fields to be developed were those of the Allegheny plateaus. Early mines were small ventures, farmers digging into the hillsides, or a small coal company in the form of a partnership. For the soft coal was easy to get at. We ourselves had seen West Virginia farmers digging out their own supplies with pick and shovel. Twenty-nine horizontal layers of coal made accessible by the deeply cut ravines and gorges of the dissected plateau. Small operators with little capital could and did lease or buy up surface land and cut right into a level coal seam whose edge appeared in a dark band on the side of the ravine.

Thus our common law, which granted mineral rights along with surface ownership; the vastness of the deposits; and the accessibility of the soft coal, together set the stage for the soft-coal drama—many operators jostling each other in their rush to get rich on a growing market.

THE ACTORS IN AN OVERDEVELOPED INDUSTRY: RAILROADS,
OPERATORS, MINERS

Coal, more coal: for the wheels along the tracks and for the smoking chimneys. The growth of America's industries was amazing. Between 1860 and 1894, from fourth place among the nations of the world in manufactures America jumped to first place. The soft-coal industry responded, but it responded too well. Year by year new mines were opened. In 1894 mine capacity exceeded the demand by 82%. This overexpansion was no new problem. It had plagued the industry from its early days.

It wasn't so much that there was more coal lying around above ground than the market could take—not overproduction in the same sense as surplus bushels of wheat piled up in warehouses. For coal is, by and large, mined only on order. But once a mine is opened, the coal might as well be on the market. It is all there ready to be dug out and loaded on cars. Since a small mine can be opened with relatively little investment, there is nothing to stop an owner in his desire to cash in on his holding. An owner of a city lot has to build a store or an apartment house on it before he can realize on his investment. Unless he is pretty sure he can rent them once they are built, he hesitates to take the risk. Likewise a manufacturer has to put up a factory and buy raw material before he can begin to make his product. But the owner of a coal deposit had no such risks to take. The coal bed was his raw material, his factory and his product all in one. The investment necessary in machinery was a relatively insignificant part of the whole undertaking. That is why there have always been too many mines. A comparatively cheap risk and a good gambling chance, with the inevitable result of an overdeveloped industry.

What role did the railroads play in the development of the soft-coal industry? Not the same leading-lady role that they did in the anthracite fields, where they were chief owners as well as carriers; but still a very important part.

Without the railroads, coal could never have reached the factories —its markets. In the early days it was difficult to interest investors in a coal-mining enterprise until they had been given assurance of reliable transportation. So the coal companies offered all sorts of bait—stock ownership, and a place on the board of directors—to attract a particular railroad to their region.

The railroads, however, were not lacking in foresight. They saw the enormous possibilities of revenue from coal traffic and soon began a scramble for the prized tonnage. Get there before the other railroad! Push into new fields—the more remote the better! That the existing mines could already furnish the country with more coal than it needed did not matter to the railroads. For more mines meant more coal to haul. More coal to haul meant more income. And the railroads not only hauled coal; they consumed it. The more coal on the market the cheaper the price. It was to the railroads' interest to have more and more mines opened.

But the faraway operators, who had to add the expense of a long haul to their costs, could not compete in the market with operators who had only a short haul. How could the railroads make sure that their new tracks would be used? They found a neat solution. Charge the distant operators lower freight rates. Let faraway southern coal reach the northern factories at prices lower than northern coal. Let midwestern coal reach the eastern market at prices lower than eastern coal. Cheaper rates for a longer haul. Why not? Keep the wheels moving! And so coal from Kentucky could undersell Illinois coal in the Chicago market.

The railroads had another great weapon besides the power to fix freight rates. They controlled the cars. Without coal cars the mines were helpless. For mining and transportation are one continuous operation. Coal at the mine opening is dumped directly into railroad cars. If there are not enough cars, the mines stop working. Here was an effective weapon which unscrupulous railroads did not hesitate to use in the early days. If a coal operator did not give the railroad low prices for the coal it bought, he found himself without enough cars. And he simply went out of business!

And last but not least, the railroads, as the largest consumers of coal —they used, in prewar days, more than one-quarter of the yearly output— could more or less dictate price, especially with so many operators competing.

Often the railroads had not enough cars. For normal demand, yes—if the term normal demand can be applied to soft coal. For the demand for coal fluctuates with good and bad times. Also the demand is seasonal. The cold of winter and the shortness of winter days greatly increase the demand for coal by electricity producers, office buildings and even railroads. And there have been almost no attempts to mine coal regularly and store it for demand, though the deterioration of the coal thus stored would be slight. Overexpansion has spread the transportation system out too thin. Much of the coal now produced in this country has been, and still is, transported undue distances, in many instances on its way to market passing across other fields producing coal of similar character.

Indiana now ships coal to eleven states and receives coal from eleven states. And so, during times of heavy demand, there are not cars enough to go round. Thus through juggling with differential freight rates, through discrimination in distributing cars and through their power as a great consumer, the railroads of the soft-coal lands have contributed to the overdevelopment and instability of the industry.

The market for coal depended, as we have seen, on the demand from factories and railroads. This meant that the demand for coal was super-sensitive to business conditions. And in those days as now, the business cycle revolved and the country went through alternate depressions and boom times.

Consider what this meant to the coal operator. Here, for instance, is a company that has bought land with capital obtained by selling bonds and stock. It opens a mine. Times are good; demand for coal is good; prices are good; profits are good. The far-scattered stockholders are pleased, for these company pens are scratching dividend checks. The success of this company does not go unnoted. Another and still another company is formed. More stockholders. More mines are opened. All are pleased as long as "times are good." But it is notorious that times do not stay good. Factories go on part time. The coal companies get fewer orders. But there are more coal companies now for these fewer orders. The first company lowers its price. Other companies lower their price. But overhead costs go on as when prices were high. The company reduces wages. Other companies follow suit. And so some mines work only two or three days a week. Some shut down for a few months, hoping that winter demand or better times will bring more orders. Some shut down altogether; some go into bankruptcy.

Few industries have had as large a crop of bankruptcies as bituminous coal. Companies have been organized, only to perish after a year or two; but the mines have remained to add to the overcapacity of the industry. For reorganizations have followed bankruptcies; when business picked up, the mines were ready to begin again. They had just changed ownership. The mining operator is a natural gambler. He risks losses for the sake of profits. And so the vicious circle began all over again with every new spurt of business activity. The history of soft coal has been a history of extremes. Times of shortage and high prices have meant profiteering. Oversupply and low prices have meant heavy losses. In the long run, it is probable that the profits of those who succeeded no more than balanced the losses of those who failed.

How could a large number of competing units with a product highly sensitive to business conditions work out an efficient industry? Several operators tried as far back as 1869 to bring order out of the chaos. They proposed to end the "uncontrollable competition" by consolidation and thus bring about "unified apportionment of production to demand." The scheme failed. Limiting coal production offers the same difficulties as crop control. Mines are scattered. Each operator is tempted to turn his holdings into cash, no matter how low prices go. For production to be "apportioned to demand," not only would nearly all operators have to join together: they would need the power to prevent others from opening new mines. This being impossible, coal operators have acted individually. They have never formed organizations by which developments in the industry could be shared, its trends studied. Such organizations as grew up were for influencing legislation or for combating a more tangible enemy than overcapacity—the labor unions.

The mining camps in the soft-coal lands had all the evils of those in the anthracite towns, to which their own particular evils were added. There were many Scott's Runs scattered throughout the Allegheny Plateau even in early days. Conditions were bad even when the men had jobs. When the mines went on part time, conditions were desperate.

In the bituminous as in the anthracite fields, then as now, mining was one of the most dangerous occupations. In 1934 the accident-frequency rate was three times the average for all industry, the severity rate nearly seven times the general average. Newspaper readers know this and have always waited breathlessly while rescue crews work after a gas explosion, a cave-in or other mine accident. But do they visualize the silent throng of wives and neighbors waiting at the mine opening? Insurance companies know that mining is hazardous. Life-insurance companies regard the miner's life as sixteen years shorter than the life of a person in a safe occupation. Printers and machinists, for instance, are given five or six times more insurance protection than a coal miner. Only a minimum amount of insurance is granted miners. And no wonder. In a hard-coal region from 1915 to 1923, 39% of deaths among miners aged fifteen to sixty-five were due to accident, as compared with 10% in the case of non-miners; deaths from influenza and pneumonia were 40% as compared with 25% in all other occupations; deaths from tuberculosis were 57.6% against 37.2% among other men of the same age. Almost 2000 miners are killed annually while working, and the estimate of the number of nonfatal accidents runs between 50,000 and 150,000 per year. And the danger of accident from cave-ins is increased by irregular operation, for water often fills idle mines. The accident rate is highest after a mine starts up again. The plight of the miners, always serious from hazards, becomes harrowing when mines go on part time.

Soft-coal miners began to organize about 1875. But no union can open closed mines. At best a union can only mitigate unemployment. Organization helped, however. For the communities without unions were even worse off than those with. Here in the soft-coal lands, as in anthracite, is a history of strikes, violence and bitterness—a fight by the workers against intolerable living and working conditions, a fight inevitable in a sick industry trying to make ends meet by the easiest way of cutting costs, that of keeping wages low, laying off men in slack times, and eking out company income through company-town tactics.

In 1897 the young union won recognition in the northern soft-coal fields and shortly sent John Mitchell to try to organize the anthracite country. The union was long delayed in other bituminous fields. The very vastness of them meant regional differences in standards of living—differences in wages, differences in attitudes towards labor—which made united action more difficult. Each region has its own particular history. But here a picture of life in one mining region must stand for the life in many. One fight in the western region must stand for many others throughout the Allegheny Plateau and the prairie regions.

"DOWN THE CANYON": LUDLOW, 1913

A thousand miles or more from the soft coal of the Allegheny Plateau were other soft-coal mines. These were canyon mines located in the steep gorges on the eastern slope of the Rockies in Colorado. Up narrow valleys from the plains cities to small valley towns ran the railroads. Up the canyons, ten to thirty miles from these small valley towns, lay the mining camps, Ludlow and others. And up valleys and canyons to the mines since the 1880's had flowed a stream of foreign laborers and their families, largely Greeks, Italians, Slavs and Mexicans.

"Down the canyon for you" had long been a dreaded remark. For it meant that a miner had been discharged and that he and his family were to trek down to the world outside, where jobs were scarce. Yet in September, 1913, some 9000 miners, with their families and all their worldly goods, of their own accord marched down the canyons. They did not seek the outside world. How could 9000 families find homes or work? Instead, they erected tent colonies. And there they lived for fifteen months through the cold of two Colorado winters.

These were strikers and their families; and this was a strike which was to involve the whole mining industry, from themselves and the 400,000 United Mine Workers in the eastern coal fields up to John D. Rockefeller, Jr.; and was to involve government, from local committees, the Governor of Colorado and the state militia up to the federal troops, the Secretary of Labor and the President of the United States.

John D. Rockefeller, Jr., was involved because, as chief stockholder, he controlled the Colorado Fuel & Iron Company, much the largest of the three chief companies of Colorado who controlled most of the coal. Not only the coal. These companies controlled the whole community, the small valley towns, their land, houses, stores, schools, churches and even the courts and local sheriffs. Far away in New York lived Mr. Rockefeller, chief of the absentee owners and chief overlord of this feudal structure. Under this chief overlord came President Wellborn and Superintendent Bowers, who had offices in Denver some 200 miles from the mines. Under them came the manager who had offices in Pueblo, 80 miles from the mines. On the field were assistant managers, superintendents, pit bosses or foremen, and finally the miners themselves. A dizzy superstructure of officials, each higher-up knowing less and less about actual conditions; until we find at the apex of the structure Mr. Rockefeller, testifying in 1913 that he had not attended a directors' meeting for ten years and that he had "not the slightest idea" of the wages, rents or living conditions of the miners. From 15,000 to 20,000 then lived in his company's camps.

Yet it was these conditions, about which Mr. Rockefeller had not the slightest idea, which caused the 9000 miners and their families to march down the canyons to tent colonies in 1913. What were they? Physically, they were much like those in Scott's Run in West Virginia. One-room shacks—a few with two rooms—in two or three rows on the narrow valley floors and clinging to the precipitous walls. Even some dugouts in the steep places. Roofs that leaked onto sick people so that they had to be moved from spot to spot to keep dry. Polluted water from the mines was sometimes all that was available. Many sick people—151 cases of typhoid in the Colorado Fuel & Iron Company camps in the year 1912-13. The death rate in coal mining was nearly twice as high as in the United States as a whole. Why did they live in such hovels? Only one reason: they had to. The company owned all the houses and all the land. They would not have allowed a private house, even if a miner could have afforded one. For the miners paid rent for these shacks, rent which was subtracted from their wages. The company owned the doctors, too, and subtracted the doctor's fees, one dollar a month, from the miners' wages. More for special services. The company made money on this arrangement. So no miner was allowed to employ any doctor other than the company doctor.

The company owned the stores. They made money on the stores, too, 20% annually, so President Wellborn testified. So the miners and their wives were not allowed to buy at other stores. The miners were given scrip with which they bought goods at the company stores. Their purchases were charged against their wages. Colorado had passed a law giving miners the right to buy at stores of their own choosing. The companies ignored it. Who was there to prevent? It was the old story—a company town. The exploitation of the miners was made easier by the isolation of the mining camps.

And hours? Colorado had passed an eight-hour law for miners. The companies ignored it. Who was there to prevent? Colorado had passed a law giving miners a right to use checkweighmen—men chosen by the miners to check the weighing of the coal by the company—an important point, since the men were paid by the weight of their coal. The companies ignored it. Who was there to prevent? Again the exploitation of the miners was made easier by the isolation of the mining camp.

Why did the miners endure such conditions? Why did they not strike? They did. They had called strikes in 1883, 1893, and 1903. But the companies were well prepared to handle strikes. At all times they had spies to report on "troublemakers." And these troublemakers quickly found themselves going "down the canyon." More than that, the companies had armed guards ready. These armed guards brought in strikebreakers, who frequently did not know that they were being brought in to break a strike. That, too, was against the law. Many of the strikebreakers deserted when they found out the real situation, and the strikebreakers of one strike became the strikers in the next. Again, why did not the civil authorities insist that laws be obeyed? The simplest of all answers. They, too, were controlled by the companies. Deputy sheriffs were maintained by the companies. Jurymen were selected by the companies. Company officials acted as election judges, with the polling places on company grounds. It was all simple, even simpler than medieval feudalism. And who was there to prevent?

Such were the conditions in the houses, in the mines, in the communities, which led to the march of the 9000 down the canyon in the snow. The men had asked for seven things, five of which had been made mandatory by law but had not been in practice in the mines and camps. The other two things were a raise in wages and recognition of the union. The union. That was the real stumbling block. Public opinion finally forced the companies to obey the laws. But the companies and in particular John D. Rockefeller, Jr., stood out for the principle of the "open shop." They maintained that the men were satisfied with their conditions but were stirred up by union agitators, that they struck because they were afraid of the union organizers. Seventy percent of the workers in the Colorado Fuel & Iron Company, they maintained, were thus intimidated by a few men to the point of living fifteen months in a tent colony. These 9000 men, they further declared, were violating the right of a man to choose his own conditions of work by trying to establish a closed shop, thus forcing the men who were contented and "loyal" to the company to join the union. John D. Rockefeller, Jr., said:

We believe the issue is not a local one in Colorado. It is a national issue whether workers shall be allowed to work under such conditions as they may choose. As part owners of the property our interest in the laboring men in this country is so immense, so deep, so profound that we stand ready to lose every cent we put in that company rather than see the men we have employed thrown out of work and have imposed upon them conditions which are not of their seeking and which neither they nor we can see are in our interest.

Here was the issue. Which workers were to choose the conditions under which they were to work? The 70% (union men) who were protesting against the company's standards? Or the 30% who were intimidated by the company's power over their jobs? Unquestionably each side was fighting for its own economic interest. On the one side were the miners living in unbearable conditions, as was afterwards admitted; on the other side were the companies, run by and for absentee owners of great wealth. Here is the way the fight was fought out.

First, with support from the state government.

The companies imported guards who were deputized by the sheriffs as national guardsmen. This was at first opposed by Governor Ammons of Colorado. For some months he tried to bring about an understanding between strikers and managers. But the managers steadily refused to meet with the strikers for fear this would be interpreted as a recognition of the union. Finally Governor Ammons himself capitulated and the state troopers were put at the service of the companies.

Second, with guns, fire and detective agency.

The Colorado Fuel & Iron Company engaged the Baldwin–Fells Detective Agency, which had already proved itself brutal and effective in West Virginia strikes, to help recruit armed guards, protect mines and suppress the strike. Up the valleys came something new. An armored automobile with a mounted machine gun constructed in the Colorado Fuel & Iron Company shops at Pueblo. The "Death Special"! Up the narrow valley went the Death Special to the tent colony at Forbes. Open warfare. Skirmishings. Both sides armed but not equally. For the Death Special could fire into the tents, and women and children were easy targets. Fighting in the towns. Fighting in the tent colonies. Finally a twelve-hour fight at Ludlow. The machine gun was mounted on the hillside, where it could rake the tent colony. Two bombs exploded on the hill. The miners were sure this was the beginning of an attack. They fired back. The fight was on. Women and children ran wildly from tents. Some escaped. Some hid in the tents as best they could. An unarmed miner was seized. Lieutenant Linderfelt in charge of the troops broke a rifle stock over his head and ordered him shot. Frenzy everywhere. The hills full of terrified men, women and children with the militia shooting. Then a new weapon. Fire. The tents were set ablaze. The women and children huddled in pits who escaped the guns were now suffocated. A frenzy. An orgy. Burning tents were looted. The scene became a massacre.

The whole neighborhood was roused. State troops could not control the situation. Governor Ammons wired President Wilson for federal troops. The fighting came to an end. Twenty-one people killed in the Ludlow attack. Thirty more in the other fighting.

And Rockefeller? He looked out of his New York office on Upton Sinclair and four women picketing. He looked at cartoons, at flaming articles of himself everywhere. He made a public announcement that his company had of its own free will granted the demands of the strikers but that the obstinacy of the strikers had continued the strike and caused the violence. The press of the nation, however, made it clear that Rockefeller had only granted the miners the five points which the state law had granted them years before. The other two demands, raise in wages and recognition of the union, the company did not grant.

Rockefeller hired a publicity agent to "educate the public." The education included many falsifications. The fight was not over yet. Finally it reached the White House. The Secretary of Labor sent out a commission to investigate. On the basis of its report President Wilson proposed a plan of settlement demanding a three-year truce in which period there were to be: (1) enforcement of the Colorado mining and labor laws, (2) reemployment of strikers not guilty of violence, (3) prohibition of intimidation of either union or nonunion men, (4) posting of current wages and regulations at each mine, (5) outlawing of strikes during the three-year period, grievances to be arbitrated by a commission of three made up of a representative from each side and an impartial member chosen by President Wilson. The miners accepted and the company refused. But in refusing they hinted that they had a better plan.

What did this plan turn out to be? It was worked out by W. L. Mackenzie King, financed through the Rockefeller Institute and called the Industrial Representation Plan. It provided in effect for a company union. That is, an organization made up of miners and managers was to meet to consider the problems. But the organization was to be controlled entirely by the company. The U. S. Commission declared that the plan

embodies none of the principles of effectual collective bargaining and instead is a hypocritical pretense of granting what is in reality withheld [and that it was] conceived and carried out, not for the purpose of aiding the Company's employees in Colorado, but for the purpose of ameliorating or removing the unfavorable criticism of Mr. Rockefeller which had arisen throughout the country following his rejection of President Wilson's plan of settlement. [And again] The effectiveness of such a plan lies wholly in its tendency to deceive the public and lull criticism, while permitting the Company to maintain its absolute power.

The fight was over. Up the canyons again. Fifteen months in the tent colonies. Bitterness of warfare and killed men, women and children. An agreement that the companies would obey the state laws. A company union. Meager results in the coal mines of Colorado. But the public had been aroused.

THE WORLD WAR AND AFTER

Then came the World War. American industries as well as American agriculture went into a boom period. Steel for munitions, food and clothing for the army, lumber for ships—all these supplies had to reach their destination by railroad. And behind all this activity was soft coal, that supplied 70% of the energy to keep the wheels turning. Eleven thousand mines, owned and operated by thousands of enterprising individuals, sought to supply the nation's needs. But with all these 11,000 mines in operation, the engines of the nation were running cold for lack of fuel. Not because the capacity of the mines was not more than equal to the demand as it had always been, but because the railroads had not enough cars to supply so many mines, with increased production. Many of these were small workings in remote places far from markets. As each demanded its share of railroad cars, the long hauls caused unnecessary delays and transport congestion. Shortage became acute. Prices rose. And as always in the coal industry, the lure of quick profits meant the opening of many small new mines. Thus the "war brides" of the Appalachian Plateau were born. The temporary "snow birds" and "fly-by-nights" appeared in the Appalachian valleys wherever coal outcropped. To open a small mine here meant almost no capital investment. These entrepreneurs gave no thought to fixed charges, depreciation, depletion and maintenance. For their stay was to be short. Many of these mines, because of inferior coal or inaccessibility to markets, would not have been worth opening under normal conditions. Yet paved roads followed them up the spurs of the mountains; and shortly, bowling over the roads, came the silk-shirt salesmen, previously unknown to these mountain folk. Around about, in these isolated hills, were families living as people must in isolated places, meeting their own needs—hardy, independent, self-sufficient. The coal companies offered wages dazzling to the eyes of these self-helping people of the hills. The mountain farmers, the "hillbillys," turned miners. And soon they were herded into miserable company shacks, spending their days underground. Negroes came up from the cotton fields to make wartime wages. They could live in even more miserable shacks. Bring them in. Dazzle them, too, with promises. Often brought in as strikebreakers, and ignorant of anything that had to do with mining, they stayed to join the union and became good workers.

The war brides flourished while war prices flourished. They closed when the war market ended. But not to relieve the industry of its greatest problem—excess capacity. For these small mines were easier to open than to keep open, and the recurring periods of shortage and high prices that accompanied the strikes after the war saw the reopening of not only the old war brides, but new snow birds and fly-by-nights. Expansion continued unabated until 1923, when the high-water mark was reached. In that year the bituminous mines in the United States numbered 15,000: 9000 commercial mines with an annual output of over 1000 tons, 6000 local workings and wagon or "truck" mines. These mines had the potential capacity to produce 970 million tons, or nearly 70% more coal than the country had ever been able to use. And at the same time that the industry's capacity was growing at such a rapid rate, the market for bituminous coal was steadily shrinking.

In 1918 soft coal furnished 70% of the nation's mechanical power. In 1929 this proportion had dropped to 55%, and in 1936 it stood at 50%.

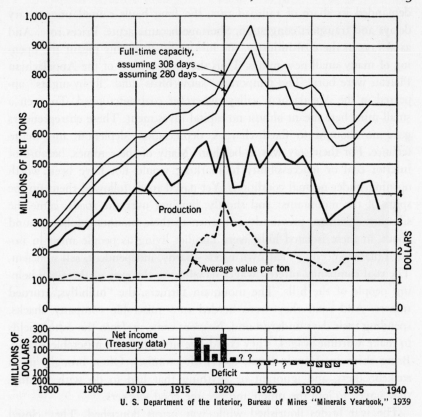

U. S. Department of the Interior, Bureau of Mines "Minerals Yearbook," 1939

BITUMINOUS COAL: MINE CAPACITY, PRODUCTION, VALUE, AND NET INCOME OR DEFICIT, 1900–1938

Coal was losing ground. Not because our total energy requirements were decreasing—on the contrary, they increased substantially between 1918 and 1930—but because other fuels were competing with coal. And because we were economizing in our use of coal.

During and following the World War, the fuel-economy movement made rapid strides. The most striking savings were made in electric-power plants. In 1899 it required 7.05 pounds of coal to generate one kilowatt hour of electricity. In 1930 the same work was accomplished with 1.6 pounds of coal. The steam railroads, the iron and steel industry, coke manufacture, etc., show similar gains. Soft coal went into a decline.

Oil and water power each more than doubled its share of the national energy budget during the ten years following the World War. Gasoline-driven automobiles and trucks encroached more and more on the domain

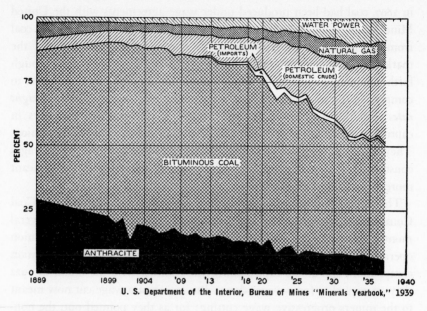

U. S. Department of the Interior, Bureau of Mines "Minerals Yearbook," 1939

PERCENT OF TOTAL B.T.U. EQUIVALENT CON-
TRIBUTED BY THE SEVERAL SOURCES OF
ENERGY, 1889–1937

of the coal-consuming railroads; and the Diesel engine, run by fuel oil, replaced many steam engines in ships and factories. Water power came into increasing use for the generation of electricity. It is cheaper than coal where it is a by-product of flood control, or if the coal fields are far away. Soft coal, which had started most of the nation's wheels, now turned a smaller and smaller percent of them. Indeed, soft coal showed signs of becoming a chronic invalid.

Does this mean that coal will come to occupy a lesser and lesser place in the production of energy? Will our invalid get sicker and sicker? Not necessarily. It may be that the full impact of these competitive fuels has been felt. It may be otherwise. We may later find that there is still a real problem in the relation of coal prices to the prices of other fuels.

At any rate, the decline of coal consumption at a time when the industry was expanding sent the whole competitive merry-go-round whirling at a faster and faster pace. In the struggle for a hold on a shrinking market, union and nonunion operators were pitted against each other.

Before the war the bulk of the country's coal came from Pennsylvania, Ohio, Indiana and Illinois, where, ever since the recognition of the union in 1897, coal had been produced under wage agreements with the United Mine Workers of America. But now, following the World War, coal from the nonunion fields of Kentucky and West Virginia invaded the markets in increasing amounts. This coal was of high quality and, though farther from the centers of industry than the northern coal, was able to compete in the northern markets with the help of *more favorable freight rates.* But the real reason for the success of the southern operators in capturing the market was the fact that they were running nonunion. They could cut wages at any time to meet market conditions. Since wages constituted 65% of the cost of production, any reduction in them meant more than economies elsewhere.

The miners had been granted their wage scale by the Bituminous Coal Commission, appointed by the President in 1919, which after several months' investigation had increased wages some 25% to 30%. Union operators, who were bound by wage agreements, couldn't meet nonunion competition, and at the expiration of the contract with the union in 1922 they attempted to force wages down. But to accept a wage cut now meant to the miners progressive wage cutting; for as they pointed out, the non-union operators would meet every wage cut by union operators with a further cut. The northern operators, however, were desperate and refused to renew the agreement. A five-month strike, in which the anthracite miners and later the railway shopmen joined, won for the miners the maintenance of the existing wage scale for another year: a precarious victory, for nonunion tonnage continued to increase. The union, knowing only too well that the union operators were at the mercy of their non-union competitors, sent organizers into Kentucky and West Virginia. But the slightest attempt at organization in the South was accompanied by murder, evictions and general terror.

In 1924, partly because coal demand was good, partly through fear of another long strike, the operators were persuaded to renew the 1923 agreement. And for three years! It looked as though peace had come to the soft-coal industry at last. But no sooner had the agreement been signed than operators began to chisel. At first secretly, and then openly, operators abandoned their contracts. The campaign to break the union was on! The Bethlehem Steel Company, acting on orders from their New York office, led off. The Rockefeller-owned Consolidation Coal Company, the Mellon-owned Pittsburgh Coal Company, and some of the railroad mines, followed by repudiating their agreements. The usual practice was to close down. Then, after a short period, reopen on a nonunion basis with a lowered wage scale. In 1924, 40% of the country's coal mines were nonunion. One year later, 60%. At the expiration of the agreement in 1927 the union called a strike against those operators who had broken their contracts. Several of the railroads shut down their own mines and ordered coal from nonunion producers, trying thereby to force the failure of the strike. Some operators claimed that the railroads and other large consumers forced them to repudiate the union by threatening to buy permanently in the South. Operators who were not opposed to working under union agreements were unable to do so because of the competition in their own fields. The large companies had started the campaign against the union; the smaller companies had to follow.

After a sixteen-month struggle the men returned to work on whatever terms they could get. The union had been broken.

Who were the real masters of soft coal? To the casual observer this struggle appeared as one between operator and operator and between operators and miners. It was not generally recognized that it was a three-cornered fight, and that the consumer, usually the forgotten man, played in these encounters a most important part. For the important consumers of soft coal are not the domestic users who fill their coal bins with a few tons, or those who buy from the "ice man" in bushel bags. The chief consumers of coal are the billion-dollar industries—steel, electric-power plants, railroads, etc., who buy in thousand- and even million-ton lots. The power they can wield is as great as their orders are large. Hear the purchasing agent for the Louisville and Nashville Railroad testifying before the Supreme Court:

It is a well known fact that the buying power of these large consumers of coal is more intelligent, more forceful, more far reaching than ever before in the history of the industry. . . . They dictate their own price. The purchaser makes it. And he makes it because of his tremendous force and influence of his buying power. Why, it is nothing these days for one interest or one concern to buy several million tons of coal.

This was the power behind the threats to the union operators in the 1927 strike!

But these industries exerted an influence on the struggle not only as large consumers but as producers as well. For these industries, in order to be assured of a cheap and plentiful supply of coal, had opened their own mines. Much cheaper to mine their own coal than to buy from independent coal operators. And so, during the war and the years following, when prices were high, these "captive" mines, owned and operated by companies for their own use, appeared in practically every coal field. To keep the cost of their coal low, they paid low wages. Hence their opposition to the union.

Now while their captive mines supplied one-fourth of their needs, these big industries had to buy the rest. And by keeping low the price of the coal which they sold to themselves through subsidiary coal companies, they beat down the price of what they had to buy. They didn't care whether they took a profit on their own coal operations, for their chief business was not selling coal. They could make their profits on their principal product, steel, electricity, or whatever it might be. And when 20% to 25% of the total bituminous production—for that is what these captive mines produced—entered a competitive market at a cut price, the independent coal operator, to stay in the market, had to cut his price too. But that is not all that happened. Whenever these captive mines had more coal than they needed for themselves, they dumped their excess on the market. This dumping, of course, came just at a time when business was slack and when all the coal operators were having a hard time to dispose of their coal. And this forced prices down still further.

So as competing producers they undercut prices, and as large consumers they bought at their own price. And the domestic consumers—users of only 10% of the bituminous production—often made up for the loss sustained on the industrial consumer and enabled mines to keep running. In 1932 when the average price of coal at the mine had dropped from $1.78 in 1929 to $1.31, a decline of 26%, the average price to domestic consumers declined from $8.85 to $7.71, a drop of only 13%. And some of the railroad and electric power utilities were buying coal as low as 50 to 75 cents a ton.

The railroads have had a greater stake in the coal industry than the coal operators themselves in that the freight charges consistently average more than the cost of producing coal. In 1933 when the price per ton at the mine was $1.34, the average freight charge per ton was $2.20. The freight charge thus represented 62% of the delivered cost of coal, a ratio higher than for almost any other commodity shipped by the railroads. In that year the average freight charge for all freight handled was 11% of the delivered cost.

These industries—the railroads, steel companies, electric utilities—were the real masters of the coal fields.

By 1930 the union had all but disappeared from the soft-coal fields. The traditional handicap no longer hampered northern operators as they entered the ring against southern competitors. But there was no winning in this fight, not so long as the mines had twice as much coal as the market could take.

Price cut had followed price cut. Mine after mine had shut down. In 1923 there had been 9000 commercial mines. In 1932 there were 5500. From 1923 to 1929, when other industries were extraordinarily prosperous, the coal industry had lost each year 20 million dollars. By 1932 the annual loss had increased to 50 million, and there was hardly a coal-mining company that was not either bankrupt or existing on its reserves.

Closed mines meant idle workers. Three hundred thousand miners had lost their jobs between 1923 and 1932. Those fortunate enough to have jobs were receiving only half their former wages as a result of wage reductions and part-time working of the mines. And at the bottom of the heap were those miners who were receiving, at the end of two weeks, from 15 to 20 cents in cash. This was not at all uncommon in West Virginia in 1931, according to evidence introduced in the Carter Coal Case. Many workers testified that for two years they had been living entirely on company scrip without seeing any cash. The prices asked for goods in company stores sometimes ran as much as 11.6% more than the same things in stores in neighboring towns. According to other testimony, average wages in one district in the Southern Appalachian region were $1.25 a day in 1931–32; $7.20 represented typical earnings for a two-week period. From this amount $2.50 was deducted for rent, $2.00 for powder, $1.00 for the company doctor, 75 cents for coal and 25 cents for blacksmithing. In all, these deductions amount to $6.50, leaving the miner and his family a balance of only 70 cents for food for two weeks. "White horses" in bituminous as well as in anthracite!

The operators, even the most hard-boiled of them, knew that starved miners meant poor and indifferent workers. But there was little they could do about it. They, too, were victims of cutthroat competition.

They were too suspicious of each other to be willing to plan together to end their own misery, let alone that of the miners. And so they spent their efforts in armed resistance to those miners who still believed in a union. The *New York Times* reported that this "resistance by the operators led to large expenditures for armed guards, munitions and machine guns; they evicted strikers, made the coal fields armed camps and the police and court records . . . were filled with tales of assaults, violence, arrests and injunctions."

This, then, was the picture of the coal industry in the third year of the Great Depression. Coal was indeed "sick." Its illness had reached a crisis

Form 182-N 6-37 3M
Colliery No. ▓ .... From .... AUG 1 1937 TO AUG 15 1937 .. Inc. Payroll and Check No. ▓ ....
Mr. ....▓................................. In Account With WEBSTER COAL AND COKE COMPANY

CREDIT			DEBIT				BALANCE	
By	Tons	@ 1.0976			To Old Age Benefit			46	
"	"	@ .8512			" Amount Assigned to Rent		2	64	
" 5008 "		@ .7199	36	29	" " " Coal				
"	"	@			" " " Physician			75	
"	Yards	@			" " " Garage				
"	"	@			" " " Wash House			50	
"	Allowance @		11	22	" " " Check-Off			65	
"	"	@			" " " Ck. w'ghm'n			85	
"	Hours	@			" " " Hosp.		2	50	
"	"	@			" " "				
"	"	@			" " "				
	Gross Earnings		47	51	" " "				
Less Supplies	Smithing		1	45	" " " Store		36	71	
TOTAL CREDIT			46	06	TOTAL DEBIT		45	06	1 00

DETACH AND HOLD THIS PART.   SIGN ON BACK OF THE CHECK BELOW WHEN CASHED

Form 182-N 6-27 3M
Colliery No. ▓ .... From .... AUG 16 1937 TO AUG 31 1937 .. Inc. Payroll and Check No. ▓ ....
Mr. ....▓................................. In Account With WEBSTER COAL AND COKE COMPANY

CREDIT			DEBIT				BALANCE	
By	Tons	@ 1.0976			To Old Age Benefit			36	
"	"	@ .8512			" Amount Assigned to Rent		2	64	
" 4012 "		@ .7199	29	22	" " " Coal				
"	"	@			" " " Physician			75	
"	Yards	@			" " " Garage				
"	"	@			" " " Wash House			50	
"	Allowance @		8	84	" " " Check-Off			65	
"	"	@			" " " Ck. w'ghm'n			75	
"	Hours	@			" " " Death fund		1	00	
"	"	@			" " " C. V. M. Hosp.		2	50	
"	"	@			" " "				
	Gross Earnings		38	06	" " "				
Less Supplies	Smithing		2	49	" " " Store		25	42	
TOTAL CREDIT			35	57	TOTAL DEBIT		34	57	1 00

DETACH AND HOLD THIS PART.   SIGN ON BACK OF THE CHECK BELOW WHEN CASHED

From the Cooperative Builder

FACSIMILE OF A "WHITE HORSE"

This shows how deductions shrank a Cambria, Pa., miner's earnings of $85.57 for one month to $2 cash: a typical case.

stage. True, all the nation's industries were run down, but their illness was of recent origin. Coal's, on the other hand, was of long standing. Other industries had enjoyed prosperity in the years following the war. But coal, like agriculture, had never recovered from the effects of the World War and had been in a decline since 1920.

THE NEW DEAL IN COAL

No wonder, then, that most of the soft-coal operators snatched at the opportunity offered by the National Industrial Recovery Act for federal

aid. Under the Act all industries were to draw up "codes of fair competition." Through open hearings the public was to be given an opportunity to scrutinize them. After approval by the President, each code
became legally binding on all members of the industry in question—and
exempt from the provisions of the antitrust laws.

Here was a chance for the entire coal industry, not merely regional
groups, to come in under one covering agreement. An agreement whose
greatest attraction was its promise to end ruinous price cutting. For, once
a code had been agreed upon by the industry and price determined by
the Code Authority, to sell below those prices would be against the law.
Competition was to be put under control. Cooperation was to be the order
of the day. Cooperation between operator and operator. Cooperation between operator and miner. For the NIRA was concerned not only with
industry but with labor as well. Recovery depended on the ability of the
working class to buy back the products of factory and farm; each code,
therefore, was to provide for minimum wages and the reemployment of
workers through shorter hours. And to back up these provisions the government gave its support and encouragement to labor in its right to
organize into unions with leaders of its own choosing.

But cooperation was a practice with which coal operators had had little
experience. And it was in anything but a cooperative mood that they
gathered in Washington in the summer of 1933. Individualists to the core,
suspicious of one another, they wrangled and argued through four days
of Washington heat, and then, true to character, produced not one code
but 27 separate codes! Only one of these offered to cooperate with government and labor. Many of these coal owners sat for the first time in the
same room with representatives of organized labor. And they didn't like
it. Typical of their attitude was the action of the steel executive who
walked out of a conference in Secretary of Labor Perkins' office when he
heard that William A. Green, President of the American Federation of
Labor, was to be there.

The dominant tone of the hearings was set by a group of operators
representing two-thirds of the total bituminous production. This group
included the captive-mine owners. They wanted no government interference—theirs was a "let-us-alone" policy. They were opposed to the
shorter work week and a uniform wage scale. And the union! They
would have nothing to do with it. They would deal directly with their
own employees, they said; it was unnecessary for the miners to join any
outside organization. Yet these employers, while refusing to their employees the power that comes through collective action, spoke at the hear-

ings in Washington through their own trade organizations—through the Northern Coal Control Association in their capacity as coal operators, and through the National Association of Manufacturers, the United States Chamber of Commerce, the Association of American Railroads and the various Boards of Trade in their capacity as steel executives, railroad officials and industrial magnates.

For weeks the coal operators wrestled with a code through one deadlocked conference after another. And when it became apparent that no agreement was possible, General Johnson, the NIRA administrator, had to write one for them. This lack of plan and common understanding revealed as nothing else could the unwillingness if not the incapacity of coal owners and managers, even in a crisis, to organize and govern themselves. They submitted finally, but reluctantly, to minimum wages and unionization in exchange for the privilege of fixing minimum prices above the average cost of production. And then began the experiment of imposing order upon chaos, under the spread of the Blue Eagle's wing.

Washington again, two years later. A strange scene this. Operators pleading for a continuation of the code. For the Supreme Court had declared the NIRA unconstitutional. What had happened to change their attitude? Simply this. As a result of the code they had a net operating profit for the first time in years. The industry's deficit had been reduced from 47½ million dollars in 1933 to 7½ million in 1934. The number of days the mines worked had been increased from 146 in 1932 to 178 in 1934. Not so strange, after all, that they should like the code!

And the miners? In 1932 only 15% of the bituminous workers had been left in the union. Eighteen months later 90% of the coal diggers carried union cards. Their average weekly earnings had increased from $14.47 in 1933 to $18.10 in 1934. In those few districts which had been operating under union contracts before the code, the code had meant no wage gain. But in some districts the increase was as much as 100% above the precode level. This extra did not go for luxuries. Families of five had gone hungry on $500 a year. Now they could have more milk, bread and meat. The miners were grateful for the code.

The code brought together bitter enemies of the past who were obliged to sit down around a common conference table. In sections of the country where collective bargaining had never before existed, operators made real efforts to enter into wage negotiations on a sincere and co-operative basis.

Then came the invalidation of the NRA, followed soon by a substi-

tute measure—the Guffey Act, which not only encouraged collective bargaining but made it compulsory! Operators and miners together fought
for this continuance of the code idea, since both feared a return to the
days of competitive chaos. Not that they had become "buddies," but the
same agreement which guaranteed a return of costs to the operator also
paid minimum wages to the miners. They knew that they could not
separately control price cutting.

But what had worked for the common good of the majority of the
industry and for labor had worked against the interests of the large
consumers of soft coal—the railroads, the steel mills, the electric-power
plants. They were no longer able to buy at bargain rates. So these captive
mine owners and the southern operators, who wanted to continue to pay
lower wages than the north, fought the Guffey bill with all the strength
they could command. The Manufacturers Association, the U. S. Chamber
of Commerce, were again on the scene, and the American Liberty League
declared the bill "inconsistent with American principles." None of these
business associations had anything to say about the dangers of an unorganized industry nor did they make any suggestions for improvements.
Those whom they represented profited from the chaotic condition of the
industry.

Despite their opposition the Guffey Act was passed. It provided for
minimum-price fixing as the code had done. It made collective bargaining compulsory, and guaranteed enforcement of the Act by imposing a
tax of 15% a ton on all coal mined, 90% of which was refunded to those
who complied with the law. But the Guffey Act never really had a chance
to work. Before the Bituminous Coal Commission, created by the Act,
could get into operation this same group who wished to be rid of any
government regulation challenged the law before the Supreme Court.
And on May 18, 1936, nine months after it had been passed, the Court
ruled the Guffey Act unconstitutional on the grounds that coal mining
does not directly affect interstate commerce and that the regulation of
wages and hours of labor in such an industry was beyond the powers of
Congress.

What would happen to the industry now? The NRA had been ruled
out; the Guffey Act had been ruled out. Could any new legislation be
passed that would be acceptable to the Court? And in the meantime
could anything hold the industry together? These questions agitated the
coal operators and the union, and found their way into the press.

Christmas Day, 1936. Another meeting. This time at White Sulphur
Springs, West Virginia. Operators wondering if the industry would pre-

sent a united front in favor of new legislation. Evidences of continued opposition by the southern operators and captive mine owners, but also evidence that considerable numbers of producers favored regulation. John L. Lewis, President of the United Mine Workers of America, telling the operators that the union would support any marketing plan written by the industry if only it assured the industry sufficient income to keep up wages. Under the Guffey Act average weekly earnings had quietly increased, through increased operating time, from $18.10 in 1934 to $24.95 at the end of 1936.

Now began negotiations for a new contract. Signed on April 2, 1937, to run until March 3, 1939, it covered practically the entire bituminous industry. For the first time in years the Minerals Yearbook of 1937 had made no reference to strikes or labor difficulties as causes of industrial disputes. Operators and miners were developing a spirit of give and take!

And in August, 1938, operators from Harlan County, Kentucky, that last stand of rugged individualism, signed up with the union. "Bloody Harlan County" had been for years the scene of violence and bloodshed. Dynamiting, bombings, shootings had been the testimony before the La Follette Committee of the Senate investigating "civil liberties." The Kentucky Governor's Commission harrowed the country with pronouncements of "reprisals on the part of bankers, coal operators and others of the wealthier class" . . . "practiced against Churches whose ministers had the courage to criticize from the pulpit"; with evidence of the "unbelievable" living conditions of union miners discharged and evicted from their company-owned homes (11 children and 4 adults in a three-room building); with evidence that the "miners' wages are cut for additional school costs"—schools in which the coal operators "have much to say in the selection of teachers"; with evidence of forcing the miners to buy $1.00 raffle tickets for "dilapidated" automobiles, a device that netted the company $700 to $800 a car; evidence on the part of the company that they cut from $1800 to $2400 a month from the miners' pay for the service of two doctors whom the company paid a total of $700. Newspapers were full of reports of the coal companies' control of the Sheriff's office, of well-paid spy jobs, of a baby's death because the coal company refused to send their doctor to his union father's home.

Out of the La Follette investigation had come a criminal prosecution by the government against twenty-two coal corporations, twenty-four mine executives and twenty-three former or present law-enforcement officers of Harlan County. While the trial was in progress three persons were killed: a former deputy on trial, a witness subpoenaed by the government, and a miner. The trial ended in a mistrial. Then came an agreement with the Harlan County Coal Operators Association. But "Bloody Harlan" was not ready for industrial peace. The long standing strife still continues.

Also, out of the White Sulphur Springs Conference came a new law— the Bituminous Coal Act of 1937. Patterned closely after the Guffey Act in its price-fixing provisions, it did, however, omit the labor provisions in deference to the prevailing opinion of the Supreme Court, but declared that the public policy of the United States recognized the right of employees to organize and bargain collectively through representatives of their own choosing. The United Mine Workers were willing to support the bill without the labor guarantee, in return for a 50-cent increase in the daily basic wage.

The new law set up a Bituminous Coal Commission to administer the Act—a commission made up of presidential appointees representing the producers, the miners and the public. It divided the industry into twenty-three separate districts. Each district determines the average cost of production for its area and recommends a minimum price below which the price of coal should not be sold. On these recommendations the Coal Commission fixes prices.

The Act recognized a neglected social group—the consumer. A Consumers' Counsel, responsible only to Congress and with power to subpoena, examine witnesses and conduct investigations, was appointed to work with the Commission. This is the first time such an office has been established by Congress. The policy of price fixing is to be balanced by this "watchdog" for the people. His watchdog qualities have already been put to the test. The Commission announced the new schedule of prices without holding public hearings as required under the Act, a course of action with which the Consumers' Counsel took issue. He contended rightly that only through public hearings can consumers, small or large, have some voice in determining the price of coal. Coal companies are notoriously secretive about the items which make up their costs and will fight to keep them from becoming public. But the Consumers' Counsel has taken an aggressive stand in demanding full publicity for the cost data on which prices are to be based. The Counsel and his staff are also doing notable work in urging the adoption of standards of classification for coals so that the small consumer may have the same information available to him as the large consumer through his own experts.

WHAT REMAINS TO BE DONE?

If the Act remains on the books—and we say "if" advisedly, for a bill for its repeal has been introduced in Congress—how far can the Bituminous Coal Act go towards correcting the problems of the soft-coal industry? What other measures must be taken? The two main goals must be kept in mind:

First, better living conditions must be provided for 470,000 miners and their families who look to this industry for a livelihood: steadier employment and higher wages for those at work; and for those who have been or will be cast off by shrinking markets or technological advances, a chance to rehabilitate themselves in other occupations.

Second, the resource itself must be conserved. The known quantity of coal underground, as we shall see in the next chapter, seems ample for many generations to come. Yet supplies will do no good unless it is practical to get them out. We must face the fact that already, in many fields, the richest and most accessible seams have been depleted. We shall soon be working thinner and poorer veins, and paying more in labor for what coal we produce (except as technical changes reduce costs for a while).

Both difficulties—human waste and waste of coal—spring from the same basic causes. Excess mine capacity, leading to competition in its most destructive form, has not only made the business generally unprofitable and decent living for its workers impossible; it has led to serious waste of the resource through closing down mines, in hard times, under circumstances that prevent future recovery of the coal left underground. Competition from other fuels has intensified these evils.

Destructive competition cannot be dealt with by the industry alone nor by state governments, for raising prices and wages only in one company or one state would be suicidal. Coal is the Nation's business.

With the NRA code the federal government belatedly assumed responsibility. In a time of desperate trouble it administered the quickest and simplest remedy possible: it raised prices, at the same time taking steps to encourage unions, raise wages, spread out employment, and safeguard consumers' interests. It did nothing directly about waste of coal nor about overcapacity. Indirectly, overcapacity was apparently encouraged, for the number of small truck mines has increased since the NRA and total capacity has grown. Under the present Coal Act, which still fixes prices although the safeguards to labor have been weakened, there is still nothing to conserve the coal; nothing to reduce overcapacity or keep it from increasing.

What can be done about excess capacity? The National Resources Board Report summarizes the main suggestions advanced so far:

1. Inclusion in the wage agreement—between operators and the miners' union—of a minimum employment guarantee in such a way as to encourage a shift of business from high cost mines to those able to operate more steadily.

If such a plan were tried, the central authority ought to consider how many mines would be drastically affected, and how great a loss of recoverable coal would have to be balanced against the resulting gains. The miners tried to get a guarantee of 200 days employment into their wage agreement of 1939 but compromised on a "union shop" guarantee, which at the time was of greater importance to them.

2. Promoters of new mines to be required by the Federal Securities Commission to state in their offerings to investors that existing capacity in the industry is already more than sufficient.

This would discourage unwise promotions.

3. Control of new branch lines of common carrier railroads in the light of their effect on mine capacity. To construct a branch line a railroad must, under existing laws, obtain a certificate of public convenience and necessity. The Coal Commission could recommend to the ICC that a new extension was unnecessary, if existing capacity was found to be sufficient.

Under the present rulings of the ICC the railroads furnish cars in proportion to a coal company's capacity to produce. If a mine's capacity is ten cars a day and the supply of cars is 80% of the total demand for cars, the mine will get eight cars a day. The only way to get more cars is to increase capacity. So the coal company opens new mines in the same seam. And the railroad builds new spurs to the additional mines. This measure might discourage new ventures by making transportation more difficult. It would not prevent the coal companies from building their own tracks to a rail connection. Nor would it affect the increasing number of mines served by motor transport.

4. A governmental agency to purchase and shut down marginal mines. A tax on all coal tonnage to be levied to pay for these mines and to re-

habilitate the miners displaced. The retirement of marginal mines would afford steadier employment in the mines remaining and would tend to center production in the lower cost mines whose savings in overhead, through steadier running time, would go far to absorb the tax.

This would be a sensible attack on technological unemployment. Mechanization came late to the coal fields, but it must be reckoned with now and in the future. Eighty percent of the coal is now cut by machine; haulage underground is largely electrified; and machine loading, in use only since 1922, accounts for 14% of production. Output per miner has doubled since 1890. That is, we can duplicate 1890 production with only half as many workers. Society should have the benefits of the more efficient mining promised by technical progress. But it will pay too heavily, through more Scott's Runs, unless such a measure for preventing ghost towns is enacted. Devising a rehabilitation program coordinately with the retirement of the high-cost mines would be difficult but absolutely necessary. This measure, while eliminating some mines, would not prevent the opening of new ones.

5. Purchase by the government of coal lands that are near railroads and might soon be the scene of new and unneeded mines. When the time came for use, these would be leased, not sold, the Nation receiving royalties.

Adding to our national coal reserves by this plan would provide a market for coal lands, relieving thereby the pressure on land owners to open more mines in order to meet taxes and interest which has always been one of the most powerful causes for overdevelopment. To make the plan work operators remaining in business would have to agree not to expand their own capacity beyond that approved by the central authority.

It is up to the public and to the government to recognize how urgent the need is for strong action. We should immediately give Congress constitutional power to act directly on production, and wages and hours as well as on price: coal is a national resource. Production quotas may or may not be desirable; Congress should at any rate have power to call for such a program, and should direct the Coal Commission to study the possibilities. We should empower the government to begin purchasing some marginal mines and untapped coal lands, as suggested in (4) and (5). We should direct a public-planning agency to devise national policies for all power resources, since the position of coal is so greatly affected by competing fuels. This agency should attack the problems of waste in all power resources and work out conservation measures to be implemented by Congress. At the same time, and coordinately with the conservation program, means for rehabilitating stranded miners must be found. To do this effectively, do we not need a planning agency that deals on an even wider front than that of all power resources? Think of the railroads' multiple relation to coal, and the enormous wastes involved in cross-haulage. Might it not be wise to save on freight rates and pay more miners? Who is to study such problems and lay a basis for action? Consider how many miners are now completely or partially unemployed, and how many more will be displaced by technical advances. Must they all go on relief? Can many be turned into subsistence farmers, when we already have a large migrant farm population to plan for? Or is there some more positive program to be conceived?

These questions, which take us out of the coal towns and beyond the coal fields, we must hold until the final chapter. Next in order is another look at coal itself: coal in the making and coal still awaiting its use.

MINERS UNDERGROUND IN A SOFT-COAL SEAM

In the days of hand mining, undercutting was a difficult and dangerous operation. Four out of five tons, in soft coal, are now cut by machine. Mechanical loading, now used for 14 per cent of production, is increasing and threatens to put many miners out of work.

Farm Security Administration—Photo by Johnson

A STRANDED COMMUNITY

Miners' homes at Scotts Run, W. Va. Note sewage.

A FRESH START

About a hundred families from Scotts Run have been resettled in the Arthurdale Homestead project: homes, farm land, chances to build and make and grow needed things; the opportunity to learn how.

TAKING OFF A MOUNTAINTOP

Strip mining is a large-scale transformation of the earth's surface. In prairie states one sees great fields turned into ridges and gorges, the parallel lines of excavations often forty or fifty feet deep.

Chapter VI—COAL: FROM COCKROACHES TO CAPITALISTS

Case History Number Two

The Age of Cockroaches

Coal Fields in the United States

Kinds of Coal

Getting Coal Out

Have We Enough Coal? Planning for the Future

Chapter VI—COAL: FROM COCKROACHES TO CAPITALISTS

Case History Number Two

The Age of Cockroaches

COAL WAS IN THE MAKING. The world was green and warm and damp. Coal plants were growing in the long-ago Paleozoic (Ancient Life) marsh, and men had not yet appeared upon the earth. There was in the world no hand with its opposed thumb, able to grasp a branch of the early conifers, and no brain to conceive of a tool. There was no mammal carrying her unborn young within her body and feeding her newly born from milk of her own making. There were no birds fluttering from the strange seal trees to giant ferns. Of color, except the lush green, there was little. No brilliant plumage, no true flowers, few seed-bearing plants in this green warm world where coal was in the making.

And yet living things already had had a long history stretching back over three geologic eras, perhaps some seven hundred millions of years. From a great swamp rose tree ferns, drooping their graceful fronds from a height of fifty feet. Still higher towered the leafless, blunt, branched seal or scale trees, destined later to disappear from the earth. Clumps like giant bamboo or cane brakes a foot thick stood near lower and finer ferns. Horsetails, ferns, ground pine—giants compared with their dwarfed descendants of today; small conifers, a new experiment in seed bearing, ranged close to the swamp. The air was filled with tiny spores blown from thousands of species of primitive plants even as now, millions of years later, mushrooms drop their spores and evergreens scatter their pollen showers of spores to the wind. Animals there were, too, some three thousand species. Many kinds of fish swam in the shallow ˙˙˙˙ ˙˙˙ over the fallen fetid tangle of the swamp, picking their way ˙˙˙˙ of their three eyes, crawled many kinds of lizardlike or eel- ˙˙˙ bia, well adapted to a world now marsh, now dry. Iridescent ˙˙˙ twenty-nine inches in stretch of wing, darted over the rank

201

marsh growth. Insects, millions of insects, swarmed in the shadow of the rank vegetation which was destined to become coal.

Scientists have called it the Age of Cockroaches when coal was in the making. Some eight hundred species of these tempting creatures, from three to four inches long, scampered freely over the earth and under the coal plants, checked neither by human emotions nor by man-made brooms. And when their happy scuttling days were over, their dead bodies sank deep into the tangled mire of swamp; and slowly their organic matter disappeared by the strange chemical process of decay, and bit by bit was replaced by deposits of carbon even while the swamp vegetation was metamorphosed into coal. Thus it comes about that the picks of present-day miners hack out fossils of these carnivorous cockroaches of the Paleozoic Era.

These cockroaches were, so to speak, the first masters of the coal fields or what was to become coal fields. But they were not absentee landlords! They lived on the land. They fought a fierce fight for life, as is the way with each ascendant form of life. But they passed away, as ancient orders do. For perhaps a hundred million years the coal fields knew no masters. The ancient swamp became buried deeper and deeper under layer after layer of sediment until, squeezed of part of its gases, fats and water under the weight of the overlying strata, it became hard black gleaming carbon. But the impress of leaves and fronds and trunks of the old vegetation still remains.

On the surface of the earth, life went on evolving. To the early carboniferous ferns and trees were added flowers of brilliant hue and seed-bearing plants of many kinds; to the early fish and amphibia were added reptiles, giant lizards, birds and finally tiny mammals. Until at last came men, men with hands capable of grasping and with brains and cultures capable of grasping. So at length, in what we now call the Age of Capitalism, came the modern masters of the coal fields, successors to these early masters in the Age of Cockroaches.

In the damp green world where the cockroaches were flourishing and the coal plants were growing, North America was already a continent. This had come about, as has all continent building, through the same earth behaviors which have given us soil—mountain building and erosion of rock. Geologically, a continent means a large mass of land which has mountain ranges on its margins and a depressed central plain. In the very early days long before there was any life on the earth, when the earth first began to cool and the crust to crumple, certain parts of the earth emerged above the primordial acid waters. These parts are called nuclear

NUCLEAR LANDS IN NORTH AMERICA

Based on map, page 458, in "Introductory Geology" by Louis V. Pirsson and Charles Schuchert

lands or shields. These areas of greatest crustal activity tend to remain relatively constant. That is, there has never been a general interchange in position between continent and sea. In North America the three original nuclear lands which first emerged (eastern Canada, the Antilles and the Western Cordillera) were so placed that erosion, uplift, erosion and uplift carried on over millions of years, eventually joined the high lands on the two ocean shores by a plain to the north, and to the south by a shallow sea. Such a sea is called an epeiric sea. After many changes in shape of land and water, in the Age of Cockroaches this shallow, inland, salt-water sea stretched its arm from the present Gulf of Mexico, flowing over Texas, Oklahoma, Kansas, Missouri, Illinois, Indiana, Kentucky, parts of Tennessee, Michigan and Maryland, over West Virginia and, most important of all, Pennsylvania. (See maps, pages 205 and 171.)

When coal was in the making, the rock layer-cake had already reached gigantic depth, and thousands of feet of sediments already lay under this Paleozoic sea. The shallow sea between the continental margins alternated with a low Central Plain as the crust rose and fell innumerable times, partly from the direct deposit of eroded sediments which caused a shifting of the crustal weight, partly from the deep subterranean flow of the hot magmas. And so the layer-cake was built: a layer of swamp vegetation, then a slight subsidence and a layer of clay or sand; then a further subsidence and a layer of shells or bones of tiny lime-extracting animals which lived in the shallow seas; an uplift, another layer of swamp vegetation; a subsidence, more layers of sand and lime and clay; until in Oklahoma and Arkansas the layers are 25,000 feet thick, lying in some places over earlier layers of sediment 53,000 feet thick! Twenty-nine separate swamps made twenty-nine layers of coal from 3 inches to 10 feet thick, averaging 3¼ feet. As the ancient swamps got buried deeper and deeper, the overlayers of the layer-cake exerted more and more pressure which squeezed out the water, fat and gases, making coals of different quality.

All this layer-cake building happened in the Age of Cockroaches, or the Pennsylvania period (a period is a part of an era): so called not because the three-eyed amphibia which slipped and slopped under the coal-making plants or the scuttling scorpions or cockroaches knew the future William Penn and his woods, but because geologists often name a period after the locality where the series was studied in detail. Not only was coal in the making in this shallow epeiric sea. Animals were in the making. The unstable environment of the shallow marginal waters, which came and went with minor upward and downward movements of the sea bottom, proved the best breeding ground for animals still geologically new. So that here came the first biological experiments which eventually led to air-breathing and land-moving animals—here, where coal was in the making.

COAL FIELDS IN THE UNITED STATES

The mountains whose disintegrated rock formed the layer-cake, the giant range of Appalachians, stretched in those days from Georgia to Nova Scotia, covering the present-day Atlantic plain and out into the ocean. Only occasional stumps of them are now left on the Atlantic coast. In the trough, the old strait, to the east of the mountains were the thickest

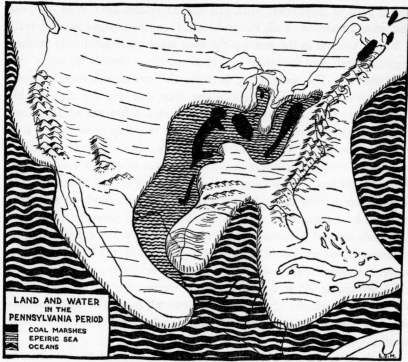

LAND AND WATER
IN THE
PENNSYLVANIA PERIOD

COAL MARSHES
EPEIRIC SEA
OCEANS

Based on map, page 511, in "Introductory Geology" by Louis V. Pirsson and Charles Schuchert

deposits. And so it was there that the earth crumpled in gigantic folds in the next great mountain movement, the so-called Appalachian Revolution. The push ran east and west. The most eastern fold formed the Blue Ridge Mountains, which have now lost their sedimentary overlay. The most western fold ended along an almost abrupt line now called the Allegheny Front, a cliff running from the present Catskills to Birmingham, Alabama. (See map, page 46.) The surface rose in four great folds (the first supposed to have been some 40,000 feet high!) carrying with them the layers of sediments of the past, among them the layers of coal. But most of the coal in these Folded Alleghenies was lost when the folds eroded to a peneplain (almost a plain) with parallel stripes of different sediments, across which flowed the rivers to the Atlantic. When the peneplain again rose and the softer of these sediments washed away, our present folded mountains remained—successive parallel ridges of different kinds of rock, with the old rivers of the peneplain keeping their old course through the ridges in what we call water gaps. Towards the northern part of the Folded Alleghenies, the northern end of the trough, the coal is still

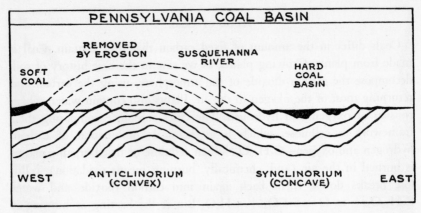

preserved, squeezed of its oil and gas and distorted by the pressure of the folding. This is anthracite or hard coal. Here the layers of coal may lie at any angle to the surface and run deep into the earth.

In the anthracite fields the coal lies in basins which represent the concave portion of a fold (sincline); the convex portion (anticline) has disappeared through erosion. On the sides of the basins or valleys, the coal is obviously nearer the surface, so near that it is now obtained by the new process called stripping. This is nothing more or less than digging a trench (sometimes 100, sometimes 200 feet deep) with a giant steam shovel to expose the coal, which is then taken out by a small steam shovel. Since within the large coal basin or valley there are many minor folds, there may be a pocket of coal left near enough the surface to permit of strip mining. These pockets of coal, which are the original layer squeezed into knuckles, may be 60 or even 80 feet thick.

The veins of bituminous or soft coal, however, lie in undisturbed horizontal strata under the Allegheny Plateau and the prairies, and are consequently flat; and if a river has cut a valley, they can be worked by a tunnel.

The coal at the base of the Rockies was made later than the eastern coal but by the same process. The beds were dragged up relatively close to the surface when the Rocky Mountains pushed their igneous mass high into the air. Consequently the tilted edges of the once horizontal sheets are found near the surface on the plains just east of the mountains. More deposits are found on the plateaus west of the Rockies, wherever the original sheets have not been eroded away. In Montana and the Dakotas and around the Gulf and up the Mississippi Bottoms are more huge deposits of lignite. At present it does not pay to mine this coal with such low carbon content.

KINDS OF COAL

Coals differ in the amount of fixed carbon that they contain. Coal is made from plants. Growing plants, as we saw in the case history of soil, decompose the carbon dioxide of the atmosphere, using the carbon and returning most of the oxygen to the air. Plants also contain water, which consists of oxygen and hydrogen. The chief substance composing their framework is cellulose, which is a chemical combination of carbon, hydrogen and oxygen—$C_6H_{10}O_5$. When cellulose or dried organic matter is burned in the air (and, chemically, burning means oxidation), cellulose breaks down, turns back again into carbon dioxide and water $C_6H_{10}O_5 + 12\ O = 6\ CO_2 + 5\ H_2O$. But if the heating or burning is without air or in a limited amount of air, the oxidation is incomplete and much of the carbon remains.

This happens artificially in the making of charcoal or naturally if organic matter decays where air cannot reach it freely, as when plants grow under water or are smothered under a layer of clay or sand. For decay, too, is a process of oxidation. In partial oxidation, some water (H_2O) is removed, some carbon dioxide (CO_2) and some marsh gas (CH_2). The decayed organic matter, which is left much richer in carbon and poorer in hydrogen than the original material, is known as peat.

Since carbon burns readily—that is, it readily oxidizes—the more carbon the decayed organic matter contains, the better it will burn. The products made from old decayed swamp vegetation arranged in the order of the proportion of gas, fats and water having been squeezed out of them, and consequently the proportion of fixed carbon they contain, are: peat, lignite, bituminous coal, anthracite, graphite. Peat contains least carbon; anthracite has from 90% to 95% of fixed carbon; graphite is pure carbon. Coke is made by partial burning of bituminous coal, which releases some of the water and gas and leaves a larger proportion of carbon.

GETTING COAL OUT

Soft-coal mining methods vary all the way from one-man hand-worked diggings in hillsides to the elaborately shored-up rooms of a large company's mine, where nearly all the work may be done by machine. Here is a description of work in a Pittsburgh Coal Company mine, taken from *Fortune,* October, 1933:

Mining soft coal is not so romantic, so dangerous, or so laborious an occupation as it has often been pictured. The coal runs in veins from five to ten feet thick and at an average depth of about 300 feet underground. There are no shafts in the Pittsburgh Coal Co. mines; the mine starts at the foot of a hill and tunnels through it. The tunnels are called "entries"; the places where the miners work are called "rooms." A room is about six feet high, twenty feet wide, maybe several hundred feet long. There are only two or three miners to a room; they work off by themselves and the foreman does not get around very often. If the miner wants to take life easy there is nothing to stop him—except that he is usually paid piece-work rates and so the less he works the less he earns. But what he does is pretty much up to him, which is one reason why coal miners often like coal mining and also why they are so individualistic. Also miners' wages are nearly two thirds of the total cost of production.

Work in a room starts at 3:00 A.M. when a fire boss, who gets $33 a week, goes in and sees that the room is safe to work in. Nobody else is allowed to enter until the fire boss comes out. Then the miners go in, each with an electric light in his hat and a battery on his hip. First job is cutting a groove in the coal vein, the groove running parallel and close to the floor. This undercuts the coal and makes it easier to blow it loose. The undercutting is done by an electric machine. Next the miner drills holes in the coal vein, over the groove. Dynamite is put in the holes and a miner known as a shot-firer explodes the charge. The result is a large mass of loose coal. Here is where the big hand-labor element comes in, for somebody has to pick up the loose coal and put it in the car. This somebody is called a loader. A fair day's work is about nine tons, al-though here there is a very wide variation depending partly on the coal and considerably on the loader. There are also mechanical loaders, the use of which is advancing rapidly and will advance much more rapidly if the miners force their wages up to the point at which the machine is more economical. In 1931, 13 percent of U.S. soft coal was mechanically loaded. After the coal has been loaded into the cars, it is drawn out of the mine via mule power or electric power.

Anthracite techniques must take account of harder coal, tilted strata, and deeper workings (sometimes 1000 feet underground). Mechaniza-tion has been developing in the hard-coal industry also: about 21% of anthracite is mechanically loaded, compared to 13% of bituminous. Strip or open-pit mining produces 6% of soft-coal output, 10% or 12% of hard coal. Its use seems to be increasing faster, however, in bituminous mining.

Surface practices other than stripping vary also. The surface of the earth in the Allegheny Plateau is entirely different from that in the prairies nearer the Mississippi. The surface soil of the plateau is not good for agriculture, whereas the topsoil of the prairies is among the richest in the world. So it comes about that in West Virginia the mine owners commonly finish mining in a particular spot by producing a "fall"— letting the surface cave in. This practice usually makes the surface unfit for any growing thing. But the prairie farms of Illinois are often carried on over the mines, and the top and underrights are owned by different people. No fall is allowed in these sections, and accidental ones are punishable. Also ground water, so necessary for surface agriculture, must be protected. These methods mean that more coal must be left underground which is permanently lost.

Anyone who explores the Appalachian plateaus in a Ford from West Virginia to Alabama becomes sensitive to the ups and downs. If he will pause at each crest and let his eye range around the faraway even-lined horizon, he will gradually discard his layman's conception that a plateau *is* a flattish, unbroken surface. And if he will stretch his layman's mind as well as he can, back, back to the geologic days before the rivers had sawed their canyons or gorges or widish valleys, he will suddenly see what this land of hills *must once have been*. Yes, this land of hills must have been like a plain and would still be like a plain if the eroded valleys were filled. For all the "ups" rise to the same general level.

Then when he plunges down the next steep grade, he will read with new excitement the differentiated deposits of the layer-cake piled thousands of feet high. Down the layer-cake to the river at the bottom and up the layer-cake in reverse order. An eroded plateau which we call hills and valleys. A layer-cake built through millions of years when coal was in the making.

And as one sees the farmers of West Virginia digging the soft coal out of the banded hillside; as one walks upright through the miles of level underground channels of the eight-foot-thick Pittsburgh seam or crawls through the thinner seams where men still crouch to dig; as one shoots hundreds of feet down a shaft in the hard-coal mines of the anthracite region to underground railroads, ventilating systems, blasting, gas testing and all the mechanisms of modern mining; or even as one peers down the perilous well of a bootlegger, one sees everywhere evidences of the old swamp life. Fossils abound. Plants and animals which lived and died in the Age of Cockroaches when coal was in the making.

HAVE WE ENOUGH COAL? PLANNING FOR THE FUTURE

In such a way was coal made, and in such ways are we of the present United States getting it out of the ground. Have we enough coal—enough for now and for the future? Are our methods of production wasteful, remembering our definition of waste as a loss, the remedy of which would not be more costly than the loss itself?

How much coal have we in the ground? Estimates vary. One geologist

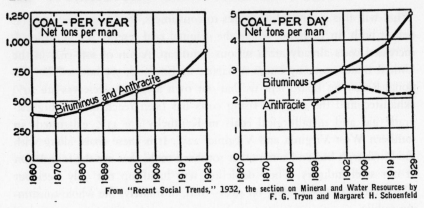

From "Recent Social Trends," 1932, the section on Mineral and Water Resources by
F. G. Tryon and Margaret H. Schoenfeld

TREND IN COAL OUTPUT PER MAN

Increases in productivity have been due to mechanization and to discovery of easily worked sources. The decline in anthracite reflects changes in demand and depletion of the most accessible supplies.

puts the figure for the total amount of coal in the United States within 3000 feet of the surface at 3,540,000 million tons. Another estimate gives: 2,271,080 million metric tons of bituminous and 22,542 million of anthracite; or a total of 2,293,622 million tons of coal, not counting subbituminous or lignite. Production of hard and soft coal combined, in the peak year 1918, was less than 700 million tons; in 1937 we took out less than 500 million tons. Of course, coal may find new uses (for example, as a source of gasoline if our oil reserves give out); but on the other hand, substitutes for coal (such as electricity from water power) may be more largely developed. Even should coal consumption increase, it looks as if exhaustion of our coal reserves lies two thousand years or so ahead!

Is this, then, one place where the psychology of "Why save when there is plenty more?" may do no harm? We do tend to think of our coal reserves as unlimited, if, indeed, we think of them at all. And yet future generations may regret this attitude and our present lack of planning even as we regret the similar attitude of our forefathers towards our country's soil. Why? What danger can there be?

Having plenty of coal in American earth is one thing. Getting it out is another. Some veins are easier to mine than others. In the haste to get the coal up for immediate private gain, the richest and most easily mined veins have been dug out. The danger is that we shall soon have to spend more for what we get. For a while we may enjoy low costs on account of technical improvements in mining. Then costs may rise seriously.

What will this mean? High prices to consumers, low wages to workers: one or both. In England, where the original coal reserve is 7% depleted, increased costs already are a serious handicap. A ton of soft coal in the United States costs 1.7 hours of labor; in England, 7.5 hours. The National Resources Board tells us that our own anthracite reserves are 29% exhausted and the stage of rising costs has been reached. The highest-grade gas and metallurgical coals in Kentucky are 11% exhausted; in southern West Virginia and Virginia, 22%. It is these coals, along with the Pittsburgh bed and some other southern coals, that are the foundation of our steel industry. Their depletion will handicap not only steel but all the industries dependent on steel—thus, ultimately, the whole consuming public.

Waste, therefore, is a matter of immediate concern. Human wastes in the coal industry—the hardships of miners, the deprivations of mining communities—have made us less sensitive to physical waste of the coal itself and waste of effort in mining. But such waste occurs, and in serious proportions.

It was reliably estimated in 1923 that the average loss in United States coal mines was 35%—perhaps 15% being unavoidable. The percentage has increased since then. (Losses in western Europe were from 5% to 10%.) This kind of waste comes largely from abandoning mines before all the recoverable coal is out, allowing roofs to collapse or water to flood.

Determining what is really wasteful—balancing one loss against another—is a task that cannot be left to individual coal operators. Even if coal men were concerned more with greatest ultimate recovery of coal than with monthly balance sheets, there would still be vital factors left out. For example, strip mining often ruins the surface land for agriculture; and so far, adequate methods of restoration have not been worked out. Thirty thousand acres in the Mississippi Valley and in eastern states have been devastated. Illinois, as we have seen, protects itself against cave-ins. But what of its 183,000 acres that offer a fine site for this open-pit coal mining? Here is a method that recovers a high percentage of coal; yet it damages the basic agricultural resource, soil, and offers fewer jobs than other mining methods. Certainly a long-sighted vision in such matters is not to be expected of the individual out to make profits and to count gains in terms of his own immediate investment rather than of people's welfare or the country's future.

The history of the coal industry left us with the belief that government planning of some sort is necessary in order to bring adequate financial returns on capital invested and decent lives to the workers involved. To this must now be added that government planning for our coal reserves and the methods of mining them, with or for the industry, is necessary to prevent waste and an avoidable increase in costs which will trail with it hardships for future workers and consumers.

WHAT'S THE PRICE OF COAL?

The nation's wheels are turning
And the merry fires burning;
Carload after carload
Away the engines roll.
And crouching in the dark
With steaming shoulder stark
Down below the daylight
The men are digging coal.
 Keep the fires burning
 Digging out the coal!

In Wall Street they're so busy
You'd think they must be dizzy.
By polished desks mahogany
Sit owners of the coal.
The Wall Street elevators
Go up a hundred floor;
The miners' elevators
Go down as far and more
 To where the men are digging
 Digging out the coal.

Clever wits are matching
Where mighty pens are scratching;
To be an owner nowadays
Is not an easy role.
The owners, troubled, sit.
Their heavy brows are knit.
No longer are they getting
Good dividends on coal.
 Tell the men to quit
 Digging out the coal!

The owners, frustrate, sit
Their purses badly hit.
Times are bad. Depression.
No profit out of coal.
And in the mining town
The mines have been shut down;
No longer are men digging.
They're living on the dole.
 They haven't any wages
 So they're living on the dole.

Down the Youghiogheny
The beds are not mahogany
For Negro nor for white,
For hillbilly or Pole.
Children of the slag heap
In broken shanties sleep
And tired women sweep
The dust and grime of coal
    And think their men are lucky
    When they can dig the coal.

Mining towns are grimy
And their little runs are slimy;
There isn't any plumbing
And typhoid takes its toll.
But up the Lackawanna
And up the Susquehanna
And up Monongahela
They want to dig the coal.
    If you had children starving
    You'd want to dig the coal.

But in Mahanoy, Shamokin,
The fires still are smokin':
The miner folk are living
On the coal they stole.
The trucks are on the highways
The trucks are on the byways
For bootleggers are busy
Digging out the coal.
    They'd rather steal a living
    Than try to live on dole.

The owners in the cities sit
And still their weary brows are knit.
What's the market? Up or down?
What's the price of coal?
Far away from where they sit
Men are dying in the pit.
Far away in grime and murk
Women weep and women work.
Far away, oh, hear them cry!
Skinny little children die
    And that's the price of coal.

L.S.M.

CHAPTER VII—OUR OIL AND GASOLINE CULTURE

The Present

OUR THIRTY MILLION AUTOMOBILE DRIVERS

THREE HUNDRED AND FIFTY THOUSAND GASOLINE STATIONS

PIPE LINES, STORAGE TANKS AND REFINERIES

PRODUCERS IN THE FIELD

PARADOXES IN OIL. A BOTTLE-NECK PATTERN

OKLAHOMA CITY: CIVIC PRIDE VS. QUICK MONEY

A BOOM TOWN: FOUR PHASES

WHAT NEXT?

The Present

OUR THIRTY MILLION AUTOMOBILE DRIVERS

Not all of America's machinery, not all of America's wheels are turned by coal. Coal has one great rival in our industrial culture. Oil and its four great products. Fuel oil for locomotives, steamers and other motors; lubricating oil for all machinery; kerosene; and, above all, gasoline. The smell of gasoline is ever in the American nostrils. If you live in a city, go out and count the cars going by. On Park Avenue, New York, 2700 pass you in an average hour. And these are only pleasure cars and taxis. Over by the water front, on West Street, more than 1600 trucks and other vehicles boom by in an hour, while overhead the pleasure cars and taxis whiz in another procession. Through the Hudson and Lincoln tubes, and over all the bridges, 237,000 vehicles come onto Manhattan Island every twenty-four hours. It is the same in Chicago, in St. Louis, in Los Angeles, in San Francisco, where the giant bridges span the great bay harbor and the Golden Gate, and the cars look down on the ferries, the onetime exclusive carriers from the opposite shores.

If you live in the suburbs, go out and count the cars on your nearest highway or pike. Pleasure cars come streaming to and from the local station, more cars streaming to and from the city, buses, trucks of every kind—delivery trucks from the near-by city, big red trucks of Grandmother's Bread (how this would have surprised Grandmother!), trucks with coal, with stone, with more autos, mysterious canvas-covered trucks, monster moving vans. If you live near enough, you can enjoy their booming all through the night, for these are owls who fly best when the garages are full of resting daytime cars, pleasure or business.

If you live in the real country, go out in your little car, Model T or otherwise. Drawn up before each kitchen door at suppertime will be a mate to your own car, even though the house roof needs shingling and long rows of ragged clothes hang from the clothesline. In the morning hours you may hear the chugging of a gasoline engine. A sawmill has moved into your neighborhood, and stumps and sawdust piles are about to take the place of the trees you have grown up with. Or if the prairie lands are your home, you may hear the whir of the new tractors where your neighbors are hurrying to get the hay harvested before the rain.

If you are a young American, all these things seem natural. You take the gasoline world for granted. You tinker with your own or your neighbor's engine, you recognize a wrong or a new sound on the road, you go to work and to play with the steering wheel in your hand. And if you are an old American, you endure the sounds and smells and the speed of the younger generation and try not to think of the accident rates or feel superior because you still enjoy walking. For you, too, take the gasoline world for granted.

THREE HUNDRED AND FIFTY THOUSAND GASOLINE STATIONS

But what do the United States drivers of our thirty million automobiles know of the work or the workers behind this familiar gasoline world? They know the gas stations and the cheerful men and women who put the hose nozzles into their gasoline tanks or pour the thick oil into their engines. Each driver has his pet brand. Families fight over them. "What made you fill her up with that rotten Shell? Don't you know it's run by a Dutchman from England anyway?" Or "Good Gulf! It ought to be called 'Good Grief'!" Or once in a while, "I wouldn't buy Standard if she never ran again. Don't you know what a skinflint old Rockefeller was?" Or even, "Tydol, please. I own some stock." Or out in the wheat lands of Minnesota or Nebraska a farmer voice, "How are the sales of the Cooperative gas coming along? We'll beat the Standard yet!" Yes, these thirty million drivers rejoice at the variety and the multiplicity of roadside pumps, would rejoice even if they knew that there are 350,000 retail outlets in the United States. How many of them realize that the fluctuating price posted on the pumps might be lower if there were not so many pumps? Some marketing experts say there are four or five times too many pumps for efficiency or profit. "How could that be?" the drivers would say. For they are Americans and so believe in competition as the savior of business.

To back up their argument, these American automobile drivers would point to the occasional pumps which appear for a short time, selling gas at eight or nine cents a gallon. Not, necessarily, that they would buy this smuggled stuff themselves. But they have noticed that the regular companies soon install their own pumps near by when one of these ramshackle, low-priced pumps begins operating. "Fighting gas" the companies call the product, and most of the motorists give it a try. "Probably better than the bootleg stuff, and cheaper than the regular." It matters little to them that the roadside pumps keep closing up. For other pumps keep coming.

Who owns them? Seemingly these 350,000 pumps represent independent small businesses; but over half of them are really linked with the big companies: 10 % of them are operated directly by the big companies and probably another 50% are controlled by these companies under what is known as the "lease and license" system. It works this way. A man—or often a man and his wife—living on a roadside think they would like to run a gas station. It looks profitable on this road where the cars are whizzing by. So the Texas Company, say, leases the premises from the man and sublets back to him the right to run a filling station, provided he will sell Texas products exclusively. By way of rental, the man is allowed to buy gasoline from the Texas Company at a lower price than independent dealers are charged. How much lower depends on whether the building and equipment belong to the dealer or to the company. It is lowest if the dealer owns the whole business and takes all the risk, and this is the arrangement the companies prefer; but often they install the pumps, many times the station as well. These "100 percent" accounts are naturally irritating to the manufacturers of special products such as high-grade lubricating oil.

The many drivers know that there is more difference in the color of the gas sold by the different companies than there is in the price. The big companies pretty much follow the price set by Standard Oil. But they compete vigorously in advertising—what American does not know this?—and in special kinds of filling-station services. Also, each company now tries to cover as much territory as possible and has since the sales of gasoline began to increase in 1927–29. Shell had been sold in the West. But in 1929 it not only expanded in its old territory: it moved into eastern territory and acquired 11,250 new dealers. The Standard Oil of New York —Socony—and the Standard Oil of New Jersey also began expanding. So everybody expanded. Then life became hard for the man and his wife who had leased a filling station. Then the pumps began to come and go on the highways. More pumps than the traffic will bear!

PIPE LINES, STORAGE TANKS AND REFINERIES

The men and women who run pumps are only the last link in the complicated work pattern of oil. Behind the 350,000 gas stations, what work and workers do the drivers of the automobiles know? They may know the great storage tanks. New Yorkers are familiar with the tanks of Bayonne, the peninsula across the Hudson, stretching from Jersey City down into the Upper Bay and linked to Staten Island by the graceful Bayonne Bridge. Hundreds of huge Standard Oil tanks, which look from an airplane like a druggist's display of pill boxes. Everyone knows that these Bayonne pill boxes were owned by Rockefeller. A few remember how he outwitted the railroad which was trying to prevent his constructing pipes down the peninsula, by getting a franchise from Town Council and Mayor, and digging and completing the pipe line across the entire city overnight with 300 men!

Though the dwellers of Chicago may not see the tanks of Whiting so often, they know they are there when the wind blows west. But neither drivers nor city folk wonder much where these tanks, ranged on the outskirts of all large centers of population, get their oil. They accept them and their smell as parts of their familiar gasoline world. Nor have these drivers any idea as they speed east or west over the highways of California or roll along from New York to Chicago or to Texas, that crossing under the roads are buried pipes carrying sluggish black oil to the refineries from oil wells three hundred, four hundred or even a thousand miles away. So oblivious are the auto drivers, of these great underground transportation subways, that few of them notice the pumping stations spaced every twenty or thirty miles according to the grade. Yet there are 250,000 miles of pipe line in the United States, 112,000 carrying petroleum and the rest gas, and *all* the railroads have only a little over 400,000 miles of track!

The refineries themselves even the layman can hardly miss, though to him these plants appear only as huge masses of complicated pipes, tanks and scaffolding, which he regards with the characteristic, lack-luster layman eye. If he went inside, he would be overwhelmed by the amount of mechanism and the fewness of the workers. Into these complex refineries runs the stream of crude black petroleum, practically useless until it has gone through some processing. Here the carbon and hydrogen of the crude oil is broken down by elaborate methods into fuel and lubricating oils, gasoline and kerosene, leaving a black mass, largely asphalt or paraffin wax according to its "base," but also material for many other by-products such as carbon black, commercial solvents, paraffin wax, medicinal oils, insecticides and road oil. In older plants, such as those at the Dorcheat Bayou, Louisiana, sulphuric acid was used as a precipitant, with much consequent damage to the surrounding country. In the great new plants, such as that at Paulboro, New Jersey, by a new process

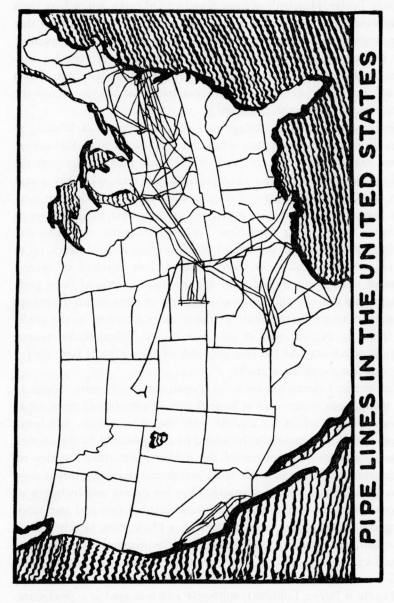

Of our 250,000 miles of pipe lines for gas and oil, 112,000 miles, costing over a billion dollars, transport petroleum.

the impurities are dissolved by a harmless chemical solvent and removed from the oil substances.

Over a billion barrels of oil produced in the United States yearly. Twelve billion dollars' capital investment in oil and another two billion and up in natural gas. Such are the staggering proportions of the oil industry. But it is here in the refineries—not in the gas stations where small and big business fight to market gasoline, not in the fields where producers, big and little, fight to produce crude petroleum—that the oil money is most consistently made. For crude oil is of no use to the consumer until refined. Yet there are only about 395 refineries in the whole country. Among these, the big money is made by a still smaller group of big companies, twenty in number, who refine 80% of all the oil. A part of the money made by these huge companies is, of course, passed on to their investors, for here again we meet the modern company financed by the money of many stockholders. But most of the profit accumulates in the hands of the few men who keep a minor part of the stock, but enough to perpetuate a substantial part of the profits into service contracts, bonuses, fees and commissions. Again we meet the industrial barons, successors to the earlier rugged individualists of the refining companies who made the great oil fortunes.

It is here, too, that we find the pattern of semimonopoly in the twenty big companies, just as we found this pattern of semimonopoly in the eight big companies controlling the anthracite fields. Keen competition has, of course, tried to keep new companies from growing to powerful size. But once in, they hang together on matters of common interest and together adjust both output and price so as to bring maximum money returns. Thus the group of giant concerns, as a whole, act somewhat like a true monopoly.

These few big companies are, however, more than refiners. They are integrated businesses. We have seen how they really control the retailing of 60% of gasoline. They also control the pipe lines—those arteries of the industry—piping 98% of the crude oil. And in order further to control price and supply, they also extend their sway back into the fields and produce half the petroleum.

PRODUCERS IN THE FIELD

For back of the refineries at the other end of the pipe lines are more work and more workers, who annually produce over one billion barrels of crude oil, half for the twenty big refining companies in their role of producers, and the other half for the 16,000 smaller producer companies. Millions of Americans are used to the derricks of an oil field; for they rise in twenty states from Pennsylvania west to California. But millions more have never seen their pointed scaffolds rising 120 to 180 feet into the air, or heard the clink-clanking of the plunging center pump, or smelled—no, almost tasted—the heavy, pungent, pervasive odor from thick black oil that lies in pools around the pumps and often in straggling streams throughout the field. In the prairie lands of Kansas, Oklahoma and Texas, the derricks show miles away silhouetted against a cloudless sky. They rise in droves, sometimes thousands of them, almost never alone. There never seem to be many men about. The few one sees wear high muddy rubber boots and are smudged with black smears of oil and mud. If the engine is not working, they sit on "the lazy bench." About 100,000 men in all fields—more or less, depending on whether it is boom time for oil production.

Clank, clank. The electric or Diesel engine has started. The rotary table begins to revolve. The swivel and square drill stem (called the "Kelly"), hooked onto the traveling block, rises and falls rhythmically in the center of the scaffold. And down below one knows but does not see that a stream of thick petroleum is rising in a hole 500, 1000, even 11,000 feet deep, rising to the opening of the pipe line and starting on its pulsing journey to a far-off refinery. If the gas pressure is great enough, the oil rises silently without a pump. It seems so easy as one stands by and watches. So easy—and yet, incredible that such depths can be plumbed, such mechanism devised to be operated from the surface to a pool of oil twice as far down under the earth as Mount Mitchell is high above the sea.

It seems even more incredible if one is lucky enough to see a well being drilled. An 80-foot pipe length made of four jointed sections, coupled to the plunging drill stem at one end, and with a drill at the other end which screws as it bores and squeezes up mud and drill cuttings along the outside of the pipe, helping to make the lining of the hole firm. Down go the first 80 feet of the pipe. A new section is added and follows the first. Then another and another. But the drill gets dull and up the whole series of jointed pipes must come, even if they are eleven thousand feet long! And after the drill is sharpened, down they must all go again. Surely an incredible sight to the layman.

Texas has produced probably the most spectacular gushers, but they occur in other fields as well. In Mexico, the oil rushes up, hot, in a black geyser. Terrifying, even when under control. Destructive, wasteful and dangerous beyond description when the gas pressure in the oil sands is so great that the gusher goes wild. Then huge pools of oil lie on the surface, adding to the difficulties of operation and to the danger from fire. In the Louisiana bayous, and off the California coast, the derricks rise in the water and the oil is drained off through pipes to the land. Even here there is danger of fire, that constant menace of the oil fields.

But why so many derricks in a bunch? No layman can help asking the question. And in the answer lies, perhaps, the central problem of the oil industry, certainly the answer to the prodigious waste of the fast disappearing natural resource which plays so large a part in our everyday American lives. The strange situation is due both to the geology of the oil fields and to an old legal concept. The old common law in the United States, as we said in the history of coal, gives the right to underground minerals to the owner of the surface property. In its application to oil this became the Law of Capture because, unlike coal, oil is fugitive. It lies in great underground "pools," or beds of sand, which may well extend under many owners' boundary lines. Along with oil is always some gas and sometimes water, all under such pressure that they rush to any outlet, though the pressure may not be sufficient to bring the oil to the surface. (See chart, page 275.) Thus an owner can sink a well on his own property and pull oil from under his neighbor's land. And the Law of Capture legalized this action!

With what results? Production fields bristling with derricks pumping oil as fast as they can. Pump while the pumping is good. That has become the practice on the oil fields. Speed! Put up two, three, as many derricks as you can and close to your neighbor's line. Get your oil out as fast as possible or the other fellow will get it. And even if you own all the land above the pool, get it out in a hurry and to the refinery, for the other fellows are producing fast and will grab the market. Speed. With no thought of how large the demand is.

This has been the common practice even though ordinarily oil production is carried on under lease and not directly by the land owner. The rental charged is usually one-eighth of the oil produced. Here is another pressure towards speed. For by the terms of the lease the owner can force the producer to keep drilling if, perchance, he is inclined to slow up in the hope of getting better prices. Caught between the landlord's eagerness to cash in on his investment and his neighbor's ability to drain his oil, the producer usually keeps on drilling. There are 16,000 producers thus urging on their hundreds of thousands of pumps throughout the country's oil fields.

Then when the producers get their oil, they are faced with selling it. And here they run into the refiners, who have practically a monopoly and set the price at which they will buy crude. They post a price and that price goes. ("They" often means a Standard Oil Company.) Not a happy picture of the independent producer. First, competition forces him to mad speed to get the oil from the ground; second, someone else sets the price of his product.

PARADOXES IN OIL. A BOTTLE-NECK PATTERN

The three activities in the oil industry—production, transportation and refining, and retailing—are related to one another in a bottle-neck pattern. At the production end we have 16,000 producers, natural gamblers, pressed to speed by the Law of Capture and their own "get-results-quick-and-clear-out" psychology, acting under cutthroat competition. Here, too, are the 20 big integrated companies in their producing role, producing half the crude. The production end of the industry is highly unstable.

From here the oil flows through the pipe lines to the refineries—the bottle neck of the industry. For 98% of the pipe lines are under the control of the 20 integrated companies, and 80% of the oil is refined in their refineries. The several hundred independent refiners handle only 20% of the refining business. This branch of the industry is semimonopolistic and stable.

Then the oil—now gasoline or fuel or lubricating oil—flows out to 350,000 retail outlets, 10% of them belonging to the 20 integrated companies, 50% more controlled by them through lease, and 40% in the hands of independent retailers. Again we find cutthroat competition and a highly unstable business. A paradoxical situation: competition and instability at the two ends, semimonopoly and stability in the middle. Such is the bottle-neck pattern of the oil industry illustrated in the chart. The workings of this pattern, with the striking conflicts among the three sets of actors, have brought about another paradox: that the supply of oil is not controlled by demand. The consumer has never been brought into organic relation with the industry.

There is still another and basic paradox in the oil industry, that of a country's giving over the exploitation of a limited and essential natural resource to the control of a few individuals. The perception that this *is* a paradox is just coming home to the American in his present-day gasoline culture. His vision, such as it is, has been clarified largely through reports of waste and fear of shortage. For the same forces which have made for speed, for disregard of demand, have made for "spectacular and magnif-

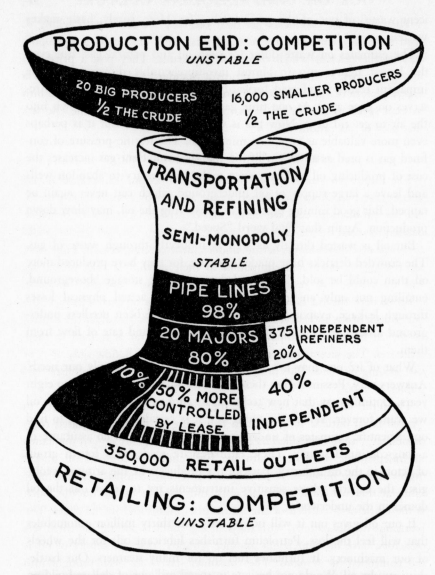

PRODUCTION END: COMPETITION
UNSTABLE

20 BIG PRODUCERS ½ THE CRUDE

16,000 SMALLER PRODUCERS ½ THE CRUDE

TRANSPORTATION AND REFINING

SEMI-MONOPOLY

STABLE

PIPE LINES 98%

20 MAJORS 80%

375 INDEPENDENT REFINERS 20%

10%

50% MORE CONTROLLED BY LEASE

40% INDEPENDENT

350,000 RETAIL OUTLETS

RETAILING: COMPETITION
UNSTABLE

BOTTLE-NECK PATTERN OF THE OIL INDUSTRY

Black is the share of production, transportation and refining, and retail marketing controlled by the twenty big integrated companies called the "majors."

icent waste" of one of the great earth gifts. Here, surely, haste makes
waste!

The estimates on waste differ for both oil and natural gas. But even
the lowest figures run to almost incomprehensible dimensions. (The
impatient reader is referred forward to the discussion of waste and reserves on page 279.) At one time gas was simply burned or blown into
the air to get rid of it. Now gas is valuable as a fuel. But it is perhaps
even more valuable as an aid in mining oil. The terrific pressure of confined gas is used as an aid in lifting the oil. Insufficient gas increases the
cost of producing oil and may even make it necessary to abandon wells
and leave a large supply of oil underground which can never again be
tapped. But good mining practice, in conserving the oil, may slow down
production. Again that fatal word "Speed."

But oil is wasted directly as well as indirectly through waste of gas.
The crowded derricks have made for waste, for they have produced more
oil than could be sold. This has led to excessive storage aboveground,
entailing not only an unnecessary expense but actual physical losses
through leakage, evaporation and fire. There have been needless underground losses due to unscientific spacing of wells and rate of flow from
them.

What of it? one may ask. Have we not enough to supply our need?
Answers vary. Pessimists say there will be a shortage within five to eight
years. Optimists say that new technical inventions will give us all the oil
we want forever. Where the truth lies, it is certainly important to find
out. Scientific estimates of underground reserves give us no assurance of
a long-continued supply. These estimates are made by a fourth group
of actors in the oil industry. Back of the producers lie the army of geologists, the experts whose sensitive instruments try to ferret out the oil
domes in the underworld.

If our oil gives out it will not be only our thirty million automobiles
that will feel the loss. Petroleum furnishes lubricant oils for the wheels
of our machinery. It furnishes fuel oil for many steamers. Our battle-
ships run by oil. We do not hesitate to spend millions of dollars building
them. It would seem logical to save fuel to run them. Our airplanes run
by oil. We look to them as a great future commercial and military force.
Yet we know that the supply of oil is limited, that the available reserves—
whether they stand at 17 billion barrels, as the American Petroleum
Institute estimates, or at more or less—are being depleted by more than
a billion barrels a year. Evidence points to increasing use. It points, even
if new processes increase the availability of what we have, to increasing

costs. And at present it points to continuing waste—"magnificent and spectacular waste." Must we add another adjective, American? Once more comes the question, Who owns the gifts from American earth which we all need to use?

We need a wider perspective on this question. The geologic occurrence of crude oil, the extent of our reserves, and waste, will be discussed in Chapter IX. We also need to know more about how oil has been "developed."

OKLAHOMA CITY: CIVIC PRIDE VS. QUICK MONEY

Such is the organization of the American oil industry, and such is the waste it has produced. What does it look like in action? Come to Oklahoma City and see. In the state capitol two civic factions, representing two civic virtues, have been fighting a bitter fight. One faction stands for the beauty of its capital city. The Statehouse, the Governor's Mansion, fine residence and good business sections, the Mall with sunken gardens, have been everyone's civic pride, a sentiment to which any hundred-percent American responds. This sentiment still dominates one civic faction. The other faction has yielded to the lure of quick oil money, for oil derricks made their appearance close to the city limits in 1929. Quick money also makes its appeal to the American heart. So the fight was on. In the thick of the battle stood Governor Marland, former head of the Marland Oil Company which, in an overexpanded condition, he sold to Morgan, the New York banking firm which we have met as the purchasers of the anthracite coal fields. But Governor Marland had also been a leader in the beautification campaign which had produced statues and shaded boulevards, parks and civic buildings. Oratory has gushed as well as oil, elections have been held, laws have been made and disobeyed, as the two factions representing the two American sentiments have struggled for possession of the city. The picture opposite page 229 shows which side has triumphed, which side the Governor finally supported. It does not show the derricks around the State Hospital, around the State University Medical School, around the abandoned homes of the rich on Lincoln Terrace, or emerging from the gardens of the Mall. But they are there. Oil saved Oklahoma City through the years of depression. The question now is, Can the city save itself after the oil has been drained from its underground pool?

A BOOM TOWN: FOUR PHASES

If we move southwest to the East Texas oil field, we shall see how an oil rush hits a smaller town. If we had driven into Kilgore nine years

Photo by Ewing Galloway

AN OIL GUSHER

AN OIL-BOOM TOWN

The main street of Freer, Texas: no paving, no sewers, no water. A "check exchange" but no banks. Flimsy buildings for hotels, bars, pool rooms, movies, etc.

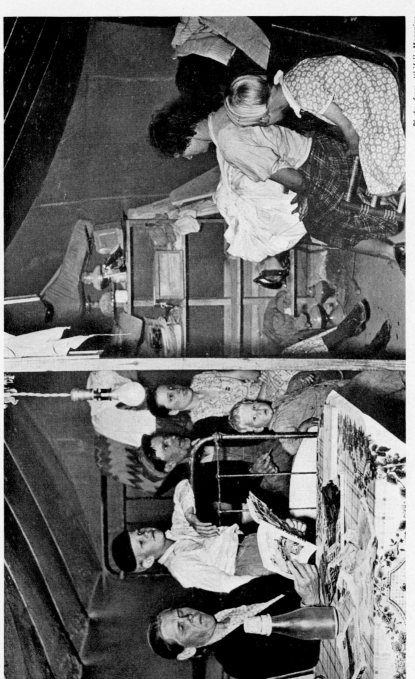

Photo from "Life" Magazine

TWO FAMILIES IN A TENT

The oil industry has its thousands of migrants—people who move from field to field as new oil strikes are made.

OIL WELLS NEAR STATE CAPITOL: OKLAHOMA CITY

ago, we should have noted three cotton gins, the normal response of a rural business center in a cotton farming district. If we had talked to the railroad agent or his one assistant, or to the men and women in the row of small stores, or to the teller of the single bank, we should have heard the typical story of cotton lands in those days. Cotton ten cents a pound, not enough to cover the cost of producing it, little credit securable from merchants or bank, deep discouragement in the tree-shaded cottages of the quiet streets and despair among the Negro tenant farmers.

And now? The boom is over. It struck the town like a squall when on a Sunday, December 28, 1930, a great oil gusher announced to the community that its farming days were over—at least for the time. It announced this fact to the world also. And the world responded the next morning and continued to respond for several years. No one who has not lived through a boom fever can really understand the excitement, the insanity of speculation, that seizes even the most conservative. Cottages and dilapidated garages turning overnight into apartment houses, rows of tents, hundreds of tiny huts like roadside tourist camps springing up on every vacant lot, men rolled up under trees beside an open fire, hordes breaking into churches to sleep on pews and floor until, fatigued with cleaning up and delousing, the Baptist Church gave itself for a jail. Cheaply constructed stores, hotels, movie houses. After typhoid and diphtheria epidemics, a water and sewage system, for Kilgore had neither before oil. A new railroad station and 26 assistants to the agent. Streams of trucks, autos, trailers roaring down the muddy road, getting stuck until the maddened drivers of the stream of autos behind help haul them out. And on the fringe around this hectic center, in the cotton fields, the clanking of new derricks, as the bits screw their way down to the "Woodbine sand" some 3600 feet below where the sought-for oil lies. Now and then an oil well catches fire and the lurid glare at night lights up the squalid, new settlement and shows red on the immense, black column of smoke. Always the gas torches flare. For the community is not equipped to take care of the gas that comes up with the oil. Separate it and burn it, is the quickest way to get rid of it! Costly flares of a precious resource. But who has time in a boom town to think of anything except tomorrow's earning? So gas torches burn and the salt water underground is allowed to flow into the oil. No time for economy, no thought for the future.

Other rural towns near by are turning into boom cities. They, too, are sending out trainloads of oil cars. Oil goes down to ten cents a barrel (it had once been over a dollar) and imported water, peddled in the streets, goes up to the same price. A special session of the Texas legislature is called. After all, this is Texas wealth that is being wasted. This is Texas oil that is bringing only ten cents a barrel. How to control a boom frenzy? "Proration. Restrict the flow of every well," say the assemblymen. "Martial law," says the Governor. State militia enter the region, and all wells must stop pumping. The producers resist. Violence. Churches are burned. A new type of frenzy in this second phase of the boom cycle.

Then begins supervised restriction of production, proration. The price begins to rise. Stricter proration. The price rises higher still. Women and children move into the community. New schools are built. More railroad tracks, stabler business conditions. The third phase of the boom town has been reached.

And the fourth phase, when oil begins to fail? or the salt water gradually rises in the wells? We can see no answer at Kilgore, for some oil still flows; and improved railroad service, better highways, and low rents help to keep business activity going. Perhaps, if the surrounding farm land has not been ruined, Kilgore will survive as a small trading center. But perhaps, like Smackover, Arkansas, like Burbank, Oklahoma, and like many another wild growth of the onrushing oil industry, the mere ghost of a town will remain, with only a few straggling inhabitants, vacant stores and silent streets. From boom town to ghost town, and the cycle is complete.

What Next?

The layman who has seen such things, perhaps even the layman who reads of them, can scarcely help asking how such human waste, such waste of America's fast-disappearing oil and natural gas can be prevented. For, with variations, the history of Kilgore is repeated at each new oil strike. He may well ask. The government, the public and even the industry itself are asking this and other questions. And so far there are no answers acceptable to all the actors in the oil drama, which includes in its cast not only the actors in the industry and the consumers, but behind both, the public or the country. Once more the question, Who owns the earth and all that lies therein?

Out of the present will grow the future, even as the present itself has grown out of the past. Before we look forward, we must look back, so that we think not merely of a static picture but of trends. The trends concern not merely prices, figures of production and consumption, numbers of workers, and all the other statistical material essential to an understanding of a great industry. The trends also concern social thinking, standards of living, standards of value for human life, for community life, conceptions of the function of government. If the present-day oil industry presents its three chief actors in its drama as numerous, unorganized and competitive at the production and marketing ends, and as monopolistic, highly organized in the bottle neck of refining and transportation, this strange picture surely has its roots in past social thinking as well as past events. Back, then, to a few historic snapshots of the industrial pioneers and still further back to the geologic making of oil which is responsible for so many of our present-day oil problems.

Chapter VIII—A FUGITIVE MINERAL AND ITS CAPTORS

History Lives in Present Oil

Drake's Folly, 1859. The First Oil Boom

Enter Rockefeller

The California Fields Come In

A Gasoline Culture Is Born. A Monopoly Is Dissolved

The World War. A Race for Supplies. Conservation Talk

Monopolistic Yearnings

The Deluge: 1928–1932

The New Deal and the Oil Industry

Present and Future

Chapter VIII—A FUGITIVE MINERAL AND ITS CAPTORS

History Lives in Present Oil

DRAKE'S FOLLY, 1859. THE FIRST OIL BOOM

THERE WAS a new oil-burning lamp on the market and a new expensive stuff called coal oil or kerosene, distilled from coal shale, when the Pennsylvania Dutchmen in the small town of Titusville began to watch the amusing performances of a newcomer, Colonel Edwin Laurancine Drake. Drake had begun his work for Samuel Bissell, a New York lawyer who had organized a company some years before. Now Bissell had found this energetic onetime railway conductor, given him the impressive title of "Colonel," and sent him off to Titusville. For Bissell was interested in the strange black stuff called "rock oil" that oozed out of the ground in this part of Pennsylvania and spread a scum on the surface of the creeks. The farmers—indeed, the Indians before them— had long treasured the thick black oil as a homemade remedy for sore muscles and aching joints. Lately it had been bottled and widely sold for its "wonderful curative powers" when taken internally, too! But now the local farmers were interested in a new use of this stuff and used to skim it off the top of the creeks or soak it up in blankets, and try to separate it when it rose, mixed with brine, in the neighboring salt wells. For this stuff could now be made into "carbon oil"—very much the same thing as coal oil, only cheaper to make. But no one supposed that there might be a way of getting the crude oil in quantities—no one, apparently, except Colonel Drake and his backer. Even Bissell's enthusiasm eventually gave out, and he withdrew his support. But Drake persisted. Therefore the Pennsylvania Dutch farmers looked at the Colonel's activities with amusement or pity and dubbed the structure he built "Drake's Folly."

On the outside the structure appeared as a sloping tower attached to a shack, both tower and shack roughly boarded. Inside was a well with a shaft going down into the ground 69½ feet. Wells and pumps were familiar objects in the salt-well regions of Pennsylvania, and elsewhere in a country where plumbing had not yet flowered. But this was a new kind of well, deeper than the deepest salt well, a well which it took three months to drill, a well which on August 21 filled with thick black rock oil. And Drake's Folly turned suddenly into the first oil boom.

Since the days of the forty-niners men had been crossing the continent to get gold. Here was another earth gift—"black gold"—nearer home. The diggers and prospectors, the swindlers and reporters, moved with a rush into the astonished Titusville and Oil Creek area. Small refineries were set up to obtain the prized kerosene. But in the process they also distilled a quantity of gasoline. No use for gasoline. How to dispose of it was the question. "Burn it" was the usual answer; sometimes, "Dump it into the streams." In small farmhouses and big city mansions all over the country people bought the Rock Oil kerosene and filled, trimmed and lighted the latest marvel, the brilliant kerosene lamp: for so it seemed to eyes used to whale oil or candlelight. And all over the country the gambling pioneers began to dream of new quick wealth. Some worked alone on the pattern of the lone western gold prospector. Some worked through organized companies (of which there were more on paper than there were in the field!). The refineries of Erie, Pittsburgh and New York, then of Cleveland, Baltimore and Boston, became famous. The oil came to them first by wagon and rail; or by wagon down to Oil Creek, then by flat boat down the Creek into the Allegheny River and so to the railroads at Pittsburgh; and by 1866 several short pipe lines were bringing oil to the refineries nearest the wells. Thus came the first foreshadowing of the dramatic role to be played by the refiners' group in the industry.

On the producing fields, too, the later dramatic roles were being developed. In the midst of a backward farming community appeared this sudden feverish activity, and the stolid Pennsylvania Dutch farmers turned overnight into avaricious royalty owners. For when they leased their poor farms, they received a definite amount on all oil taken from their properties. Booms and royalties. The patterns which were to curse the oil industry had begun.

Up and down the Oil Creek ran lease hunters, buying the farms if they could, leasing if they couldn't. In June of 1859 had come the great frost, destroying the farm crop. And here was an underground crop which sent the prices of these farms soaring. One farmer sold the oil rights on his 180-acre farm for $1500 and one-fourth of all oil recovered. Three men got $10,000 for a one-third interest in their yet unsuccessful well. Wells sprang up everywhere. Farms were bought and sold, leased and split up. In 1865 a farmer sold his farm for $280,000 and within two months the purchasers had leased out ninety sites on it with cash bonuses of $315,000 and royalties besides. A well on one farm was producing 800 barrels a day and the farm was estimated to be worth three million dollars. Booms and royalties had surely arrived.

The inevitable aftermath of a boom followed swiftly. And with the aftermath came other patterns which were to curse the oil industry—price fluctuations, uncertainty, *overproduction*. Until the January following Drake's first well, the price of crude oil at the well was $20 a barrel. Wells, and more wells on every side. By the end of 1861 the price was down to 10 cents a barrel. There was more oil than could be sold even at that price. Oil flowed faster than barrels could be made. It seeped uselessly into the earth or down the creeks; and even where storage holes had been dug to hold some of it, much was lost through evaporation and seepage.

Two years from the first oil well, and the producers were in a dilemma which was to persist. Some enterprising characters tried to persuade all operators to combine—to agree on shutting down their wells and stopping their drills in times of oversupply. Most of these price-raising combinations remained mere talk, though their aim was ambitious enough: nothing less than to monopolize the supply of oil! Occasionally agreements were reached; and to enforce them, vigilance committees patrolled the country-side. Once, in 1873, there was actually a ten-day period when not a barrel of oil was produced. Soon an association of refiners contracted to pay the producers' combine $4 a barrel for their crude—provided that the total output be held down to a certain figure. Yet this effort, like the ones before it, crumbled. Output ran over the limit, the agreement was voided, and prices tumbled again. Why?

Oil men had the same urge towards production that coal operators have: the drive to cash in on an investment that cannot be turned to other uses. In the case of oil, special factors aggravated this urge. For one thing, there were the royalty owners. Many leases were valid only as long as oil was produced. The same Pennsylvania Dutch farmers who had sneered at Drake, who had invested neither work nor time but had happened to own some poor agricultural land, could force the flood of oil to continue even if the operators were ready to hold back.

Second, there was the Law of Capture. This was not a piece of legis-lation. Rather it was an unhealthy mixture of an unalterable fact and a deeply rooted property conception. America had taken over the English common-law assumption that subsoil minerals belong to the owner of the land over them. But the fact was that oil did not stay put under the small parcels of land that the owners leased out. It moved, under hydro-static and gas pressure, towards any opening. When a well was brought in, neighboring properties were immediately riddled with wells; and likely as not, some of the oil under the discoverer's leasehold would migrate to the new openings. Woe to him, therefore, who delayed drilling or held back the oil once it had started flowing! Haste made waste—not only waste of capital in technically needless drilling, but waste of oil above-ground as it outran the demand or the transportation facilities. Yet caution meant an empty pocket.

Although kerosene quickly became a commodity of national and inter-national importance, and the business grew to imposing size, almost no one seriously questioned this method of exploitation. In 1889 the Pennsyl-vania Supreme Court confirmed the situation with dramatic clarity. Oil, gas, and water, said the Court, are "minerals ferae naturae." Oil moves as do wild animals. And like wild animals belongs to him who can capture it. The only right of an owner is to drill on his own land. He must cap-ture the oil and gas to gain possession of them.

Thus the urge of both royalty owners and producers to cash in became a chronic fever. Stories like the following one have tickled the pride and glee of oil producers ever since the great gamble began:

Back in the early Pennsylvania days when oil was selling at 10 cents a barrel, and only selling when the well was near a railroad, an operator went out about 40 miles from a railroad and drilled a 150-barrel wildcat well.

His No. 2 was nearing the sand and the operator decided that he would go to the city for a rest—he couldn't sell his oil anyway, and there was nothing for him to do but rest.

The day after he got to town he received the following message from his driller: "No. 2 is making 500 barrels. No. 1 has increased to 300 barrels a day. All running on the ground. Rush timbers for No. 3."

No wonder that curtailment proposals made little appeal to such temperaments! And no wonder that, when prices were so ruinous as to bring about shutdowns, the first signs of improvement brought a new deluge.

Enter Rockefeller

Eleven years after the first well at Titusville. The citizens of Cleveland had grown used to the smell of petroleum from the refineries, to the long line of oil cars, to the sailing ships with special oil tanks. They had grown used to the new wealth which kerosene was bringing to their city. Among them was a thin narrow-faced young man of thirty-one, recently a partner in the produce commission business, whose father had trained him "to be sharp" by cheating him as a child. Of all the people in the United States at this time, this young man was to prove the most important to the growing oil industry. He had dabbled in the oil business in 1862 and gone into it completely in 1865. The young man was John D. Rockefeller. Now, in 1870, he was Cleveland's largest refiner and could reorganize his business under the name of the Standard Oil Company of Ohio, with capital of $1,000,000. By 1879 this company, with assets later estimated at $80,000,-000, was to control practically the entire refining business of the country.

The narrow eyes looked out from the long shrewd face and saw the chief problem of the young oil industry. Competition was producing instability; it was producing waste. Not only in the producing fields but in the refineries as well. By 1870 Cleveland alone had a refining capacity of 12,000 barrels a day—enough to handle nearly all the oil produced in the oil regions if the other refiners in New York, Pittsburgh, Erie, Philadelphia and Buffalo didn't refine a gallon. The price of kerosene had fallen from 70 cents in 1865 to 23 cents in 1870.

Rockefeller's answer was simple. Do away with competition. Establish a monopoly. And what the producers talked about and wrangled about, Rockefeller did.

Here entered a new pattern in the oil industry. By 1879 Rockefeller had risen to dominance. In 1882 he strengthened his control by reorganizing Standard Oil into a "trust," in which nine men voted the stock of the forty companies in the agreement. To the gambling excitement and cut-throat competition of the producing fields was added the monopolistic control of refineries and pipe lines by the greatest as well as the first of America's trusts, presided over by the greatest of the industrial pioneers known to us by the irreverent name of robber barons.

How do away with his rivals' competition? It must be done in secrecy. For there were other clever refiners—and it was through control of this end of the industry that he saw future money. Rockefeller, several jumps ahead of his competitors, saw that control of transportation was the essential weapon. He had already gone to Cleveland's chief railroad, the Lake Shore. In those days, before railroads were regulated as common carriers, rebates were often given to favor big shippers or to encourage longer hauls. Cleveland's refiners were not so near the oil fields as were others. If the Lake Shore wanted to hold its traffic in crude oil from the fields to Cleveland and in refined products from there eastward to the main markets, it would have to give cheaper rates. And cheaper rates, argued Rockefeller, to just *one* of Cleveland's refiners! Either all would be destroyed by competition—from Pennsylvania refiners and among themselves—and there would be no more Cleveland oil traffic; or the railroad could help Rockefeller to dominance and enjoy his business. If the Lake Shore should refuse, there were other railroads. The Lake Shore acquiesced. Thus Rockefeller could undersell his rivals. More business meant larger rebates; larger rebates meant more business. By 1870 he could guarantee regular shipments of 60 carloads a day—something no competitor could begin to approach. A few of them had got on to the rebate game. But as largest shipper, Rockefeller easily beat them all.

Then came "drawbacks." For in 1872, with the formation of the South Improvement Company, Rockefeller gained this still deadlier weapon. This company was an association of three chief oil-carrying railroads and several of the most important refiners in Philadelphia, Pittsburgh, New York—and in Cleveland, Standard Oil. The combine was to act as "evener" of shipments among the railroads, thus saving them from rate wars. In return, not only were the roads to give rebates of 40 to 50% on crude and 25 to 50% on refined oil shipped by these refiners; they also agreed to pay them a "drawback," at the same percentages, on every barrel of oil shipped by *any* competitor! No rate wars; on the contrary, in order to pay the drawbacks, rates on oil were to be doubled!

The monopoly ball had started rolling. It had rolled over the small Cleveland refiners first. It increased in speed and weight during the short life of the South Improvement Company, for in less than one month after its formation Rockefeller bought out 20 of Cleveland's 25 remaining refineries. But it rolled on in secrecy. Each refiner admitted to the combine signed a solemn pledge of secrecy. No wonder! For no more powerful and no more unfair business tactic than this drawback scheme had ever been thought of. But a minor railroad employee, right in the oil region whose refiners were about to be ruined, blundered. The whole secret plan leaked out.

Rage now made the unruly oil producers unite. It even made them join with their neighbor refiners against this outside monopoly scheme. Their protests thundered from the press and resounded in the halls of the legislature in the shape of bills to revoke the company's charter, to abolish railroad discrimination, and to establish free pipe lines. They sounded even in the halls of Congress, where hearings were held that resulted in the denunciation of the South Improvement Company as "one of the most gigantic and dangerous conspiracies ever attempted."

Its charter was revoked. However, the company was already extinct, for at the first angry outburst the railroads had backed down and restored the old rates. Rockefeller, though taken aback by the violence of the public outcry, was unperturbed by the company's collapse. His associates, less quick than he in using the brief chance to seize control in their cities, were left about as before. But Rockefeller emerged with the whole oil industry of Cleveland securely under control. He was now in a position to invade—and subdue—other refining centers. Pittsburgh first; more gradually the oil region itself, New York, Philadelphia, all of them.

Rockefeller saw that loose agreements such as the producers tried would always fail. His method was to absorb or annihilate. He could do this because he managed single-handed to wring from the railroads every necessary advantage. He alone could guarantee large and regular shipments. He alone was keen enough to sense both the weakness and the strength of the railroads: to choose the exact time and place of an impending rate war to offer a rational plan—in return for some concession.

Yes, the railroad in Pittsburgh could say it had no cars for a certain refiner's shipment. Yes, the Louisville road would find it necessary to raise a rival company's rates. Yes, the railroads would give an accounting to Standard of all oil shipments, quantity and destination. Rival refiners did not know why it was that there was always a Standard agent at the right spot to underbid them. Neither did they know that Standard Oil received thousands of dollars a month on the oil *they* were shipping. They did know that Mr. Smith sold out for a third of his investment, Mr. Brown for a half. Mr. Jones refused to sell: his business fell to zero. Secrecy. Competition must be done away with.

Rockefeller had still other methods of gaining his dream of monopoly. His company's huge New Jersey refineries stood at Communipaw and Constable Hook. The Pennsylvania Railroad carried the crude oil to Bayonne, and from there the New Jersey Central brought it into the refineries. Why pay the New Jersey Central for this haul? It would pay to install pipes. But though Rockefeller persuaded the Common Council of Bayonne to grant him a franchise to lay the pipes, the Mayor at first stood with the railroad and vetoed it. In a few months Rockefeller had persuaded the Mayor. But he knew that if the franchise were granted openly, the New Jersey Central would at once get out an injunction and block his plan. Again Rockefeller resorted to secrecy.

Secretly he had the route surveyed and marked. He assembled all materials and tools and loaded them into carts in the company's yard, each cart with its exact instructions. On a certain night 300 men armed with picks and shovels appeared, commanded by engineers who had worked out "the attack" in detail. At the same time the Common Council was assembling in its chamber and the Mayor sat in readiness in his office. In a few minutes the ordinance was passed; a few minutes later the Mayor had signed it. A few minutes more and the 300 workmen were digging a trench, lowering pipes, refilling the trench, and repairing the streets. By morning, and before either citizens or the New Jersey Central knew what had happened, Rockefeller's oil was flowing under the streets of the city to the Standard's refineries. Monopoly could be established with swiftness as well as with secrecy if the efficiency of Rockefeller commanded.

Control of pipe lines was as essential to the Standard monopoly as domination of the railroads. Many times bills to make public carriers of the pipe lines were introduced in the Pennsylvania legislature. Occasionally one might be reported out of committee, might even pass one house; but none ever became law. There was always a friend of Standard in the right spot.

In the course of his career Rockefeller used many devices, from hiding behind bogus independents to setting up temporary grocery stores to ruin "rebel dealers"—for such were they called who dared to buy any but Standard kerosene. Rockefeller's business talent was as ruthless as it was efficient.

For he did develop an astoundingly efficient business organization. An acute judge of people, he assembled the shrewdest brains in the business under him. He took large risks, borrowed largely when times were ripe for an expansive stroke, and gained as largely. He had a genius for organization. Also a genius for thrift. He got reports on the smallest details, down to the feed of the horses. He made his own glue, hoops, barrels. It was infinite care in little things, as well as boldness in bigger ones, that built the Standard empire.

The larger the empire grew, the more vocal its victims became. Again and again there was excitement in the press. Democracy was being threatened.

Process servers began to hunt the great man. Two lawsuits in Pennsylvania. Then in New York State, in 1879, the Hepburn Committee was appointed to investigate the methods of railroads and trusts. Standard Oil came in for its share of investigation. Public hearings with Rockefeller and Archbold sitting silent, refusing to answer, or jesting—always indifferent. More excitement in the press. Chauncey Depew, counsel for the railroads, defended them by blackening all business practices. His voice rang out to the listening public. "Every manufacturer in the State of New York existed by violence and lived by discrimination." Not in New York alone. In every state of the Union. Still the narrow eyes were indifferent. Why worry over the public excitement? In 1879, with a nominal capital of $3,500,000, Standard Oil paid dividends of $3,150,000. "Hide the profits and say nothing." That became the slogan. In his organization, so said John D. Rockefeller, he wished "only the big ones, those who have proved they can do a big business. As for the others, unfortunately they will have to die."

And die they did. But the world was getting used to their deaths. It was getting used to gigantic fortunes. There was something thrilling about these industrial pioneers, who had been poor boys. Railroad barons —Vanderbilt, Gould, Fiske, Hill, Harriman; the industrial barons—Pullman, Armour, Rockefeller, Carnegie, Mellon, the Du Ponts. America became proud of her millionaires. See what opportunities there were in a democracy! And yet America believed in competition. The press was divided. People were restless. Depressions. Inflations. Stock-exchange panics. Runs on banks. Investigations. Indignation. Acceptance. Let's have millionaires but competition, too!

Finally a law. Competition must be preserved. Democracy was based on competition. Trusts were threatening the rights of individuals, they were prospering through restraint of free trade. The Sherman Antitrust Act was a repudiation of the new American pattern of monopoly. More excitement. More discussion. "After all, these men have developed the industries of our country." "Rockefeller has effected real economies in the oil industry and lowered the price of kerosene." But the law was passed. Trusts were declared an illegal form of organization. And big business took on new outward patterns, new paper organizations. "Trusts" disappeared. "Holding companies" took their place. But the big fortunes continued to grow. Kerosene lamps and kerosene stoves burned throughout the land and the world. And their kerosene still came from the refineries of the Standard Oil. The oil still came to the refineries through the Standard's own pipe lines. And the price of Standard was the market price.

THE CALIFORNIA FIELDS COME IN

1896. A forty-year-old Irishman, with a single dime in his pocket, arrived in Los Angeles, an old prospector by temperament and trade. "Mexican Pete" he was called. It was twenty-four years since he had left his frontier home in Wisconsin to prospect for gold in Indian Territory and later in

Mexico. He found it. Doheny was always finding things. He made his pile and lost it. Doheny was always losing things. That was the life he loved: big risks and big gains. That was the life it was easy to find in Mexico. Even if you had to teach school for a while, in order to earn enough to live on. He was an active member of the Vigilance Committee, for he liked fighting gunmen. He liked guns; he liked fighting; he liked power. Power. Over things or over men. Power was what he craved. Now, he was "broke" and in a country new to him. What would it hold for him? That was always the exciting question to Doheny. A Negro goes by with a cart full of darkish earth. Doheny stops him, looks at the earth, feels it, smells it. Where did he get it? On a useless patch of land near the Rancho la Brea asphalt lake on the outskirts of Los Angeles. Doheny puts up his claim sign; goes to the government office and registers it; returns with a pick-ax and falls to. A gusher. An oil gusher! Again, Doheny had found something.

Doheny in new store clothes was shortly calling on the rich citizens of Los Angeles and Pasadena. He found eager ears for his story. Professional men, broken-down business men from the east, the get-rich citizens always found in a mild climate where real-estate booms can be launched, they all listened, formed a company, bought up land. Yet Doheny was not impressive; though his eyes had a fever glow, and his walk as well as his temper had an energy, and his words were convincing even if his voice was squeaky. Both convincing and impressive were the derricks that began to rise around the City of Angels. The rich citizens on the hill sold their luxurious homes and their view to make room for the forest of derricks, and bought oil stock. More convincing still was the oil that began to flow as the thick smell of crude petroleum floated through the hot southern air. Most convincing of all were the dividends that began to flow into the bank accounts of the discerning stockholders. The single dime of a few years ago was multiplying into a fortune in the pocket of the enterprising organizer. Power. He saw it coming. The old business men nodded with satisfaction. They had not judged wrong. Edward L. Doheny was a coming man. And the California oil fields were coming in.

A GASOLINE CULTURE IS BORN. A MONOPOLY IS DISSOLVED

Model T was almost ready and Henry Ford was an excited inventor. For some years his strange little horseless carriages had snorted down the streets of Detroit to the amusement and astonishment of the citizens. The driver sat in front behind the onetime dashboard, and behind was tucked in a new engine. The internal-combustion engine run by that hitherto useless by-product of petroleum, gasoline.

At first Henry Ford took in partners and went out for stockholders. But then he had another idea. Here was something big. Here was something on which to found a family fortune, and Henry Ford was a family man. He bought out his partners, paying 40 millions to one of them. Three stockholders were enough: Henry Ford, Mrs. Ford and Edsel Ford. Did the echoes of his small snorting engine reach along the Lake front to Cleveland to the keen ears of Mr. Rockefeller? For the days of kerosene lamps and stoves were almost over.

Another laboratory, years earlier. Another inventor, working on a bulb, an electric-light bulb. Now it was making its way in the market. Thomas Edison did not found a trust. He did not found a family fortune. But he did change the habits of America by his invention, and he might have changed the destiny of Rockefeller himself. Except that when the country put away its kerosene lamps, pressed a button in the wall and burst into floods of unprecedented light, the horseless carriage was a commercial reality. The age of gasoline had arrived. Rockefeller and his refineries responded.

Ida Tarbell had been working on a book. Her determined mannish face with its kind eyes had been seen wherever there were facts to be gathered about the Standard Oil Company, its business organization, its rebates and drawbacks, its spies, its fight against competition, its secrecy. And now the book was off the press. It burst like a giant firecracker and reverberated through business offices, Wall Street banks, professional gatherings and domestic dinners. The world divided into two camps, both indignant. "Muckraking," pronounced the rich. "It's easy enough to criticize. But, after all, Rockefeller hasn't done anything that isn't legal. It's up to the country to make and enforce laws—not to an individual. What's more, he has opened up the greatest American business, and given employment to thousands of men. Why shouldn't he make a fortune? He started poor like his critics. He's smarter than the rest, that's all." Other voices. Academic voices. Church voices. "Look what he gives away. Where would the University of Chicago be but for him?" And once more Chicago hummed the Doxology to the words "Praise John from whom oil blessings flow. . . . Praise Bill and John, but John the most." "He is a God-fearing man," said pious voices. "He is always warning against drinking and gambling. A great example to youth." And the Baptists, who had cheered him at their convention a few years before,

once more recounted his lavish gifts. From the pulpit in Cleveland came
these words: "People charge Mr. Rockefeller with stealing the money
he gave to the church but he has laid it on the altar and thus sanctified
it."

But there were other voices. "Tainted money," they said. Some of them
were the voices of the thousands of business men who felt they had been
cheated when his monopoly ball rolled over them. Some were the academic voices of those who disapproved of the dismissal of John Commons
from Syracuse University because its donor, John Archbold, did not
approve of his views concerning the rising labor movement. The voices
of the workingmen themselves, at least within the Standard Oil Company, were seldom protesting. Good wages, even under extreme paternalism, kept these voices but a faint murmur. The voices filled America.
When they came to the ears of the great man himself he answered
simply and feelingly, "God gave me the money." Oil flowed in a magnificent stream from the fields; and money flowed into the bank account
of Rockefeller and out again to the missionaries in China, to an Institute
for Medical Research, to colleges, schools and churches. "I believe the
power to make money is a gift of God," said John D. Rockefeller, "to be
developed and used to the best of our ability for the good of mankind.
Having been endowed with the gift I possess, I believe it is my duty to
make money and still more money and to use the money I make for the
good of my fellow man according to the dictates of my conscience." But
though the inner voice of his conscience may have been stilled by this
philosophy, the outer voices kept muttering "tainted money."

1909. A three-year trial had been going on. The Bureau of Corporations
had been established in 1903 under the new Federal Department of
Commerce and Labor and three years later had handed in their first
report on the Standard Oil Company followed by a two-volume report
on the whole petroleum industry. As a result the Standard was again
and again in court under various charges. Now the federal government
itself was suing for the dissolution of Standard Oil of New Jersey. Again
the voices. Was the Standard Oil violating the Sherman Antitrust Act?
Business shrewdness was one thing. But breaking the law was another.
Perhaps trusts were undemocratic after all. Perhaps competition was
healthier, more democratic. Still . . .

Local courts decided against the Standard Oil. The world gasped. A
decision against the mighty John D.? Would it hold? The company
appealed to the U. S. Supreme Court. Another two years. Big money

versus competition. The public waited breathlessly. In May, 1911, the morning papers reported the decision of the Supreme Court. The aim and practice of the Standard Oil trust, it said, had been by unfair means "to drive others from the field and to exclude them from their right to trade." Therefore it was illegal and must be dissolved! America breathed again. Competition could now save democracy.

Those who hoped that the Standard empire would crumble, however, were to be disappointed. The form of the dissolution decree actually made it certain that the many companies which made up this empire would still work together. It directed that the stocks of the parent company, Standard of New Jersey, should be exchanged for a pro rata share of stock in each of the thirty-odd subsidiaries. Thus the same important stockholders—the "Rockefeller interests"—continued to shape the policies of all companies harmoniously.

But the multiplication of the automobile accomplished what the courts failed to do by division. An expanding market for oil, plus new sources of supply, opened new opportunities—which the Standard companies were finding it impossible to corner even before the famous decree. In 1900 there were 8000 daredevil Americans who owned an automobile. In 1909, the year Ford launched his fateful Model T, the number had grown to 312,000. By 1916 not thousands but millions had been added: there were 3½ million motor vehicles registered!

And oil gushed forth plenteously from American earth to fuel and lubricate these thirsty engines. No longer were the derricks concentrated in Pennsylvania. Before the turn of the century other parts of this Appalachian field were producing; also the comparatively small Lima–Indiana area. Soon even greater fields were flowing: Gulf Coast, Midcontinent, Rocky Mountain, California. Crude-oil production averaged about 100 million barrels annually in 1901–05. In 1910 it was over 200 million; in 1916, 300 million.

Out among the derricks Standard's future rivals began to emerge. Near the Texas coast in 1902 when the Spindletop gusher blew in, the forerunners of Texas Company and Gulf were formed. Harry Sinclair struck a pay well in 1904 which got him $100,000; in the next five years he drilled $1,000,000 out of Midcontinent oil sands. Humble Oil Company and Cities Service originated in wildcat wells. In California Doheny's Pan–American Petroleum Company had prospered, and in Mexico he ruled great oil fields. Princely powers and princely imagination. He played at pulling down one Mexican President and setting up another, and revenged his Irish soul against England by giving a fortune to help

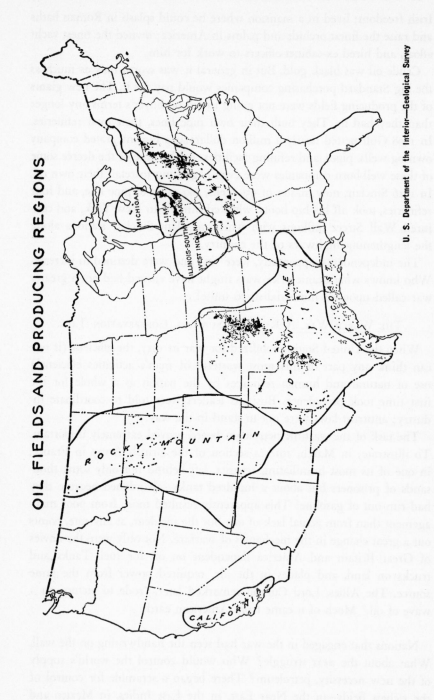

OIL FIELDS AND PRODUCING REGIONS

U. S. Department of the Interior—Geological Survey

Irish freedom; lived in a mansion where he could splash in Roman baths and raise the finest orchids and palms in America; owned the finest yacht afloat, and hired ex-cabinet-officers to work for him.

Crude oil was black gold. But in general it was worth only as much as the big Standard purchasing companies would pay for it. The new giants of the producing fields were not going to sell on buyer's terms any longer than they had to. They built their own pipe lines, their own refineries. In 1908 Gulf netted nearly a million dollars as a big integrated company owning wells, pipes, and refining facilities. At the time of the decree some of these well-born companies were even beginning to retail their own oil. In 1916 Sinclair, now master of 550 wells, 500 miles of pipe line, and four refineries, took off his hip boots, whisked himself to New York, and conjured Wall Street millions with which to plant Sinclair stations along the lengthening highways of the country.

The independents, apparently, were "in" and were destined to increase. Who knows what titanic price wars might have ensued had not a greater war called upon all industrialists to unite!

THE WORLD WAR. A RACE FOR SUPPLIES. CONSERVATION TALK

When the United States mobilized for war in 1917, the efficient (if one can think any part of this most wasteful of man's activities efficient!) use of natural and human resources by the nation as a whole for the first time took precedence. Business leaders were told to coordinate industry; antitrust laws were not to stand in the way.

The task of the wartime petroleum board proved extremely important. To illustrate: in March, 1918, a section of the British Army in France, in one of its most humiliating retreats, left behind not only some thousands of prisoners but about a hundred tanks—abandoned because they had run out of gasoline! This apparently resulted more from poor management than from actual lack of oil; but the incident, at any rate, points out a great change in the mechanics of warfare. Not only were the navies of Great Britain and America dependent on oil for fuel. Tanks and trucks on land, and planes in the air, required power from the same source. The Allies, Lord Curzon remarked later, "rode to victory on a wave of oil." Much of it came from American earth.

Nations that engaged in the war had seen the handwriting on the wall. What about the *next* struggle? Who would control the world's supply of the new necessity, petroleum? There began a scramble for control of the richest fields—in the Near East, in the East Indies, in Mexico and

Venezuela. The impoverished Central Powers could not take much part. Neither did Russia—it had its own rich sources, now operated by the Soviet government, under which no private capital was left to seek investment abroad. This oil war was largely a battle between British and American capital, a battle fought with letters and contracts, in which the careful phrases of diplomats played as big a part as the activities of oil men themselves. One might wonder why the United States, producing from its own wells 67% of the world's supply, should add the voice of its State Department to the oil companies' demands for yet more sources. A naïve question; for American fortunes had long since begun to find investment abroad sometimes more profitable than at home, and the government was bent on making the world safe for American investors no less than for American merchants.

Moreover, even though our production of oil had been increasing remarkably, how could we be sure we would always have enough? Already, during the war years, use had outrun production and forced heavy withdrawals from stored stocks. This fact grew into a specter of scarcity.

The British got the lion's share of the concessions through their Anglo-Persian and Burmah Oil companies allied with Sir Henri Deterding's powerful Royal–Dutch Shell. Nevertheless, Americans did in the postwar years gain some foreign holdings, particularly in Venezuela and Mexico (the latter recently expropriated by the Mexican government, to the chagrin of oil men and State Department).

Aside from these sources abroad, there still remained large unproven areas within the country. No time was lost in trying them out. In the year 1920 alone 33,911 wells were drilled, 24,273 of them producers, an unprecedented number.

The wealthier companies also collected large staffs of technicians (incidentally luring from the Bureau of Mines and the Geology Survey many of their best men) to improve methods of exploring and drilling. And they invested largely in new refining equipment—great cracking units in which crude petroleum molecules were broken up to yield a greater ratio of gasoline.

Rapid drilling continued. Crude-oil production doubled between 1919 and 1923. For three years ending 1923, 100 million barrels a year were added to the stored surplus of crude and its products. A more familiar specter—overproduction—now haunted the oil men.

Meanwhile the fear of scarcity had jolted America's largest landowner, the government, into action. There was a great to-do about conserving the nation's oil supply.

The call for conservation had first sounded in Washington fifteen years earlier. Theodore Roosevelt and Gifford Pinchot (head of the Forestry Service) had aroused the country to some concern over the reckless, wasteful, often fraudulent way in which timber and other resources of the public domain were being exploited. "The time has come," Roosevelt said in 1906, "when no oil or coal lands held by the government . . . should be alienated. The fee to such lands should be kept in the United States Government . . . and the lands should be leased only on such terms and for such periods as will enable the government to keep entire control thereof." Here was an attitude new in America and a suggestion momentous in its implications. Americans had been consuming their inheritance like true prodigal sons. One countryside despoiled, they moved on to the next. There was always more "out West." But beneath Roosevelt's words lay a somber fact: the last West had been reached. Careless confidence that American resources were somehow bottomless and endless would have to make way for other and harder thoughts. It was time to take stock, to consider future as well as present needs.

When Roosevelt spoke, public oil lands were salable under mining-placer laws, the only restriction being one of size, in line with the nation's traditional anxiety lest large holdings fall into the hands of a few owners. Congress until 1920 refused to act on Roosevelt's suggestion that these lands be leased rather than sold. Thus, until then, the net result of the conservation movement relating to oil lands was that a few million acres were withdrawn from sale. This was irksome to many oil men, to whom the reserved oil looked like dollars underground, much better pumped up into their pockets.

Conservation, therefore, unfortunately came to signify nonuse, in the minds of many Americans. Of course, Roosevelt's suggestions implied much more than setting aside a reserve. They implied, through leasing policies, judgment and control over the rate and manner in which the resources of the public domain were to be exploited. They implied, to speak boldly, some national planning and increased government super-vision. However, outright reserves of oil were certainly part of the pro-gram, especially because of America's new big navy. Oil-burning ships were the thing. In 1912 President Taft reserved some 68,000 acres for the Navy. Wilson added 9500.

After the World War and its inroads on aboveground stocks of oil, conservation talk revived; likewise the eagerness of oil men to dig into the five or six million acres of public petroleum land still withheld from entry. The Leasing Act of 1920 embodied but hardly reconciled these two urges. Leasing rather than selling, and the provision that the Secretary of the Interior should include in the lease proper regulations as to drilling, etc., could have made for conservation; that is, for better use of the available supply. But either the administrators lacked technical knowledge of the harm done by overdrilling, or they did not have enough conviction to go against tradition and the oil developers' demands; for these powers were used but lightly through the middle 1920's. That the real drive behind the Act was the headlong desire of oil men to "cash in" is illustrated by this provision: the Secretary was *required* to lease out Indian lands at the rate of 100,000 acres a year, no matter whether it seemed wise from the point of view of the Indians or of the nation.

Those who advocated rapid exploitation argued that government oil was being drained by wells on adjacent property, even on the reserves themselves by individuals who had claims (true or fraudulent) dating before the withdrawals. Since, therefore, the oil was bound to come up, shouldn't the government at least get royalties by leasing the rights to responsible men? So Uncle Sam gained some royalties, but his oil disappeared in ever faster-flowing streams. The quick fade-out of the scarcity bugaboo made this haste the more questionable, as the flow of oil soon merely enlarged an embarrassing and wasteful surplus.

In the scramble for leases naval reserves were by no means spared. Reserve No. 1 at Elk Hills, California: 38,000 acres; No. 2 at Buena Vista Hills: 30,000 acres; No. 3, Teapot Dome at Salt Creek, Wyoming: 9500 acres. Buried treasure.

Suddenly, with the advent of the Harding Administration in 1921, a reversal of policy. Navy Secretary Denby ordered control of these reserves transferred to the Department of Interior, noted for its sympathy with eager exploiters. Denby consulted none of his colleagues formally. One officer, questioned casually, remarked that if this transfer were completed the Navy "might just as well say good-by to its oil." It was completed. And thus Secretary Fall came into the picture. Also Doheny and Sinclair. For the three turned out to be friends.

Secretary Fall was deeply worried over private drainage of oil from the reserves. True, No. 3 was practically intact, though one or two experts thought it might eventually suffer depletion. Only a small portion of No. 1 was under private claim, but the major claimant was Standard of California, with a well at the very heart of the reserve which was depleting the reserve considerably. As for No. 2, it was honeycombed with claims and wells; the best the nation could do was to let out quick leases and get some royalties.

It occurred to Secretary Fall that fuel oil in storage tanks would be more useful to the Navy than crude oil underground. He asked bids for construction of tanks at Honolulu, plus some fuel oil, all to be paid for in royalty oil from No. 2. Doheny's Pan-American got the contract, and in the process made peculiar refinements on the announced plan. For Mr. Doheny had been looking with envious eye on the Elk Hills reserve. His vast holdings elsewhere were not enough. Nothing was enough if there were more to get. Doheny looked. Secretary Fall looked with him. And there evolved a complicated series of agreements that not only presented Doheny with extensive leases at Elk Hills and Buena Vista, but actually amounted to the government's underwriting him in a tremendous expansion of his refinery business. The Navy was to get somewhat more than the originally specified storage space and fuel oil. It was also to part with much more of its underground crude. To pay for storage facilities out of the very reserves intended to supply future needs was at best a mistaken policy. Under the new plan this mistake became one of the most brazen frauds in our history.

There remained Teapot Dome, the third reserve, the least in danger of drainage. This time it was Sinclair who looked with envious eye. For why should Doheny be the only one? Again Secretary Fall looked with him. And Sinclair received a lease under which, out of about 25 million barrels of oil underground, the Navy would get probably 2 million barrels of fuel oil and some tanks.

Doheny made $100,000,000 out of his deal. And Secretary Fall got $100,000 in a "little black bag" delivered to him by Doheny's son just before the contract was signed. Why not? wondered Doheny when questioned at the Senate investigation. For Fall was an old friend who needed money, and Doheny was not a man to go back on an old friend.

Yes, there was an investigation. Doheny casual and jesting most of the time. Occasionally emotional, not about the gigantic fraud on the country but over the death of Mr. Fall's children and over his employees killed in Mexico. Probably emotional, too, when Fall went to jail six months for accepting the little black bag. Sinclair was there, too. Massive, bald, poker-faced, answering only when his lawyer thought it wise. But later he, too, went to jail for contempt of the Senate. The leases were, after much litigation, revoked. Yet when "justice" was done, nothing could bring back the oil already taken from the Navy's reserves. And nothing could take away the fortunes made out of it by two of the country's most rugged individualists, Doheny and Sinclair.

MONOPOLISTIC YEARNINGS

The World War, besides giving an impetus to production and invention, had another important result. Leaders of the oil industry had found it advantageous to work together in certain directions without fear of antitrust prosecution. After the peace the American Petroleum Institute was formed to continue the benefits of cooperation. It has performed many useful services for its members, not the least being to present the activities of oil men to the public, through speeches, articles, advertisements, in the best possible light.

Though open to all, it was dominated from the beginning by the big men, the major companies. For now a new division among oil companies was developing. They were no longer divided into Standard and independent but into integrated and nonintegrated: into "majors" and small independent producers, refiners, jobbers, as described in Chapter VII. Not only were the comparatively new giants of the producing business building up their refining and marketing divisions, but the older giants in refining and marketing—chiefly the several largest Standard companies —were absorbing other companies with producing facilities as well as leasing large acreages themselves. Why this departure from Rockefeller Senior's dictum that oil producing was a good business to stay out of? With Americans buying cars by the millions, high crude prices were making production unusually profitable; and besides, the more controllable the flow of crude into the stills, the more certain became refinery profits. In this expansive time community of interest among major companies was being furthered by a complex structure of holding companies owning stock in several competing companies, and by jointly owned patents and pipe lines. The old oil monopoly was being reborn in new and complex form.

Wartime coordination by business leaders with the encouragement of government left a residue in the minds of some federal officials, too. At the end of 1924 President Coolidge appointed the Federal Oil Conservation Board, made up of the Secretaries of War, Navy, Interior, and Commerce, to consult with leaders of the industry about "ways and means of safeguarding the national security through conservation of our oil."

This invitation to share their thoughts with a government agency alarmed the oil men considerably. The President had suggested that "the oil industry itself might be permitted to determine its own future." But not all of his letter was so soothing. It raised the question of a future supply, pointing out that supremacy among nations, likewise domestic prosperity, hinged on this vital resource. It questioned the sanctity of the law of capture by observing that current leasing and royalty practices led to wasteful methods of recovering oil. It pointed out that over-production, far from making concern for the future unnecessary, was itself wasteful: for example, in lowering prices to where oil, limited in supply, was in some fuel uses replacing coal, apparently "unlimited" in amount.

Thoughts like these seemed, to the oil men, to point down a thorny path. The President evidently saw a connection between conserving oil and changing the methods of producing it. Change? How could this be made to happen except by control? And where would control end? A production policy implied a price policy. Any public agency meddling with prices would sooner or later be fussing over profits. The leaders saw at once that they must charm such thoughts from the mind of government. When hearings were held early in 1926, the American Petroleum Institute was there, well equipped with a book-length report on the future supply and with the impressive voice of Charles Evans Hughes, then its counsel.

The gentlemen of the Board took pains to put the visitors at their ease. The government, they said, was there to learn. What had the oracles to say? First, in the report by the Institute's Committee of Eleven, that "waste in the production, transportation, refining, and distribution of petroleum" was "negligible." That worry over future supplies was super-fluous, since their availability obviously depended upon "adequate incentives." What people would pay for, business would always supply. All would be safe if the "play of competition and the free operation of the law of Supply and Demand" were left unhampered.

Such phrases do not always carry their full meaning to the listener. At the hearings, the following paean reinforced them:

"By price the consumer casts his economic vote. The commodities of the world are candidates. Each has its manifold uses. The consumer by price elects goods to their proper offices. A commodity adapted to being town crier is never elected mayor. [So much for the President's unfortunate reference to oil as fuel!] Knowing his own mind, and with unerring judgment, the consumer pursues through price the economic initiative, referendum, and recall. He votes every minute. He changes his politics hourly. His mutations are the essence of economic wisdom. Commerce is democracy. And democracy meets each day as it did at Athens. Its constitution, its laws, its legislative and judicial power are all made, interpreted, and enforced by a single ballot—price."

After such lyricism it remained for Mr. Hughes to speak more sternly. There might be, he said, some underground waste of oil. It had even been suggested that there was other waste, due to untimely production. Since these matters had been brought up, it was necessary to consider the implied remedy, production control. Obviously it was impossible. The federal government possessed no power to prescribe methods of oil recovery. Perhaps the states had such power to a limited degree. Neither could the federal government legally control the rate of exploitation, except in its role of landowner; and since its policy of rapid development under the Leasing Act was being continued currently, who could question its wisdom? And surely it was unimaginable that a state, if it had the power to limit production, would place its citizens at a disadvantage by exercising it. However, there was this possibility: private leaseholders having separate interests in an oil property might wish to plan its development cooperatively. At the moment they would be hampered from doing so by fear of the antitrust laws. If government wanted to do something positive for the oil industry, here was the point at which to do it. But, in sum, regulation of production could in no way reach serious proportions. If it should, prices would rise and consumers would resist.

Amid such calming counsels only one intransigent voice was heard, that of Henry L. Doherty, himself a prominent oil man, a member of the American Petroleum Institute, and president of the huge Cities Service Company. There *was* waste in the production of oil, he insisted. Scandalous waste. If his colleagues regarded as "negligible" all the senseless duplication of drilling equipment and work, surely they could not so dismiss the actual loss of reservoir energy. He pointed out what was scarcely recognized at the time: that oil is propelled to the surface chiefly by gas pressure, and that the more wells were drilled in a new field the more leaks there were through which to lose this natural pusher. What was the answer? Nullify the law of capture. Operate each pool as an engineering unit; make it legally what it was in geologic fact. Surely somewhere, in state or federal government, there lay the power to accomplish this; otherwise the United States must admit that it lacked power to conserve a mineral absolutely vital to the national defense.

The leaders thought this idea interesting but Utopian. Technical knowledge was still insufficient. If government, as landowner, wanted to give unit operation a trial, well and good. But force it on private producers? Impossible.

The complacency of these men's views reflected temporarily stable conditions in their business. Since 1923 no huge new fields had been

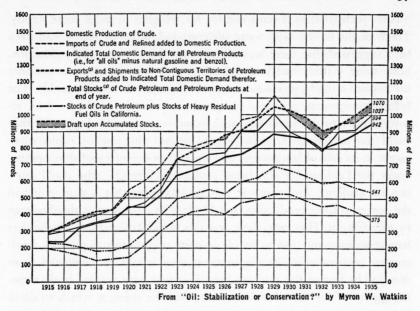

From "Oil: Stabilization or Conservation?" by Myron W. Watkins

PETROLEUM PROCUREMENT AND DISPOSITION IN THE UNITED STATES, 1915–1935

brought in. Throughout most of 1926 the dangerous surplus was being carved down. Prices were good. But some months after the hearings, flush production burst out in the incredibly rich Seminole area of Oklahoma. Impossible things began to happen.

THE DELUGE: 1928–1932

Other huge fields came roaring in: Kettleman Hills, California, in 1928; Oklahoma City in 1929; biggest of all, East Texas, where Kilgore began its boom-town cycle, in 1930. Great "gardens of gurgitating gushers," to use a pleasant old description of oil fields. From 1927 till the present moment a terrific excess of productive capacity has not ceased to bear down on oil prices, threatening the ruin of this important industry.

The Conservation Board urged voluntary cooperation to ward off disaster, and some of the big companies began to think the unit plan worth a tryout. Many of them were busily leasing large tracts; and where control was not too much divided—for example, in the small Sugar Land field in Texas which was entirely under lease to the Humble Oil and Refining Company—unitization was put to the test. Results proved the importance of Mr. Doherty's advice on gas pressure. This and similar experiments led to startling estimates of waste in other fields. Operating profits at Cromwell field could have been $134,500,000 instead of $50,000,-000—under a unit plan. At Seminole, according to a 1930 report, one well in three need not have been drilled; development and operating costs could have been reduced 40%; net income could have been 28% greater.

The first unit development of a large field was at Kettleman Hills North Dome in California. It required cooperation between a number of minor leaseholders and two major ones: Standard of California and the United States Government, which in 1930 at last amended the Leasing Act to permit the Secretary of Interior to enter for the government into unitization agreements. Although cooperation was something less than perfect, the benefits were plain to see. Within three years the annual waste of natural gas in the field was reduced from over 100 billion cubic feet to less than 3 billion, with resulting gains in the amount of oil available by natural flow. And oil from this large field, which under competitive drilling could have demoralized California prices if not others as well, came to sale in more rational amounts.

In very few fields was control centralized enough to allow voluntary unitization. As cheap oil from the new Texas and Oklahoma fields flooded the market, vested interests were endangered. The major companies and other leaseholders deeply involved in older fields, looking for a way out, started down the path that in 1926 had looked so forbidding. They asked —and got—state-enforced curtailment of production in the two states. This straitjacket was to be applied in flush fields but not, they hoped, in their own chief hunting grounds. It was the rage of the victims—the independent producers whose dreams of wealth from the new discoveries were thus darkened—that led to such violence as the church burnings at Kilgore.

So curtailment started in the new fields. Proving ineffective as well as unfair, it was made state-wide. Still overproduction and price drops continued. A conference of oil-state governors met, but only Kansas joined Texas and Oklahoma in the agreement which resulted. Meanwhile the Federal Trade Commission had sponsored a "fair competition" agreement among whatever companies wanted to sign, limiting destructive practices in the struggle to get rid of refined products. The Federal Oil Conservation Board decided to help by publishing forecasts of demand and recommending state production quotas. This Board even looked with favor on the attempts of major companies to enter into an international apportionment of world marketing quotas, to ease the sting of the world-wide

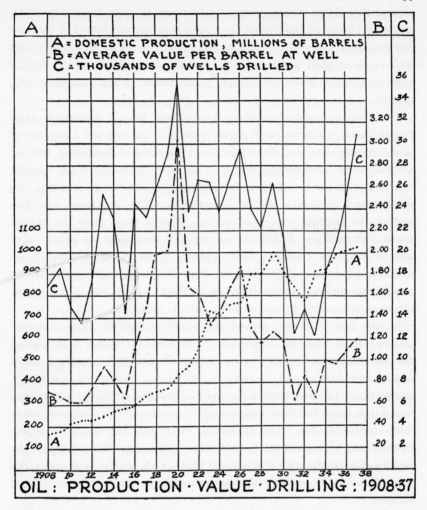

A = DOMESTIC PRODUCTION, MILLIONS OF BARRELS
B = AVERAGE VALUE PER BARREL AT WELL
C = THOUSANDS OF WELLS DRILLED

OIL : PRODUCTION · VALUE · DRILLING : 1908·37

battle between Anglo–Persian and Royal–Dutch Shell on one side against
Standard of New Jersey, Socony, and Vacuum Oil, chiefly, on the American side; but the Department of Justice threatened prosecution under
antitrust laws.

In the wild 1860's vigilante groups had policed the producing fields
trying to enforce shutdowns. Now in a worse chaos the armed forces of
state were brought to bear in Texas and Oklahoma; martial law reigned
at Kilgore and elsewhere. These unprecedented restrictive measures were
superficially effective. Production dropped from a billion barrels in 1929
to less than 800 million in 1932. Stocks were reduced. Prices were expected

to rise. But on the contrary: they sank—to the ruinous point, in July, 1931, of 23 cents a barrel! Why?

There was a more potent reason than lower purchasing power due to depression, perhaps even than the incomplete scope of the quota program; a reason inherent in the very basis of the restrictive methods. The flow of oil was reduced by proration: by limiting the rate of flow from each well to a fraction of its potential. There was no ban on drilling. Consequently, although low prices made for less drilling compared to past records, in no year were less than 12,000 new wells drilled. Not all of these were in unprorated states. The very producers whose output was being restricted drilled more new wells, in the hope of adding to their current allotment and their total share of the capturable oil. The real threat, therefore—the potential oversupply—kept increasing. Like the stored surpluses of cotton and wheat, it weighed on prices. And when the Supreme Court in 1932 refused to sanction using martial law to hold back production, the dam broke. Cheap "hot oil" (oil produced contrary to state regulations) flooded the market. By February, 1933, Mid-continent crude sold for 45 cents a barrel. A conference of oil-state governors and leaders of the industry was quickly called. It disagreed as to whether federal action—specifically, a prohibition against transporting hot oil in interstate commerce—was needed. But by May crude was down to less than 30 cents and the morale of oil men was down to zero. When the National Industrial Recovery Act became law in June, they decided to come in under the blue eagle's wing. No wonder! In 1931 the eighteen largest companies had lost $76,000,000; 1933 promised similar tragedy. "There are obvious dangers and disadvantages in government intervention," wrote the *Oil and Gas Journal,* "but could a federal partnership be worse than dictatorship by bootleggers and price cutters?"

THE NEW DEAL AND THE OIL INDUSTRY

The entire series of experiments in industrial control under the NRA suffered necessarily from being planned in the haste and turmoil of a national emergency and administered by overburdened officials. The Petroleum Administration shared this handicap, but less than the others. Some federal and state machinery had already been functioning. And the oil industry was not added to General Johnson's many responsibilities but became the problem of Secretary of the Interior Ickes, whose department included, in the Bureau of Mines and elsewhere, many oil experts.

The NIRA opened the way for great industries to set up codes of "fair competition," the terms to be drafted by business men themselves, acting in conference through their trade associations upon the principle of majority rule. As approved by the President after open hearings, these codes were to become legally binding not only upon those who had sub-scribed to them but upon everyone in the industry; and action taken under them was declared exempt from antitrust laws. Recognizing that recovery efforts would be futile unless the purchasing power of the general public, normally represented to the extent of about 65% by wages, were improved, the Act expressly guaranteed to workers their right to bargain collectively through representatives of their own choosing in regard to wages, hours and working conditions. The Act also carried a special amendment relating to oil. The President was empowered to initiate proceedings before the Interstate Commerce Commission in regard to pipe-line rates; to take action (through what channels was not men-tioned) against any holding company and its subsidiary pipe line that he found tending to create a monopoly through exorbitant rates or unfair practices; and to prohibit the transportation of hot oil in interstate com-merce. Only this last power was used.

The Petroleum Code proper evolved from proposals agreed upon—more or less!—in conference by delegates representing the American Petroleum Institute and other trade groups of varying strength and aims. Their proposed code was followed to Washington by another embodying the hopes of a group of small independent producers and refiners not satisfied with the conference results. From these and the many conflicting demands brought out in public hearings a final code resulted. What did it say and how did it work?

Ultimately, entire responsibility for the way things worked rested on President Roosevelt; but to Secretary Ickes, as his Administrator, were delegated all powers given to the chief executive. As in the case of most other codes, an administrative board chosen from the ranks of industry exercised considerable power in practice. In this instance it was called a Planning and Coordination Committee.

The oil code provided for supervision of production curtailment by "a federal agency." The Administrator appointed a Petroleum Adminis-trative Board of five to do this. As existing state boards were permitted to allocate quotas in the states where proration was already in effect, it was provided that elsewhere suitable machinery should be set up.

The Planning and Coordination Committee, composed of twelve voting members representative of the industry, supervised transportation, re-finery, and marketing operations. The balance of power among its members lay with major-company representatives.

Other boards and innumerable subcommittees functioned. An important group was the Petroleum Labor Policy Board, which advised the Administrator in labor matters, mediated disputes, watched for violations, and protected the workers' right to organize.

The prevailing, though not unanimous, drive was towards nation-wide curtailment. In addition, most major companies and many others having "stripper" wells (operations in old fields, yielding but a small quantity of crude, and that only under costly artificial pressure) wanted a fixed minimum crude price that would cover costs in such cases. Independent refiners, who could thrive only on low crude prices (based on costs in flush fields) which would enable them to undersell the big integrated refiners, were opposed. Major companies wanted strict control of drilling. Independents and wildcatters wanted no such restriction. Small producers and refiners, having practically no foreign sources or large tank farms, wanted imports and withdrawals from stocks prohibited. But major companies wanted to make use of their foreign output and stored supplies.

The big companies gained at one point: the Administration was empowered to set a minimum crude price. This was kept at one dollar a barrel—enough, apparently, to make production generally profitable. And the independents gained this: no restriction on wildcat drilling or on development in fields already discovered. In case new fields came in, they were to be developed only under plans approved by the Administrator. Here was a small area in which conservation measures could have been taken; but little was done except to limit the rapidity of drilling. As to the third conflict, the Administration was given power, but no very definite instructions, to control imports and withdrawals from storage. In practice these items were kept at about the level of the years just preceding the code.

Concerning the main point, output curtailment, the code provided that the federal experts should forecast total consumer demand by months and recommend to each producing state its share of the output required to meet such a demand. If a state went over its quota, the Administration might prohibit the movement of the excess oil in interstate commerce.

Now, being national in scope, curtailment was more effective than it had ever been. Yet it was not leak-proof. Bootlegging did continue. More than a year went by before successful means of enforcing the ban on interstate commerce in hot oil were worked out. Soon thereafter this delegation of congressional power to the Administration was found unconstitutional. Congress, however, promptly passed the Connally Act to avoid this pitfall, and retained the machinery that had proved most effective. Despite some flow of hot oil, surplus stocks were steadily reduced. (A great boon to the major companies, for the excess stocks were almost entirely theirs. Some had been accumulated when scarcity seemed likely to recur and make the surpluses salable at a handsome profit; some later in a desperate effort to divert supplies from the independent refiners who threatened to get a start in new fields. The deluge threatened heavy losses on these stocks. But under the code fairly severe curtailment of current output, while the price of crude was pegged reasonably high, served to bail out the majors at the expense of independent producers.) As to other methods: since the allocation of suggested state quotas to various fields and individual wells was left entirely to the states, there was little change in the basis of proration. Nor did the federal agency, in making its quota suggestions, improve much on methods used by the Federal Oil Conservation Board before it. The basis was changed from "market demand" to "consumer demand"; that is, speculative buying was not encouraged. But no innovations were made in the direction of conserving the total supply by attention to the varying reserves of each state or to engineering problems in the fields.

Code provisions relating to the "bottle neck" of the industry, carrying and refining, were short and vague. Pipe lines, although control of them is as important strategically now as in the days when monopoly was born, were not definitely mentioned. A committee was empowered to study transportation rates and practices and to recommend action, if it saw fit, to the President, who could then act if *he* saw fit. Nobody saw fit. As to refining, the obscurity of the few provisions was no obstacle to the Planning and Coordination Committee. It controlled refinery operations as it pleased, and suggested code amendments to confirm the powers it took on. The Administrator, with whom final authority clearly lay on account of his power of amendment, permitted this high-handedness. Its result was further tightening of the major companies' control where they already, of course, dominated. Wholesale gasoline prices were controlled. Complaints were not that they were too high but—from independent refiners—that they were too low. Unquestionably these could not operate on so narrow a margin as the integrated companies could, and therefore lost ground.

Previous agreements sponsored by the Federal Trade Commission served as model for the marketing provisions of the code. They stated in great detail what did or did not constitute fair practices. Parking service and tire covers, for example, were things of value and could not be given free; whereas water, compressed air, maps, and windshield wiping were considered "of no intrinsic value" and might be given free of charge. Some rules were quite unenforceable, such as that integrated companies should equalize profits from each branch they were engaged in. All were very hard to enforce on 350,000 retail outlets ranging from large city garages to roadside hot-dog stands.

The chief wish of independents was that lease-and-license contracts, the bulwark of major-company marketing, be prohibited. Code provisions about this were evasive; no clear action was taken. Among big companies the paramount aim was to establish a wide and uniform dealer margin—in other words, to make retailing stable and profitable. Efforts to accomplish this through the code administration were changeable and not very effective. As refinery control waxed stronger, marketing control became less important to the majors, since independent brands were being cut off at an earlier stage. In so far as the wide-margin program succeeded, it encouraged the wasteful multiplication of retail outlets in an already overdeveloped business.

In the code first proposed by leaders of the industry labor provisions were most innocuous. They stated that "existing wage schedules should not be reduced but both employment and wage schedules should be increased as soon as business conditions permit." That labor finally gained anything was due chiefly to the presence of labor spokesmen at the hearings and to the energetic actions of the Labor Policy Board after the code went into effect. The approved code shortened working hours considerably and set minimum wage rates at somewhat increased levels.

The oil industry employs few workers compared to an industry like coal, and labor problems had never been of tremendous proportions. Drilling is skilled work, relatively well paid—at $10 a day in California in 1929, and this might go as high as $16 or $18 in rush times. The driller leads a nomad life and an exciting one. He may work long stretches, 12 hours a day and often 7 days a week; but the spirit of adventure, the gambling excitement of bringing in a well, compensate. In refining and transportation, machinery does most of the work. Labor per unit of output is less than in any industry but printing and publishing. Here, too, hours have been long—10 to 12 hours a day for a 6-day week. In retailing, where 60% of the industry's workers are employed, the 1931 average work week was 60 hours. Depression brought many layoffs and wage cuts. Between 1929 and 1933, 42% of those employed in production lost their jobs; 22% in refining. Shortened hours under the code gave back their jobs to many of these. Considering all branches, the changes in employment, hours, and wage rates under the code approximately offset each other, so that total labor purchasing power hardly changed. No exorbitant toll, therefore, was taken from employers.

In addition oil workers gained power through unionizing under the Recovery Act's guarantee of this right. The Labor Policy Board worked zealously to make it effective and was of particular service in seeing that workers were not forced into company unions.

What was it worth, this brief experiment halted in less than two years by the Supreme Court's decision in the Schechter case? Its aim had been to stabilize the petroleum industry on a profitable basis by adjusting supply to demand. It did this temporarily. The price structure sustained was high enough to remunerate everybody with the exception of the least efficient refiners and some independent jobbers. To rescue these would have meant higher gasoline costs to 30 million automobile drivers.

As has been shown, code operations increased the scope and temporary effectiveness of controls already begun by chiefly private means in refining, carrying, and marketing, and by state intervention in production. The only real innovation came in the gains to workers. If for this alone, the code experiment was worth while. It will prove the more valuable if the nation can recognize and remedy its shortcomings, one being the lack of protection to consumers. If the controlled prices of refined products were not exorbitant, this was not due to any guarantee provided in the code.

One unhappy result was that the abused word, conservation, was obscured for the public by a further confusion. It had long before been mistakenly identified with nonuse. Then, in the shortage scare of the early twenties, it was used as a synonym for rapid exploitation. Under the code, it became entangled with the concept of stabilization. Although the NRA in oil was an emergency undertaking, both government and business leaders claimed that it would work wonders towards conservation.

In making such claims, the leaders doubtless forgot that other resources than underground crude were involved. Some of the greatest wastes are economic ones: the extreme duplication of equipment and work in production and retailing. These are incompletely expressed when one points out that development costs in a certain field could have been reduced, say, 50%. Waste through competitive duplication is a social concern, not merely a matter for the private investor. It is a human waste. It means a poor life for service-station operators and their families. It means ghost towns in worn-out oil fields. It means that 30 million consumers today pay not only for what they get at the gasoline pump but for a lot of essentially unproductive enterprises. This kind of waste, temporary stabilization actually increased. It stimulated further drilling of worse than needless wells, further sproutings of unprofitable retail outlets. The long-run causes of instability were aggravated.

Nor did code operations do much to conserve the physical resource. Accidentally, by holding back the flow in flush fields, some waste was undoubtedly prevented. But the essential factor, control of production according to engineering principles, was left out. To conserve the potential energy in a pool, the number and placement of wells must be determined by geologic factors special to the pool, not according to leasehold. The flow from each well must be regulated not to a fraction of its greatest potential but to the minimum gas-oil ratio at which it will flow. That is, the natural propulsive forces in the pool must be utilized to bring about the greatest ultimate recovery.

Present and Future

Neither all the state governments nor many of the oil men were willing to lose the benefits of NRA "stability" after the Recovery Act had been declared unconstitutional. Therefore the federal government was asked to keep on estimating the total demand and suggesting state production quotas. It has done so. Congress was asked to continue the ban on interstate commerce in hot oil, which it did. Surface results indicate that with this much help, regulation by the states from 1935 on has been having some effect, but a diminishing one. For a time, stocks continued to shrink; supply, it seemed, was fairly well adjusted to demand. However, some states failed to cooperate fully—Illinois, Louisiana, Michigan. Increasing supplies of crude oil came to market at less than posted prices. The latter had to be lowered. As this is written (August, 1939), a second cut of 20 cents has brought Midcontinent crude to 82 cents a barrel. Oil companies say they have been losing money for 18 months. In response to the price cut, six producing states have joined in a 15-day shutdown of all wells—the most drastic curtailment ever undertaken. The old chaos is on its way back.

Stabilization will always break down periodically as long as the basic cause, overcapacity, remains. It does remain, at the moment, and is increasing. About 31,000 new wells were drilled in 1937, and the unlucky high record of 1920 may be surpassed in 1939.

What is the federal government doing? The conservation movement seems quiescent. Besides lending aid to state boards and business leaders

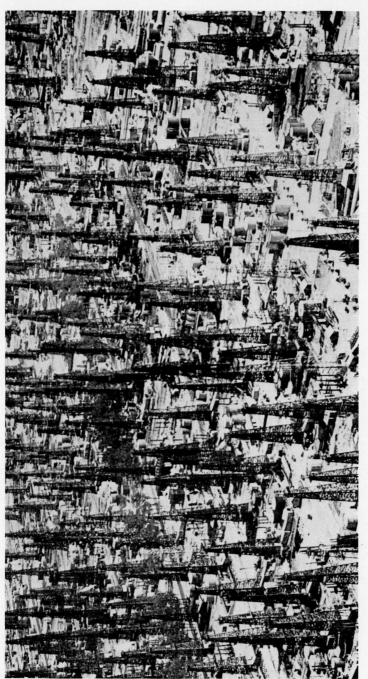

Photo by Ewing Galloway

CROWDED DERRICKS NEAR LONG BEACH, CALIFORNIA

The number of producing wells in the United States is roughly the same as the number of retail outlets: 350,000. Thousands of oil producers rush to capture as much crude as they can.

A WELL ON FIRE

This well near Los Angeles burned for five weeks. The operators finally
stopped it by tunneling down 50 feet and cutting and capping the pipes so
that the fire died for lack of fuel. So much gas had been burned that the oil
then had to be pumped up.

Esso Marketers Photo

CONTINUOUS GASOLINE-TREATING PLANT

Oil refining is highly mechanized and employs relatively few workers: about 100,000. By contrast, between 500,000 and 600,000 are employed in the very competitive, overdeveloped field of retailing refined products.

PROPANE PLANT AT THE BAYWAY REFINERY

The Standard Oil Company of New Jersey, owner of this refinery, is a billion-dollar corporation. It is the largest of the twenty big integrated companies that dominate oil transportation and refining.

in their not always unanimous efforts to keep up some crippled form of stabilization (which really implies, as the NIRA recognized, shelving antitrust laws) the federal government seems to be starting in the opposite direction at the same time. There are signs of a new trust-busting campaign. Several major companies have been convicted at Madison, Wisconsin, of violating the Sherman Act. The conviction has just been reversed on a technicality, and a retrial is in prospect. The appellate judge's opinion points up the confusion we are in. It states that even if a conspiracy to raise prices had been proved, the jury should have taken government NRA policies into account in determining the "character of the restraint of trade and the good faith of the defendants." Instead of a clear policy, we have an NRA ghost that can neither live nor die! * The Temporary National Economic Committee announces a coming investigation of the whole oil industry in order to see whether and what kind of monopolistic practices exist and what kind of action should be taken. Will clarity result? Meanwhile the government, shuttling back and forth between help and hindrance to private control in industry, reflects confusion and conflict in public opinion about the issues involved.

The social gains possible through concentrated control are easy to see, when it comes to petroleum. One has only to contrast the overdeveloped producing fields with the much more efficient refinery section of the industry, which operates at about 85% of capacity. And big companies, largely a result of changed and changing technology, are also likely instruments for extending technical progress. Oil history, however, illustrates that the prime energy behind the growth of large corporations has been the drive towards profits of the captains of industry. In other words, not all of the possible public gains have been realized; on the contrary, a large part of the benefits has obviously gone to enrich the few at the expense of the many. Have social gains, then, been negligible? We think not. For one thing, the profits of big business have constantly provided ready capital for new productive industries. Was there not a long period when the resulting Niagara flow of goods seemed (and was, for those who could buy) a great general gain? Today we count the cost in terms of exploited human lives and depleted natural resources. We are aware of social wants that the simple drive to produce more and more goods and accumulate more and more profits cannot supply. We see profits piling up faster than they can be reinvested profitably, and so lying idle, the flow of goods interrupted. We see that the tendency

* This case finally reached the Supreme Court, where an earlier decision against the oil companies was upheld.

of big business to pile up capital rather than to lower prices and increase wages makes trouble even for the business leaders themselves (since corporations cannot flourish without customers), besides denying large numbers of the working and consuming public their due share of the goods produced—or producible. There remain, nevertheless—in the oil industry, and in many businesses—potential benefits to society through large-scale operations under centralized control. The problem is to find ways of socializing the control and distributing the gains more fairly. This will require more positive action by public agencies than is included in the antitrust program of policing business to prevent discriminatory practices and "restraint of trade."

Yet public gains have resulted from the antitrust movement. Regulation of railroads as common carriers has brought improvements that make the old days of rebates and drawbacks seem barbaric if not criminal (though chances are still open, in railroad financing, for private gain at public expense). Big business should be prevented from using unfair means which give it an advantage beyond whatever superiority in efficiency it may possess. Control of oil transportation by major companies is still used unfairly. The lease-and-license system is unfair.

Government should use its big stick at such points. It should also encourage concentration of control where this can contribute to the public interest, as it did when the government entered into the Kettleman Hills unit plan. But it must at the same time find new ways of making sure that the gains from concentration of control are not outweighed by public losses. In a democratic society natural resources and the industries built on them are national resources, basic to the life of the whole people. The highest control must be democratic rather than autocratic. Under the NRA a dangerous amount of power was given to—partly taken by—a small private group, without effective control in the interest of the consuming public. Business leaders were allowed, essentially, to control the distribution of crude, its price, imports and exports, the supply and the wholesale and retail prices of refined products. That there was no check except to uphold better labor standards argues that the legislators and public officials either did not recognize the public nature of the powers they delegated or else lacked understanding or time (or the support of public opinion!) to work out ways of making public interests count. Whatever the case, present needs point not to a relaxation of federal concern and a return to uncoordinated policies, but rather in the opposite direction. The immediate need is for an expert federal agency to plan and suggest ways of coordinating federal and state activities so that they shall tend with least conflict and duplication in the direction of democratic control and shall be based on thorough study, not hurriedly patched up in moments of emergency. Such an agency must deal with social and economic policy on the broad front of all basic industries rather than with one alone. Oil is a nationally used fuel and should be considered in connection with other fuels, especially coal and gas. Moreover, only by broad planning to open up new channels of production and consumption can efforts wasted in overdeveloped businesses like oil retailing be transferred to better uses. Such an agency should also devise steps for getting at the basic cause of physical waste, uncontrolled drilling. Until this is accomplished there will be not only waste of oil but instability in the whole industry.

Has government any known powers which would enable it to regulate drilling? Would it not always run into the danger of injustice through saying to one leaseholder, "Drill!" and to another, "Abandon your investment"? There seem to be two possibilities. The federal government, by using its right of eminent domain, can appropriate all oil-bearing lands by purchase. Then it would have complete control; without injustice to owners, since these would have been remunerated. Or state governments could pass laws compelling all owners or leaseholders to join in quasi-municipal corporations, analogous to drainage districts, by means of which production could be put on a unit basis and methods regulated in the interest of physical conservation.

In view of the difficulty in getting various states to act together, the first program seems more complete and more likely. Not that it would be easy to put through, or that it is on the point of happening. But an enlightened program concerning this and the other vital aspects of our oil problem can happen. It *will* happen if the people who use petroleum products wake up to the urgency of the need to conserve and the nature of the difficulties to be met!

Chapter IX—OIL: ANCIENT DECAY TURNS MODERN WHEELS

Case History Number Three

THE PAST: OIL IN THE MAKING

THE PRESENT: TECHNIQUES AND PROBLEMS DUE TO GEOLOGY

THE FUTURE: SHALL WE CONSERVE WHAT IS LEFT?

Chapter IX—OIL: ANCIENT DECAY TURNS MODERN WHEELS

Case History Number Three

The Past: Oil in the Making

How was oil made? How did it come to be in big underground pools, a characteristic which has proved such a cruel jest to a culture whose mores and laws depend upon surface property lines? What makes salt water fill the wells when they "go dry" of oil? When is oil found alone? Who were the masters when oil was in the making? For answers we must again turn back the geologic clock to the Age of Cockroaches or even a little further back. The geologic case history of oil has much in common with that of coal. Both coal and oil originate in living matter. Both have been brought to their present state through the pressure of overlying strata. That is why coal, oil and gas are so often found together. But not always. (See maps, pages 171 and 248.)

Little oil that was made before the Age of Cockroaches is still left. But much of the oil that was in the making when the giant cockroaches scuttled under the coal plants still lay in black subterranean pools when Colonel Drake sank his first well eighty years ago. For along the shores and in the warm waters of the shallow Paleozoic (Ancient Life) seas and swamps which came and went over various parts of the slowly rising and slowly subsiding central lowlands of the North American continent, lived trillions and trillions of tiny creatures. (See map, page 205.) Not even the three eyes of the sharpest amphibian of those days, not even the multiple eyes of the dragonflies could see these living organisms, they were so small. Indeed, only the man-made eye of the microscope could have seen them then or can see them now where they are still carrying on their life. These tiny creatures we now call bacteria. Down at the bottom of the shallow salt seas and along the shores, these microscopic bacteria lived on the bodies of dead animals and plants which had sunk into the matted mire much of which was to become coal. Their living, we call decay of the bodies upon which they exist. The decaying

273

organic ooze of these plants and animals sent off tiny globules of fat, which rose through the muddy waters and got caught with particles of clay, caught and preserved from reaching the air and so from becoming completely oxidized (burned), caught in the preserving salt brine of the shore waters. Much oil is still in this state. Still caught in clay deposits which later were pressed by other overlying deposits into the oil-bearing shale of Colorado, Utah and Wyoming.

But most of the little globules of fat eventually left the clay. First, through the same earth behaviors that laid down the rock layer-cake over the old swamp vegetation, they became covered with a layer of sand which in time became covered by still more layers of rock, porous and impervious. That is, eroded rock from adjoining mountains washed down over the oil-saturated clay. Then the bottom of the sea sank slightly, carrying with it the oil-saturated clay with the layer of super-imposed sand. Again the sea was shallow; again the tiny bacterial crea-tures attacked dead shellfish, worms and crustacea. Again the globules rose and got caught by clay particles; again a layer of sand. And so the layer-cake was built just as in coal, only the cake filling was differ-ent and led, later, to different behavior of the filling with different re-sults.

As the pressure of overlying strata got greater, water and gas, being lighter than rock, began seeping up through the rock. For a layman must always remind himself that rock is not solid but composed of crystals with intervening interstices. One of the constant changes which is going on in the earth is this rising through semiporous rocks of water and gases often carrying chemical agents. Thus, for instance, was some iron deposited. Now in some of these subterranean waters and gases went the globules of fat released from decaying organic ooze. They were carried along until they reached the layer of sand above them. If above the sand was a layer of impervious rock, the oil globules stayed imprisoned in the sand. Above them the layer-cake continued to grow until in places it was many thousands of feet thick. In the heat produced by this over-lying weight and the friction of slight earth movements, the globules of fat turned into oil.

Now if these oil-saturated sand strata were compressed, filling the interstices and making slightly wavy sheets, the water would sink to the lowest dips and the oil would gather in the upper domes. If there were enough hydrogen present, the oil would turn into gas which, being the lightest of all, would seek the uppermost parts of the domes in the wavy sheets. And here the oil and gas would lie in pockets imprisoned by

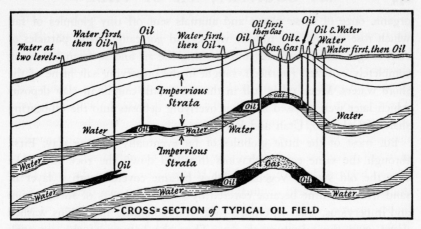

overlying strata of impervious rock; now sometimes below 15,000 feet of rock layer-cake.

But if the movement of the earth were severe and the wavy sheets of oil-saturated sands were much crumpled, the heat would turn all the oil into gas, which would seep up through the cracks caused by the violent folding or faulting and escape into the atmosphere. And so it comes about that the oil and gas that was in the making at the time of the cockroaches has most of it escaped. What remains lies in fairly horizontal sheets, as does bituminous coal. That is why it has been preserved. Such is the oil in the great sheets of oil sands which lie under the Allegheny Plateau and under the central lowlands of the United States and in the Gulf Coastal Plain, made in the Paleozoic (Ancient Life) Era. For over these lands, in the days of the cockroaches and coal plants, lay long warm shallow seas cut off from the Gulf of Mexico by mountains which then rose in southeast Texas and Louisiana. And there were laid down layers of organic mud and interbedded sands, now from 1000 to 3800 feet deep, which were never crumpled much during the 200 to 400 million years that have passed, and so still lie imprisoned under impervious sheets of rock in slightly waving sheets of oil sands. Much oil throughout these regions has been discovered through drilling salt wells. In the Gulf Coastal Plain in Louisiana, the oil fields are closely related to salt domes or great salt plugs which have been forced upward from great depth through the Gulf Coast sediment. As they pushed up they dragged with them sheets containing oil. But on the ocean shores of North America there was so much crustal movement that whatever oil was made in the Age of Cockroaches or earlier turned to gas and escaped.

Now we turn the geologic clock ahead some 200 or 300 million years, to the Cenozoic (Recent Life) Era, still 7 to 19 million years ago. In the long intervening era—the Mesozoic (Intermediate Life)—had come many changes. Not only had the waters come and gone over different parts of North America. Not only had mountains risen and been eroded level. The creatures who lived on the surface had changed. Many had come and gone. The small amphibia of the Age of Cockroaches, contemporaries of the first masters of the coal fields, had developed into monsters of unbelievable size, and passed to extinction. Yet only a small amount of oil had been made during the long Mesozoic Era, when the land knew dinosaurs, long-necked or duck-billed or armored, some dragging 38-ton bodies around, some munching plants or animals according to their habits, some even walking on their two hind legs, some sluggish, some spry, but all monstrous, incredible. The air, too, had seen new creatures. Winged reptiles, "the dragons of the air," had flown on their giant batlike wings. Birds with their mouths filled with teeth, birds that swam better than they flew. New animals in sea, on land, in the air, developed and disappeared as mountains and seas came and went through the long Mesozoic Era. Then came the Cenozoic Era, when mammals came into their own and much oil was made.

But all the time, at the bottom of some sea which has long since disappeared, the tiny bacteria throve on the bodies of dead animals, and were making oil for future American masters. For the tiny globules of fat from these decaying bodies rose and again got caught in the small particles of clay and later became covered with sand and still later with impervious rock. This happened in many places throughout the Mississippi Valley. But later disturbance of the crust turned the heated oil to gas which escaped. It stayed undisturbed in patches in the Rocky Mountain regions. Here dinosaurs (Intermediate Life Era) were masters of the land when both oil and the Colorado coal were in the making.

Still later, when grasses had appeared on the surface of the earth tempting the newly developed mammals to descend from the trees, oil was made in the California region and preserved in some undisturbed pools. The man-ape (Recent Life Era) was master then and preceded Doheny by perhaps a million years. California, the continental edge, was and is a land of earthquakes. The marine deposits in the Los Angeles basin contained great quantities of petroleum. This area was gently folded late in the Cenozoic Era. As a result of the crossing of two sets of folds, low domes were formed in which the petroleum gathered. One small fault (a slipping of the crust) cracked the earth open to a pool of petroleum which oozed to the surface and lay in a large lake open to the sun. A natural process of refining took place. The kerosene and gasoline evaporated and left an asphalt lake, crusted on top but sticky far beneath. Here was caught the elephant, the giant wolf, the saber-tooth tiger. And here, close by, Doheny swung his pick-ax and tapped the oil not released by the early fault.

Thus the oil fields were in the making under the seas when the land had many masters, stretching in time from the cockroaches through the dinosaurs to the man-ape. Made in the shallow muddy seas from the decay of dead plants and animals, stored in layers of comparatively young rocks, preserved only where the earth's crust suffered no great convulsions, lying in wavy but comparatively horizontal sheets with oil or gas in the domes and water in the depressions, oil and gas waited for the modern masters, Rockefeller, Sinclair, Doheny.

Such is the geologic case history of oil and gas. It has dominated the techniques and dominated the problems of the gasoline culture of the last quarter-century.

The Present: Techniques and Problems Due to Geology

Thus when the geologist surveyor starts out to look for oil, he follows the standards laid down for oil geology. Redford of the Bureau of Mines says oil can be found only in "areas of sedimentary beds, at least in part of marine origin and not older than Cambrian or younger than Pliocene." Further, oil will be only "in successions of alternating porous beds" and in "moderately folded or faulted beds." There is no use looking in igneous or excessively folded, faulted or overturned regions. This sharply delimits the places where it is geologically possible to find oil. The geologist surveyor, therefore, first seeks a place which long ago has been covered by a warm shallow sea and later covered by a layer of sand. These past seas have been plotted fairly accurately in the United States so that oil possibilities are now limited. If there are no surface indications of a past sea, and there are none in the thick deposits of recently underwater land like that around the Gulf of Mexico, the surveyor sometimes takes a boring. That is, he sinks a well for the sake of examining the rock layer-cake closely. If he finds evidences of interbedded muds and sands or salt water, he will then use his detecting instruments, above all the seismograph. Indeed, he will probably use this before assuming the expense of sinking a boring well. The seismograph gives records of the sound waves passing through the earth. The waves are long or short depending upon the density of the substance through which they pass.

Seismographs are the instruments which give us the records of earthquakes or of sounds under water caused, perhaps, by a submarine. The surveyor, however, must make his own sound waves. This he does by an explosion of nitroglycerine on the surface. The seismograph record shows if there are more dense subterranean areas, called "domes," in the underrock caused by a slight warping of the strata. Here there *may* be oil.

Surveyors use other extremely sensitive instruments. The torsion balance shows the pull of gravity at the earth's crust upon the density of subsurface masses. The densest rocks exercise the greatest pull. The torsion balance, by measuring these gravitational pulls over a given region, lets the geologists discover underground formations. The instrument is sensitive enough to record a change in density as small as one part in a million million. Various rocks also exercise different magnetic pulls. Minerals and igneous and metamorphic rocks have a strong pull upon the magnetic needle. Sedimentary rocks are poor transmitters of the earth's magnetism. The magnetometer is an instrument which records these pulls. An expert can interpret its records into both structure and depth of subsurface foundations.

When the surveyor finds a favorable condition, he recommends the sinking of trial wells. The diagram shows that the well may strike water, oil, gas or merely rock. It also shows why so many derricks appear in an oil field which is controlled by the law of capture.

Gas is always found in smaller or larger quantities with oil. It is made from heated oil. The trick in mining oil is to keep the gas pressure forcing the oil to the surface. If the gas is exhausted, the well must be pumped or repressured, a much more costly performance. Also if the gas is gone and the oil nearly exhausted, salt water in the lower dips of the wavy sheets will rise to the dome and eventually come up the well. When only water comes, the well, paradoxically, is said to be "dry."

Wealth from oil is sudden and great—when it comes. So the United States has been thoroughly tested for possible fields. Testing for oil is now carried on on a large scale. In the Gulf Coast area in 1934, 60 seismographs were in use, 40 torsion balance parties were operating 117 instruments, and there were eleven other parties using magnetometers, etc. The shallow fields in this area had already been worked: the top of the producing horizon was less than 3000 feet in fifteen fields that were four years old or less. Of the six 1934 discoveries, one yielded oil at 5000 feet, one at 6000, and four at 7000. Similar activities go on in other areas.

Yet in spite of the tremendous advance in determining oil sites, the proportion of dry wells is surprising and increasingly larger. The risks get greater; the activity seems not to diminish. This is more largely due to wildcatting or other drilling that is not based on preliminary scientific survey than to the inadequacy of the oil geologists' techniques, though improved methods will undoubtedly make their calculations more reliable.

The Future: Shall We Conserve What Is Left?

No new major fields can be found in the United States. With the present knowledge of geologic conditions under which oil can or cannot be found and the extent of scientific surveys of possible areas, there is literally no room for huge unknown fields to exist. In most areas the wells now go as deep as geologists say that oil can be found. The deepest is 15,000 feet.

How much oil have we left in the ground? Many calculations have been made about oil reserves in the United States. They differ widely. But they are all depressing, even the most hopeful. In 1934 the National Resources Board made a scientifically calculated guess. They estimated the underground reserves available under present methods of recovery at 13 billion barrels. These would last approximately 15 years at the 1933 rate of consumption, which has since increased. "But since some of the oil included in these reserves cannot be produced until 20 or 30 years hence . . . a shortage during the coming 15-year period can be prevented only by discovery of new fields."

We are now taking from the ground about a billion barrels of crude a year, at the expense of stupendous underground waste—using waste as we have before to mean a loss the prevention of which would have been less costly than the loss itself. Physical losses have come about through leakage, evaporation and fire; through defective wells which have allowed the oil and gas to migrate from productive strata or have let water into the oil sands; through abandonment, because of unstable prices, of many wells before exhausting the oil, which now can never be recovered; through waste of gas which, if conserved, could have brought more oil to the surface.

The estimates on waste of natural gas are appalling. At one time, one billion cubic feet of gas was daily blown into the air in the Texas Panhandle alone. This, translated into other units of heat energy, would be equivalent to pouring on the ground 62,634,000 barrels of oil each year or of throwing away 14,600,000 tons of coal. "In 12 years in California," says the Report of the National Resources Board, "the quantity of gas known to have been wasted was about one-third of that produced for commercial use, and in 1929–30, the heating value of gas wasted from the Kettleman Hills field was equivalent to the expected energy output at Boulder Dam during a like period." In the fifth report of the Federal Oil Conservation Board the statement is made that in the Oklahoma City field alone the wastage probably averaged 300 million cubic feet of natural gas per day for 1931 and 1932. It must always be remembered, moreover, that gas is not only valuable as a fuel but as an aid in mining oil.

This "spectacular" waste in the production of oil, the most striking of which has been the blowing of gas into the air, has been lessened in recent years until now there is no appreciable waste aboveground. But waste underground has had only little attention from the industry. For instance, if an oil pool contains 100 million barrels of oil of which 20 million barrels can be recovered by one method but 50 million barrels can be recovered by another method at no greater cost, then to use the first method will waste 30 million barrels of oil. This is no overstatement of the extent of waste that has taken place. True conservation should be concerned with every kind of preventable waste, which is utterly different from merely reducing the amount of oil taken out of the ground to meet market demand. Obviously genuine conservation can come only through comprehensive planning which will include the amount of production and methods used in all fields.

Before exhaustion, will come shortage with an inevitable rise in price. Even the most optimistic of the calculations show an approaching shortage. It is conceivable that the shortage will be postponed by more inventions. Polymerization makes usable certain fractions of crude formerly wasted. The process of cracking, which is the breaking down of the heavy molecules of petroleum under tremendous heat (850 to 1200 degrees) into more gasoline molecules, approximately doubled the amount of gasoline obtainable from a barrel of crude. Cracking delayed the shortage of gasoline by raising the average yield of gasoline obtained from a given amount of crude oil from around 23% to about 45%. Hydrogenation, a still newer process, makes possible 100% conversion of crude to gasoline. However, lubricants can be made only from petroleum, in our present state of knowledge. There may come an invention by which the vast oil shales of Utah and Wyoming can be made to yield gasoline. This experiment is being tried in Scotland. But even if all these "ifs" should turn into realities—*if* we should find unexpected new reserves, *if* inventions continue to enable us to get the products we need out of whatever oil we may be able to produce—eventually the cost per unit seems certain to rise.

Still another "if." If gasoline, fuel and lubricating oils do cease to be available for our millions of engines, what then? Perhaps a new fuel, or new power, or new type of engine will turn up to save our machine culture. "Sufficient unto the day is the evil thereof." So speak the optimists. And the alarmists continue their Cassandra prophecies, that the evil day is almost at hand. Whichever is right, the waste in oil remains an undisputed fact. Stupendous, incredible waste. We may get by, like the old man who said he noticed that if he got by March, he lived through the year. We may. And again we may not.

Surely even the most conservative-minded—unless his own personal and immediate profits are involved—must agree that the situation demands some action—immediate, sweeping, effective. Where else can one look for such action than to the government? For history, including the present history of the oil industry, shows that unregulated private control of the nation's oil reserves cannot bring about the operation of our oil pools as units, which, because of geologic formation, is indispensable to true conservation of the oil. It shows that private control results in such physical and economic waste that, in a future not far removed, we may be crippled in our peacetime pursuits and perilously handicapped in any war.

Chapter X—WHAT TO DO ABOUT IT

Chapter X—WHAT TO DO ABOUT IT

WE COME to the last chapter. No longer can we escape from promises made from time to time to readers—and more to ourselves. It is time to face the question, "What to do about it?" This must involve both our own best thinking and that of the reader. For whoever has traveled about the country and back into history with us, watching the development of three great natural resources, may or may not share our misgivings over the wastefulness—both physical and human—with which we have used an incomparable endowment of natural wealth. His attitude towards these assembled facts, like our own, will depend not entirely upon the validity of the facts themselves. It will depend partly upon the philosophy by which he interprets these facts—what he wants his country to be and what tools he regards as both desirable and efficient in achieving the ends he desires. In other words, since this last chapter must be a chapter of opinion, our readers will inevitably be called upon to match our opinions with their own.

Our National Drama: American Culture

Throughout the preceding pages, we have watched the unfolding of a great national drama. First of all, we have the stage set—the background against which the drama has been enacted. The stage set is the resources which form the basis of natural wealth—soil, metal ores, coal, oil, natural vegetation and animals, water, climate—all the things which were once piously called "God-given." Certainly they are not man-made. They are the fruits of the geologic and biologic drama enacted on the earth for incalculable millions of years. They are the earth forces which men find. They constitute the stage set for the drama of culture.

Second, there are the actors: Indians, pioneers, Yankees, southern plantation owners, slaves, industrialists, workers in fields and mines and factories, "builders of the nation" and "robber barons," bankers and sharecroppers, CCC boys and Justices of the Supreme Court—the procession of people who have crossed our stage.

It was our impressive natural wealth, our stage set, that drew our human wealth, our actors, to us originally. The value of human wealth has led to the somewhat startling plans of Hitler and Mussolini for increasing the population of their nations by bribes or law. The United States is as impressively rich in human wealth as it is in natural wealth, though we are now approaching the stage of a stationary population which may lead to a shrinking populace and eventually give us the anxieties that France has long suffered from.

Natural wealth and human wealth: stage set and actors. What men do to the earth and what the earth does to them is the play itself. It has a plot which is history. It has rules and sanctions and conventions, like any play. These are our social and economic habits and standards which form our culture—using the word always as the ethnologist does, to mean the sum total of a people's habits of work and of play, the things they care about, the things they believe in, the human relationships they approve of or sanction. We have seen that our American actors live according to social institutions, inherited and changing, such as the family, schools, laws and courts, art, religion, the organization of work, the use of tools. We have seen a people developing characteristic food habits, house habits, road habits, clothing habits; developing attitudes towards private property, standards of living, and the use of their agent, the government. We have seen them developing new ways of using natural resources; and, as we said in the beginning, the characteristic use of natural resources is one of the most sensitive measures of a culture. We have seen them behaving with heroism and with greed, with imaginative courage and with wastefulness. Until now, the actors in our play behave according to the rules of that special form of modern Western culture that we call American.

What makes the plot of a play? Not the random collisions of unfeeling objects, but the interaction of living people, who have desires and purposes often clashing with one another and with the environing earth forces. Conflict is a *sine qua non* for drama, and certainly there is no lack of it in the play of cultural evolution we have been watching. When conflicts become general and great groups array themselves against each other, the play comes to a turning point. We have watched such a crisis in Revolutionary times; again in the clash between North and South. We seem to have come recently to another such turning point in cultural evolution, perhaps even deeper in its significance.

It may be that each generation thinks of its times as a turning point in history. "I don't know what we are coming to!" has certainly been the complaint of many a passing generation. What justification have we today for believing that the United States has taken on a new pattern in her development, and taken it on with such suddenness that we are full of cultural inconsistencies, the old order and psychologies persisting incongruously in the midst of the new? We are used to hearing ourselves spoken of as a young nation. How old are we? A little over three hundred years if we reckon from the time our homemakers began to settle a new land; half that age if we reckon from the time we achieved independence and began governing ourselves. A more significant question, however, is: How mature are we? For age and maturity are not synonyms. Years are easily counted. But what are the earmarks of national maturity anyhow? Psychologically, an individual is spoken of as mature when he is socially adapted to cope with his problems. A nation, too, has its psychological maturity. But it also has other patterns of behavior, both economic and social, which in our Western culture mark a nation as young or mature.

From Youth to Maturity: the Turning of the Arrows

We find ourselves in a different stage of culture from the one which prevailed when a group of amazingly able men drafted that great national plan known as our Constitution. One evidence of the ability and sagacity of these men was their realization that profound cultural changes were bound to occur which would make changes in the Constitution desirable. They therefore provided for amendments, one of the smartest things they did; though less wise later generations have tended to think of any change as an irreverent repudiation of the wisdom of our forefathers. The following brief listing of the chief of these cultural changes shows how startlingly the problems we now face differ from the problems we faced when the thirteen onetime colonies laid down rules for governing themselves as an independent nation. Indeed, as we line up our national tendencies now and a brief historic time ago, we see that many have completely reversed themselves. Our history could almost be pictured in a series of charts in which the changes are symbolized by arrows that have veered from youth to maturity. Some turned gradually, and no date can be named to say, "At this point we grew up." In other things maturity came suddenly, and we can say, "We grew up during the World War," or during the great depression that followed. And in some ways we are not yet grown up. But the arrows are wobbling!

Work patterns have changed. We began with the pioneer self-sustaining work pattern, shown in the chart on page 51. The self-contained unit was sometimes an individual, sometimes a family, sometimes a town. A fairly direct relationship existed between the consumer and the large natural resources he made use of—particularly soil. The consumer was related to little work outside the unit. This is the pattern of youth. We now function with an elaborate interrelationship pattern as shown in the chart on page 5. Each consumer's needs are now met through work relationships that reach far outside the bounds of his own work. This is the pattern of maturity.

The change in work patterns is closely related to other familiar changes. We added industry to agriculture. When our industries were in the "infant" stage, we built tariff walls to protect them. The infants have long since grown up, but the tariff walls remain. We turned from a rural to an urban culture. We developed larger and larger organizations for producing and selling goods—organizations which have burst the bounds of the states that grant them charters and even of the nation. We created a huge credit structure for financing big business. In these processes, we amassed great individual fortunes. We developed monopolies and organized "trust-busting" campaigns. We now live in a changeable age, under great technological pressure continually causing still other social reorganizations. All these changes indicate not merely a local growing-up process in the United States but a transformation in the whole Western culture with the coming of the Industrial Revolution. These changes have brought about an interdependence among the various industries undreamed of in our youth.

Land and labor frontiers have closed. We began with an immense undeveloped supply of land and with few people. That was young. Our settlers have long since gone westward clear to the sea. There will be no more startling conquests of mountains, forests and prairies to open up new resources of land and build new markets. That is mature.

Distance was conquered by highways and railroads. We may expect new records for airplane flights from coast to coast; land travel and communications may be extended to bring more people closer together; but the most spectacular and far-reaching progress in this direction has already been attained.

The "labor frontier" is closed, too. There is no longer too much work and too few hands to do it, as in the days when we tempted Europe to come to us at the rate of a million a year. We established the quota in 1921: in 1932, emigration exceeded immigration. Instead of needing more workers, we now have from 12 to 8 million out of jobs. Unemployment is a problem of maturity.

Our startling growth in population was not due entirely to immigration. Families were large. The number of children per family has fallen

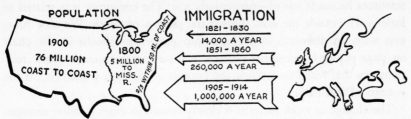

WE NEED WORKERS · WE HAVE LAND · PLEASE COME TO US!

NO MORE JOBS · NO MORE LAND · STAY OUT!

from 3.6 in 1850 to 1.5 in 1930. Our population is approaching the stationary point and may begin to fall after 1960. Also people live to greater age than they did fifty years ago. So the average age of our population has increased markedly, which changes the social picture and affects the labor market. Another arrow has veered. Another sign of maturity.

Trade and investment reach beyond our own boundaries. We have become a world power, and a nation of world traders. No major problem that confronts us today can be solved without taking directly into account conditions in other countries. Our wheat competes in a world market so that our western farmers are linked with Russia, Australia and the Argentine. American capital is struggling with England, France and Germany for a share of the oil in the Near East. Many of our industries seek buyers the world over; others seek raw materials. A nation of traders must be concerned with the fate of the world it sells to and buys from.

Foreign debts have changed direction. That we are now responsibly involved with the fate of the world is all the more true because of our changed position in world finance. We built our railroads, opened our mines, developed our industries with European capital. Now we have unemployed capital. We emerged from the World War with Europe owing us 16 billion dollars. We are now, suddenly, a mature creditor nation, wielding more heavily than any other nation the "power of the

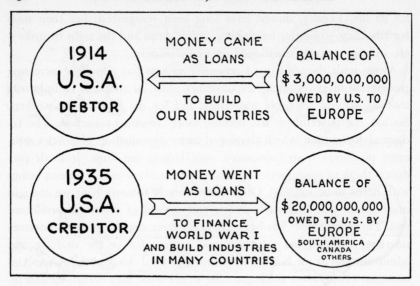

purse." As such, we are now, whether we wish to be or not, greatly responsible for the direction of world affairs.

Economic groups have formed within the nation. The closing of our land and labor frontiers, the arrival of the machine and the city have in a large measure shifted our groupings from primarily regional groups to economic groups. These changes split a relatively homogeneous people into great groups with sharply conflicting interests in the use of natural resources: (1) owners, enterprisers, managers, and (2) workers, numerically the larger group. In the original pioneer agricultural pattern, owner and worker were largely one and the same. How widely the workers even in agriculture have become separated from the owners is evident from tenancy figures. As industry grew in extent and intricacy, owners not only came to form a separate class but knew less and less about the needs and desires of workers. The younger Mr. Rockefeller's testimony in the Colorado Iron and Fuel strike shows how completely an owner may be unaware of the conditions of the men who work for him and may even feel justified in his ignorance.

Both of these groups have developed organizations. The organization of owners came first. Gradually the workers developed unions, though they were bitterly opposed by the owner group. Among the miners, the idea of a union started, as we have seen, about 1842. Farmers were slow in getting organized and still have no adequate unions. The Southern Tenant Farmers' Union was organized only in 1934 and is now fighting for its life. Legally, unions have long been recognized; but their tools for efficiency—collective bargaining, union shops and the right to strike—are still aggressively questioned by many owners.

Along with the growth of economic groups has come an increasing recognition of government responsibility alike for methods in industries that use natural resources wastefully, and for the lives of the workers. So, too, the government has become more consumer-conscious. The Industrial Revolution which developed factory production of articles separated producers from consumers, once largely the same. It made producers think of consumers statistically, as a market—not as human beings with needs to be satisfied. Only comparatively recently have we thought much about consumers from *their* end instead of from the producers' end. The government has begun to take active steps to protect consumer interests, as when the consumer was represented in the drafting and administration of the NRA, the Bituminous Coal Act and the AAA. And consumers themselves are organizing to get what they want—various information services; cooperatively produced gasoline, food and textile products; retail and professional services of many kinds.

Two American myths that persist as "historic lags" are being challenged. Concomitant with the reversal of so many national economic patterns have come disquieting changes in the social scene. Our inherited patterns of thinking, which came about as natural products of our early pioneer economy, are struggling to adjust themselves in this new and rapidly changing economy and social scene. Two of these inherited beliefs might well be called American myths. The first is the myth of unlimited resources; the second is the myth of rugged individualism. Current American psychology presents the adolescent picture of incredulity or "shock" consequent upon the blasphemous questioning of these sacred myths. Yet these myths are difficult to maintain in the face of what it is fashionable to call "reality." Erosion, depleted soil, floods, dust storms, depleted oil reserves—such are common newspaper headlines. Yet it is still called "un-American" to question the myth of unlimited resources. This myth has produced the habits of waste of our good earth and all that in it lies. Though habits of waste yield slowly to habits of conservation, there is surely a trend in this direction. In some resources we have reached only the stage of anxiety; in others we have expressed our anxiety through legislation.

So, too, with the closely allied myth of the rugged individual as the hope of national prosperity. He is tied up with our most precious national memories—with the cowboys, the forty-niners, Daniel Boone, Abraham

Lincoln, with the braving of great hardships and the making of great fortunes, with the opportunity for every boy to become the President of the United States. Admiration for him persists in the novels and movies called "Westerns," in Wall Street, and probably, sub rosa, in Al Capone and his fellow gangsters. He is heroic; he is romantic; he is successful. He is youth, he is All-American. No wonder he dies hard. No wonder that the popular imagination is captured and forgets that he may no longer fit the American life any more than do other romantic, heroic individualists of the past—the Vikings, the medieval craftsman, or the pioneer, who also belong to an economy that is gone. No wonder, too, that the popular imagination should somehow believe that we are repudiating the wisdom of our forefathers, going "un-American," if we question the myth that national prosperity depends upon rugged individualism.

And yet the social scene presents us daily headlines about the malfunctioning of individualism in terms of stranded populations, bootleg coal, low standards of living. Just as we have grown up thinking that the United States is a land of unlimited resources, we have grown up thinking that it is a "land of opportunity" for everyone. And it still is, as compared with Europe. But not as compared with even our recent past. Who could have imagined in 1914, a year when we welcomed over a million new people, that this land of opportunity would have fifteen million people unemployed in 1932 and twenty million human beings on relief in 1935? The myth that national prosperity depends upon rugged individualism has developed legal and moral habits of protecting the individual even when it involves exploitation of other human beings. And habits of legal protection for individual initiative and of property rights yield slowly to a conception of a high standard of living for all. Is it possible that another arrow may be quietly swinging towards psychological maturity, that we may be becoming socially adapted to cope with our national problems, in the subtle redefinitions of "democracy," "equality" and "freedom"?

Quietly? If there is one word which fits our present doings least of all, that is it. We have come to a loud and unhappy moment in the national drama. Everybody is dissatisfied. Our banks are filled with idle money; Wall Street is unhappy. Our most marvelous plants are running at a mere fraction of capacity; industrialists are unhappy. Not enough carloads move on steel tracks, not enough sales checks pass over the counters; dealers in all kinds of services are unhappy. As for labor, unemployment figures tell only part of the tale. Many are employed only part-time; income for many is meager and uncertain.

All this, we are told, is unnecessary. It was estimated by Harold Loeb in *The Chart of Plenty* that if this country were to set in motion all the idle resources in plant and man power, it could produce the equivalent of an income of $4400 for every family. The difference between our actual and potential production, with no plant improvement, estimated in 1929 dollars, was 42 billion dollars. If we knew how to do away with this national waste, this loss of potential goods and services, we should gain an amount sufficient to do away with poverty and meager living for all, without taking anything away from the fortunate 8% possessing in 1929 incomes of $5000 or more per family.

Here is the crowning paradox of our culture, the painfully familiar poverty amidst plenty. Even with our actual production we are told that there is "overproduction" in agriculture, coal and oil, at the same moment that we find millions of people lacking sufficient of the goods these industries produce. The quantity of goods needed by our country should be measured by our capacity to consume, not merely by our capacity to buy. Only after the needs of everyone are satisfied can we speak of genuine national surplus of goods. In short, the real economic jam which is keeping everyone dissatisfied is not simply *overproduction* but *underconsumption*. Business cannot recover by producing more because it cannot sell more: consumers cannot buy more because they have not enough income. Plants and men are idle. Instead of the happy hum of production and enjoyment, we have idleness and complaints.

And the "worst is yet to come" if we may believe current newspapers, magazines and books. They all warn us of impending disasters, but such a variety of disasters that at times it seems as if the United States could never work towards a unified aim concerning the future use of our national resources. This is due, of course, to the basic conflicts among the economic groups that make up the present-day United States.

No wonder that this is not a quiet moment in our national drama. Aside from the noise from overseas, it is hard to say who shouts loudest in the daily news: business leaders, labor, or government. Indeed, their voices are mixed, if not blended, in almost every article; for these conflicting groups are not separate but organically related in our present ways of making America's living. No one group can go its way to the injury of another group without being hit by a boomerang rebound.

The Meaning of Planning in a Democracy

Now we are convinced that government must take, increasingly, a conscious and planned share in determining the use of our physical and human resources. The emphasis is on "conscious" and "planned"; for, by the nature of the case, government plays a leading role in the drama of natural resources by what practices it permits or prohibits.

Planned—a terrifying word to the American ear. The popular idea of planning is still of an arbitrary putting over of some plan without consent of the individual or group planned for—a kind of dictator invention which undercuts democracy. Now our thesis in this last chapter is that the essence of democracy is planning *for* the majority which shall lead to planning *by* the majority, with representation but not control by minorities. That means that our task is to determine the interests of the majority in the use of our national resources and in the current economic and social problems involved in such use. We shall assume, not argue, that this planning for our national resources which furthers the interests of the majority is democratic planning for the nation. The government must transcend narrow group interests. From the broad point of view, all the groups are so intimately interrelated that the nation cannot thrive— certainly not as a democracy—unless all have some measure of the good life. Further, we feel we have established that *natural resources are national resources,* and therefore assume that planning for our national resources involves not merely the conservation or restoration of the physical resources themselves, such as we have outlined at the close of many chapters, but for the people involved in the production and consumption of these resources. That is, national planning must attend to both physical and economic waste and human waste. It must face the situations which are keeping everyone from Wall Street to Tobacco Road dissatisfied. Or more explicitly, it must study by what means we can use what we have with less waste of men and materials, and more complete use of what we know.

Our American culture expresses our plans. The striking thing about American history has not been its planlessness but rather that its planning has resulted in a crazy-quilt pattern expressing the haphazard drives of this or that small but powerful group. As long as we were young enough, with enough unused resources, particularly unused land, we got by with this crazy-quilt planning. But now that we have no golden West beckoning our malcontents and our downtrodden, we shall have to create —through national planning, which alone can really liberate our now rather frustrated productive energies—new jobs, new frontiers.

The play of American life continues to evolve, as we have said, not in random style but according to the wants and purposes of people and groups of people. Dissatisfactions have always resulted in new plans, many of them government plans. Look at our past. We became a nation, in the first place, because we had a plan for our own development which could not be carried out under England's plan for our development. And we stated our first plan in the Articles of Confederacy. That plan didn't work. We came out with another plan called the Constitution. "Planning" may smell wrong to 100% American nostrils. Yet the very hundred-percenters who now shiver at the word are the strongest adherents to the plan called the Constitution. (This plan, it is worth repeating, wisely provided for its own continual revision through democratic amendment. It was not the founding fathers who arranged the freezing of the plan—and, indeed, its virtual amendment—by Supreme Court dicta not subject to democratic review.) The real resistance of hundred-percenters is not to planning but to a new planning which reckons with the present-day United States, which takes into account the veering of basic economic and social arrows. New plans are always opposed by someone, usually by the group who are doing well under the old plan. It is simply a part of the human mechanism which acts in its own economic interests.

Look at some of the plans that Congress has passed; for Congressional action is our way in the United States of stating a plan and getting it into action. Take tariffs. That was a plan which the northern would-be industrialists expanded after the Civil War because it jumped with their economic interests. The agricultural South had another plan—no tariffs or low tariffs because they had no "infant industries" to protect. Instead, they had cotton to sell abroad and wanted cheap manufactured goods. We know all this, and we know that these two opposing plans played a large role in bringing about the Civil War. The whole war, indeed, was a conflict of plans. Slavery is a plan. The rights of states to secede is a plan. After the Civil War, the high-tariff plan was put over on the South, greatly to its economic disadvantage. That is, high tariffs have been a *plan for one group,* and another group was injured by that plan. We have always been a nation of planners from the time we drafted our first great plan, the Constitution, through the days of plans for controlling trusts down to plans for prohibition and relief and international trade agreements. Laws and plans. Too often plans for a group rather than for the nation.

It is the same situation today. Each economic group is working for plans that will further its interests. National planning must strike a fine balance among these conflicting interests. But it must go beyond this spot planning to planning for the nation as a whole. It must also take into account those intangible interests usually ignored by the economic groups which, for lack of a better word, we call the interests of the *public*. Such planning we conceive to be an efficient tool for democracy.

We repeat that it is our conviction that through government planning lies our best chance to liberate our now frustrated productive energies; that since we no longer have huge unused resources, no longer find domestic and world markets opening as if by magic to take up the slack of unemployed men and unemployed capital, it is through expert planning that new jobs, new frontiers, better living for all, must be created.

The Role and Rights of the Groups in our Democracy

But what kind of planning is needed, we can tell only after looking more closely into the present broil, which has as its basis the conflict of our economic groups. All groups give lip service to the pronouncements of "self-evident" and "inalienable" human rights contained in the declaration of our own right to independence. These inalienable rights were the new nation's interpretation of a good life. The attempt to secure them for all was (and is?) America's claim to democracy. Every normal person is striving for a good life. In our Western culture a good life is usually translated into money—means wherewith to buy things or power.

Desire for a good life is the basis of the workers' fight concerning wages, hours and working conditions. But this will help us not at all in trying to think towards a program, unless we know what a man and his family need in order to live a good life. As a minimum, he must have an income sufficient to meet basic needs of food, clothes and shelter. What does a man need? What does a family need? What does a child need? Your answer and mine may seem to be objective, and in a measure they may be so. But inevitably, anyone's answer will bear the imprint of the standards of his culture. Any answers that we give must be in terms of present-day American culture, which might include an automobile or a radio as well as the basic physical needs. There is a disparity of standards among different Americans. Setting aside the disparity between the lady who in "hard times" bemoans the loss of her "third man" as she calls the third male servant, and the relief agency that at the same moment calculates that a family of five in New York City needs $18.30 a week, let us ask what is the income needed in the United States for a "decent" standard of living.

In the United States, standards of living for various groups have been studied through income statistics. For the groups who are well enough off to pay income taxes there are the income-tax returns. Obviously these have to be interpreted, since men like J. P. Morgan, Thomas Lamont and other Morgan partners paid no income tax for the years 1931 and 1932. No one expected these men to go on relief because their returns showed losses greater than their taxable incomes. Indeed, no one was surprised that Mr. Morgan spent about 2½ million dollars on a yacht during one of the very years when he claimed to have no income. In the same way, the bare facts at the other end of the scale have to be interpreted. The needs of lower-income groups have been studied largely through information regarding their expenditures, their "budgets." In some ways this would seem to be arguing in a circle, a sort of chasing one's tail, which identifies "needs" with "income." The people who have translated mere budget data into terms of "a living wage" have attempted to break this vicious circle of reasoning by introducing a standard of what is "desirable" or "reasonable" or "decent" in the way of basic physical and also "pleasure" needs, and making a corresponding expense allowance. Obviously this throws us back on judgments as well as on facts. For example, it has been claimed that a living wage is lower in the South than in the North. The assumption is that a dollar buys more in rent, food, and other necessities in the South. Thus some of the NRA agreements allowed a lower minimum wage there than in the North. So does the present Wages and Hours Act. On the other hand, an examination of what a southern sharecropper family lives on suggests that the discrepancy between southern and northern is not so much the difference in prices (what the dollar will buy) as a difference in standards of living, which means both what people are accustomed to have and what they are accustomed to go without, including not only fresh vegetables, milk, a roof which holds out rain, shoes, etc., but schools, hospitals, doctors, telephones, radios, automobiles, etc. The difference here seems to be regional.

Inadequate incomes are found among a wide range of workers. We have seen that many, perhaps most, farmers no longer earn enough income to provide a good life for their families in terms of diet, medical care and schooling. We have seen that mining towns have an abnormal percent on relief (if *any* on relief deserves to be called normal); and that the standard of living among mining families is too low to maintain health. What of the United States as a whole?

According to a 1935 WPA estimate, $1261 would cover a year's "maintenance" budget for a city family of four. This budget would provide for no frills such as savings, and could scarcely give what many of our readers would consider an adequate standard of living. With this measure in mind, look at actual incomes in 1935–36. The total received by our 29½ million families was about 47½ billion dollars. Had it been evenly divided, every family would have had $1622. But the division was far from equal. Nearly 7 out of 10 families received less than this average amount. More than half got less than the "maintenance" budget. The most fortunate 1% (395,000 families and single individuals whose incomes were $9100 and over) received 14% of the total income—an amount that, for the less fortunate, was divided among 40% of the families. *One-third of the nation's families and single individuals had incomes under $750. Their average income was $471.* Think of trying to keep a *family* going on that amount! Nearly one in every three American families had to do it.

The program we have laid out for ourselves as a nation involves communities which can furnish their inhabitants health, education and pleasure. These things are over and above physical need. But they are not above "life, liberty and the pursuit of happiness" according to American standards. They transcend the worker-owner relation. They involve the government, which surely must take a hand if these inalienable rights are to be secured for all citizens.

"Unrest" among workers will unquestionably persist so long as their incomes are too low to permit decent living standards. We certainly *hope* it will persist. For the only alternatives are exploitation of the dole, or a lethargy due to undernourishment. We have samples of both in our democracy. We feel this is point number one in considering a planned society. Workers' wages must be high enough to permit a decent standard of living in terms of our present-day American culture.

This nation is a democracy in its set-up. Workers and their families are the vast majority. Why do so many of them not have these inalienable rights? Why do they not get wages which permit them to support their families in decency and privacy? Why do they not get healthy educational communities? Why do they not get security? Why do they not get civil liberties? The only answer must be that minorities, acting through their various economic, political and social groups, and with the help of the "barons of opinion" who speak in our papers, magazines, and broadcasts, are more powerful than the majority in the sense of getting laws passed and of maintaining, putting over on the public, attitudes that support their group aims.

But employers, after all, admit that workers need food, clothes, and a house. Even slave owners acknowledged this and accepted the responsibility for keeping their slaves alive. The same sense of responsibility led later to various forms of paternalism, from a complete town such as Pullman to the occasional mining-company town in which decent houses, clinics, libraries, and a hospital are provided. Even when paternalism succeeds in satisfying basic needs (and reference to pages 143 and 176 will show that it has often failed), even when it goes further and provides certain "advantages," it involves an undemocratic situation. Workers demand that the essential conditions of their lives shall not depend entirely upon an employer's sense of responsibility.

It is the workers' demand for a measure of genuine control over wages, working conditions, security of income, that arouses most opposition and indeed gives rise to the fundamental conflict of our time. For at this point the workers run against the traditional attitude that looks upon a producing establishment as property—the property, of course, of the owners. This attitude relegates the worker to the position of a person coming at call to do a job for which he is paid, and subtly denies him any effective interest in the industry except the acceptance or refusal of this job. The sanctity of private property is deeply ingrained in American psychology. "My bench," says the shop worker. "My plant," says the owner. Tradition and the force of law are overwhelmingly behind only one of them.

In the South many, perhaps most, Negroes have been disfranchised, denied the right of political vote. But millions of workers, north, south, east and west, have suffered "economic disfranchisement"—denied the right of a vote in the situation which controls their very lives—their jobs.

The state of our laws, and of the administrative and judicial policies through which they become effective, which have in the past so overwhelmingly supported control by owners, now begins to reflect a change in public opinion. The government has gone beyond emergency measures such as relief to attack the fundamental issue. The right of workers to bargain collectively through representatives of their own choosing was recognized by the courts nearly a hundred years ago. The Clayton Act of 1914 recognized that this included the right to strike and to engage in peaceful picketing. At long last the National Labor Relations Board has been created to defend these rights from the powerful and subtle evasions through which they have been denied. Not that the change is complete. Judges can still issue an injunction against a striking union, on the ground that no such thing as "peaceful picketing" does or can exist!

There are other respects in which justice is still less sure. For although the long-run efforts of our unions are undoubtedly in the direction of a more genuine democracy, there is, of course, no certainty that the demands of a union in specific disputes will always coincide with the public interest. We need to make sure that, as employers and workers bargain on more equal terms, the welfare of the entire community will be guarded. New York's mayor recently stepped in, when the milk supply was cut off in a dispute between farmers and distributing companies, to mediate. Other public concerns less obvious than food supply suffer during strikes, and too often no official takes the initiative to protect the public. Our haphazard machinery for this job needs to be overhauled and strengthened.

Consumers, as such, are a poorly organized group. The voice of the consuming public is, as yet, feeble and its remarks confused. For consumers include all groups; and the narrower group interests, being more organized, speak more loudly and more clearly than the all-containing unorganized group. The short-term interests of consumers demand low prices and high quality of goods. But how can they really distinguish the difference in worth among variously priced commodities? It is difficult for them to know what they are buying. Gadgets and advertising still further confuse them and make it additionally difficult for them to determine whether they are receiving adequate returns for their money. Government has stepped in to help these "forgotten men." Nearly every federal department offers specific consumer services. The Children's Bureau publishes advice on how to bring up babies; the Home Economics Bureau on menu planning; the Agriculture Department on grades and prices of foods and textiles; other bureaus on how to finance a new home, how to wire a farmhouse, how to budget your income. The presence of a Consumers' Counsel on NRA and AAA administrative boards and on some of the succeeding commissions marks a new advance. If the powers of this representative have been only advisory and his accomplishments rather limited, it is because consumers are slow to realize that better goods and services can be theirs—for the asking. As they learn the trick of amplifying their voice through organization, government response will increase and improve.

Consumers have a long-term interest in the conflict between workers and owners, which should and does increasingly make the public uphold workers in their drive to obtain better standards of living, though in particular cases it is often difficult for them to determine where their interests lie. In so far as the public is made up of buyers it will tend to resist the demands of a particular group of workers. But this same public has a concern which goes far beyond any particular controversy. It is the public, it is all of us, who pay in dozens of ways for the stoppage of production due to strikes, for losses to trade when workers' wages are cut off, for the decrease in public revenues which follows both, for the expense of maintaining order in periods of violence, for the cost of relief to jobless workers. It is the public who, through the agency of the government, must look beneath the surface conflict to find a just and workable program. And it is the public whose interests project into the future. Long-term consumption is a public concern. It is a public concern that undereducated, undernourished children will not make good citizens. It is a public concern that widespread unemployment means the loss through disuse of skills which it has taken years to develop and of machinery built at great cost.

Owners, too, want a good life. This is usually not a matter of a decent standard of living. It involves not the next meal but, more likely, the next payment on some debt: the upkeep of a living standard, or the maintenance of some enterprise, undertaken at a time when profits were good. The concern of owners lies in profits and power—one might say profits and the hope of profits.

The obvious way for an owner to protect profits is, in the old phrase, to "buy cheap and sell dear." Owners today are sometimes slackening, sometimes intensifying their policies on this score. Farmers have had little control over either the cost of materials and labor or the prices at which their products sell. Oil refiners manage to control prices in their interest rather effectively. Coal owners make price agreements, but their scope is restricted because of a shrinking market. In oil and coal, before the NRA, there was little check on the owners' desire to pay low wages, and in coal the results were serious: the history of coal shows American owners at their worst in fighting labor unions with gangster methods. Among other owners generally, attitudes vary. Cut prices and sweat shops go together, and examples are found among huge corporations as well as among small establishments. On the other hand, some owners now advocate high wages and even union contracts as part of their "public relations" policy; others because they realize that industries of nationwide scope cannot "sell dear" and forever pay low wages: workers must be able to buy. The same considerations often temper the desire to raise prices.

The leaders of our great businesses through which the nation's resources are turned into consumer goods (the necessities and pleasures of us all)— the generals under whom our productive and distributive capabilities are mobilized—resist having their leadership looked into and encroached upon. They regard the good fortune of the United States—both the wealth we own or can produce, and our world-wide power—as the result primarily of their own imagination, courage, and executive ability. They feel that their personal success is simply due to their wiser and more energetic use of opportunities equally open to all. They mistrust the ability of workers, and even of public agencies, to use wisely any control over business. As government agencies prove themselves efficient, however, owners do not relax their demands for control. They insist that the nation's industries and resources are properties, to be managed by the owners in such a way as to give them a "fair profit." There has been in the past a widespread feeling that the prosperity that continues to lurk around the corner depends exclusively upon owner prosperity, and that therefore everything should give way to owner plans. But increasingly consumers, workers, and the public now ask, "What price profit?"

And the leaders, though periodically they profess to be too fearful to proceed with much of anything, insist that theirs should be the initiative. They are dismayed when groups of consumers form nonprofit organizations to get something they want. They object when the federal government sets up a river-control project including the manufacture of electric power. Perhaps a possible owner has been deprived of a possible profit! But consumers, whether of electricity, or of houses, or of plays, music, and other art works, may well question why they should wait for these things until someone decides he can probably make a profit by supplying them.

Under business leadership Americans are presented with a dazzling supply of products which they can buy if they are rich enough. In addition they are presented with stupendous waste of resources, with idle machinery, with idle human energies and deteriorating human skills, character and even health. Why have we tolerated this kind of management?

It is because we have been behind the times, and deeply confused, in our conception of ownership. We inherited from the English colonizers a system of law based on private property. In the early days of our history when, by and large, ownership applied to a small piece of land which was equipped and worked by the owner and his family chiefly in production for their own use, this seemed just. Particularly so because, with our huge supply of land, possession was widely distributed. As we became more industrial, and met our needs more and more through specialized and ever larger industries, we might have questioned whether a business which exploited God-given resources and the ability of many workers—not primarily to meet the needs of consumers but first of all to bring a profit to the owner—was property in the same sense that a self-sustaining farm was property. Still, the value of the business and the profit to the owner seemed to have a fairly just relation to the energy and thought he put into it. We did not question much. But as time went on and big business grew bigger, the forms of government began to recognize the not-entirely-private nature of business. In the separation of functions once closely knit (ownership and direction, labor, consumption), the interests of workers and of the consuming public were insufficiently met. We began planning that should protect these interests. We began to have laws limiting hours of work, laws protecting consumers from dishonest labels, laws regulating transportation rates. And today?

Today it is obvious that private property is not the sole pillar of society. Ownership is in terms of money, and the value set on a business expresses its dynamic character rather than its tangible property. Ownership no longer means inevitable control and responsibility. People who, through stockholding, have claims to a fraction—it may be only a millionth—of the hoped-for profits of a business, do not make its policies. Control may come from ownership of majority stock, from various devices of pyramided holding companies, or merely from a particular form of administrative set-up without ownership at all. Whatever the case, any big business in order to operate effectively must be able to use large sums of money, some temporary, some long-term. Thus, considering business as a whole, the real and effective control is vested in the money-lenders. Many of our richest coal fields, our oil lands and refineries, even some of our farm lands, and certainly many of the great food industries founded on their products, are in the hands of giant corporations ultimately controlled by a few financiers. The same is true of all the businesses that answer—or fail to answer—the most vital needs of modern America: power, light, transportation, communication.

Private control of natural resources and the businesses through which they are made usable is a habit. People do not change age-old habits unless some crisis shows them to be outworn and foolish. One would think that a sweeping tragedy like the recent (and still present) depression would make us question our ways of doing things down to the very foundation. It certainly has changed some of our ways. The difficulty is, of course, that they are so complex. The woman struggling to keep her family alive on a relief allowance of $18.30 a week knows nothing of the farms, nothing of the long chain of processes that grow the wheat and make the very bread she buys. The farmer who grows the wheat may know little about the conditions that determine whether and at what price he can sell his wheat. We think little about the forces that determine our incomes and set the prices of what we need. We do know that the things we buy become our own, to use as we please. So we are sure that if J. P. Morgan buys a coal mine, it should be his to use as he pleases.

We are sure—until a crisis comes. At this very moment certain miners in Mahanoy City are taking coal from idle mines—Mr. Morgan's coal— and selling it to keep themselves from starving. The whole city, police, bank president and all, approve this violation of private control. For the whole city lives on the income of the miners. And the government of Pennsylvania, whose duty it is to protect Mr. Morgan's property, refuses to send troops to drive the miners off. For the government of Pennsylvania has another duty: to safeguard the welfare of its citizens.

The people of Mahanoy City have been taught by hunger to repudiate age-old habits—temporarily. Very likely when times are good again these people will again accept Mr. Morgan's right to run the coal mine or not to run it, as he pleases.

This is a single dramatic event. More important are the changes which have registered, the country over. For our troubles and dissatisfactions have resulted in a remarkable outburst of new plans—some well thought out, some overhasty—called the New Deal. We have seen the benefits and shortcomings of these plans as they related to farming, coal and oil.

Times have improved a little. The present point in our national drama represents a moment of retreat—a backtracking from the increased government control brought by the depression crisis. Increased government control in coal and oil under the New Deal was effected because business leaders were in desperate straits and actually sought government "help." Now that they have benefited somewhat, they are inclined to repudiate government "interference." Since the Blue Eagle was shot down by the Supreme Court, the administration has shown a tendency to defer to business leaders. Control of oil production, for example, has been left largely to the states. And the newspapers daily tell us the story of the oil industry's gradual return to the very kind of chaos from which they have so recently been rescued. With recovery, there is the tendency to return, on every hand, to the old careless neglect of the long-term concerns of the consuming public.

A democracy promises every man a vote. It can thrive only as every man, or at least a majority of men, uses the vote intelligently. The public interest in national resources can be protected only if the public is aware and active. What keeps the public from knowing its own interests?

The public listens to what it hears. Such facts as it hears are spoken predominantly by our business leaders. About bread we know just what the National Bakers' Association, or some such group, wants us to know. Newspapers, and even more the radio, are constantly occupied with teaching us to be grateful for the good works of our great corporations.

Public officials also listen to what they hear. And they, too, hear oftenest the voices of organized business leaders—from the local Chamber of Commerce to the National Association of Manufacturers.

True, the public is learning. As a nation we are more intelligently aware of national problems than ever before. But we have made only a beginning! And there is one more tremendous obstacle in the way of our thinking. It is the language in which these problems are expressed. When we study the farm problem, how do we study it? In terms of dollars and cents. Money is our universal language. It is because money fails to express some of the vital factors that we are so confused as to what to do about our national resources.

The plot of our national play has thickened. The actors are in conflict, that we know. The government is more aware of the nature of the conflicts, more ready to assume an active responsibility in helping the nation to come to democratic solutions. This is the turning point we now face in our national drama. The chief problem, as we see it, is: What role will the public ask the government to play?

THE GOVERNMENT'S JOB

And now the last of the last chapter. We are a mature but not a decrepit nation. We still have much of the energy and many of the ideals that made us the wonder of the past centuries and built a wilderness into a world power, with not only great national resources but also developed techniques for using them. Our problem is not how to get enough for our people. The problem is how to get our "plenty" to those who have not enough. Moreover the task that lies before the United States of building a planned society does not mean the creating of a new ideal. We organized ourselves into a separate nation with that very ideal in mind, and expressed in matchless words. Rather our task is now to summon up the ideals of our courageous past and place them alongside our present and decide which we want. For our present national economic and social picture certainly does not match the ideals stated in various historic national plans—Declaration of Independence, Constitution, education for all, votes for all, civil liberty for all. For life, liberty and the pursuit of happiness for all must, in the most conservative interpretation, mean a living wage, an opportunity to earn.

A program for a planned society in a democracy is—let us not shrink from the word—some sort of collectivism. It means a willing recognition by the people and their leaders that we do live collectively: that the fate-threads of 130 million Americans are woven together in a crisscross of working, selling, buying and living. It means, to recall another image, acting on the knowledge that the wheels of national life are geared together—imperfectly, as our present troubles show. The job of national planning is to release individual initiative—both for working and for enjoying—by constantly improving the social gears that collective living demands.

Will planning be carried out with efficiency and disinterested motivation under government leadership? Historically our government has given both positive and negative answers. Under war emergency a common national concern supplanted group interests, and organization of business for the common end was efficiently managed. In peacetimes many departments have issued printed material, from pamphlets for the use of farmers to geodetic survey maps, with scientific standards and zeal. The Post Office, despite the well-known distribution of political plums, has performed a public service with great business efficiency. These and many other examples answer "yes" to our question of the efficiency and disinterested motivation of government leadership. On the other hand, the Teapot Dome scandal gave a startling "no" as an answer. And many other instances of exploitation of official power for personal gains could be cited. Men do not change their standards and mores by sitting in a Washington office, and we have elected many unworthy to hold the public's welfare in their hands. Yet to discredit the integrity and ability of our government as a whole is to discredit the foundations of democracy. Either we must admit ours beaten and stop the farce of continuing to acclaim democratic principles, or we must take steps to make democracy work. We have the power, and we believe we are acquiring the vision, to make a planned society work in the United States. But our thinking must be brought up to date. The program for a planned society that we launched in 1781, and to which we have added from time to time, when translated into modern conditions means a national program that will include the following social objectives.

Permanent and Current Research

We believe that everything is the government's business that is the nation's business, and that everything is the nation's business which affects its citizens. Let us say, once again, that in the matter of national resources this means not only the physical resources such as soil, coal and oil, but the human beings engaged in using these resources directly as workers, and those using them as consumers. We believe it to be the government's job to be currently informed on all matters touching national resources. For example, we have been much hampered in making intelligent plans, through the lack of a usable land classification. We have as yet no mechanism for accurately measuring unemployment. National planning cannot be efficient if we lack data on which to base our plans. Permanent and current research must be carried on under nonpolitical specialists. Unquestionably, the current studies would have to be made by a federal board, but local state boards would have to function cooperatively with this federal board. A beginning has been made in the federal National Resources Board. And 46 of the 48 states have established state boards. These boards are advisory in character. Their activities, up to date, have been concerned largely with the physical aspects of our resources, though the federal board is keenly aware that the problems of physical waste and conservation cannot be attacked without including economic problems which involve our whole business structure. We need wide-ranging research as a background for planning. Otherwise our planning will be impromptu when we are caught in an emergency.

Restoration and Conservation of National Resources

Our irreplaceable natural resources are not unlimited. To make the best possible use of what we have is imperative. This must be part of a program of national planning, brought about through control measures depending upon the conditions in each resource. Specifically, as to the resources we have studied, we believe that the program of soil conservation (in the broad sense that includes farmer conservation!) should be continued energetically; that federal control of oil-bearing lands should be obtained by purchase and by supervision of the essential processes; that federal regulation of the bituminous coal industry should be pushed farther, and especially that the government should at once begin a program of purchasing marginal mines and adding to the national reserve of coal lands; and that anthracite fields should be bought and administered either by Pennsylvania or by the Nation. Our arguments for these beliefs have been developed in the chapters on each of the resources. Such control we believe to be in the interests of the public and consequently a part of the government's job.

But in no case can physical and human waste be remedied fully by action limited to a single resource or even to the industries built on it. So far we have made incomplete suggestions, or none at all, about what to do with superfluous farmers, superfluous land, superfluous mines, miners, oil wells, grocers, gasoline retailers, cotton spinners, grain traders. How can opportunities be opened for such victims of the great paradox —men idle, resources wasted, while millions of families lack the comforts of living? How can Americans get what they want?

Increasing the Nation's Income

The simple answer, to give low-income families more purchasing power, is only a half answer. To redistribute the national income more equitably will become practical only if the total can be increased. With all the actors in the national drama dissatisfied, any plan to help some at the expense of others will generate overwhelming resistance. Luckily this need not be the case. Social thinkers are already working out ways to make the "Chart of Plenty" a reality. The suggestions that seem to us most promising involve a step ahead on the basis of NRA experiences— an undertaking much more carefully planned than that emergency program, broader in scope, with more effective expression of public concerns. A central planning board would begin, as we saw the Petroleum Administration begin, by estimating what people would want and could buy; but this time on the assumption that recovery will happen. Their estimate would not cover everything anybody might want, but would include the demands to be made on great basic industries such as agriculture, food processing, textiles, transportation, coal, steel, construction and others. The estimates would assume certain prices, also a certain increased level of purchasing power to result from increased employment. The planners would then work out agreements, to be entered into by the industries and by the federal government, scheduling simultaneously in all the industries a step-up of production and of employment to meet the estimated demand. By setting a lower limit to wages and an upper limit to hours, the agreements would guarantee workers a fair share of the increasing national income. Rather than merely shift all insecurity to the business enterprisers, government would extend certain guarantees to them too. The plan itself would reduce business losses from underuse of plant capacity. Possible errors in the demand estimates could be miti-

gated by the government's agreement to buy articles produced according
to schedule but unsold.

This is a big program. It calls for active and responsible public control
in price and wage policies, international trade and investment—fields that
government has entered with hesitation. The courage to take these steps
must come from the power behind the government—the people. We believe that there are social experts in America today capable of such planning and leadership. It is up to all of us to call them to the job.

Although it is a program that cannot be shaped overnight, it implies
certain lines of action that must be carried on now as well as in the
future.

Economic Enfranchisement of Workers

Government must continue and strengthen its guarantee of labor's
right to bargain collectively, sanctioning the union shop and the right to
strike and to picket peacefully. Labor organization is necessary to a program aiming at better distribution of the national income. It is one way
towards the only goal worthy of a democracy: high standards of living
for all; working and living conditions that will supply not merely the
necessities but also those intangibles we think of as making a good life
—education, a share of control in your work, time and opportunity for
some play.

Social Security

Emergency-relief needs are still urgent. There are still (1939) ten
million unemployed. The public-works program has been prematurely
curtailed and should be reconstituted as a permanent way of easing unemployment, which is bound to occur sporadically even after recovery.
Rehabilitation and resettlement for marginal farming and mining communities will be urgently needed for a good while to come. The national
program of insurance against unemployment and old age should be continued and improved. Nation-wide limits on lowness of wages and length
of working hours must be kept. These measures are all absolutely necessary for sustaining general purchasing power and so keeping the national
economy healthy.

Economic Enfranchisement of Consumers

Consumer representation on government planning and administrative
agencies must be strengthened. In employer-labor disputes and in any

other matter involving availability, price, and quality of goods important to all, the interests of the consuming public should be implemented.

Revising Concepts of Ownership

A program of national planning means changing our old ideas of ownership to fit our modern economy. The development of our national resources must be evaluated in terms of use, not merely of profit. In some ways our laws and government methods have been adjusted to meet modern conditions; yet old traditions persist, trailing injustice and uncertainty. A clear national policy on the relations of business organizations to the public and their agent, the government, is essential. Confusion over the issue popularly described as monopoly against free competition is the core of the trouble. It runs through our patent and tax laws as well as through the newer efforts at planning. Here is an immense task for social pioneering.

We believe the nation must recognize that modern technology is bound to breed large business organizations with centralized control, and that a simple effort to legislate and prosecute them out of existence will be futile. It must also recognize that big businesses, drawing on the nation's man power and resources, and filling nation-wide consumer demands, can no longer be considered private property. Government need not buy them out, any more than it should prosecute them out; for legal ownership, as we have pointed out, is already largely separate from control. What must be done is to invest them with social responsibility by means of control methods such as we have outlined. Competition will persist, but in more socially useful form. Its evils—abuse of national resources, denial to workers of fair wages and to consumers of fair prices and quality—will be checked, whether they result from control by large organizations of resources and credit or from competitive overdevelopment.

Civil Liberties for All

Civil liberties, we have seen, are most often denied where economic enslavement is worst. National planning towards higher standards of living is thus the best guarantee of those liberties our Constitution promises. But we cannot afford to lose sight of them as we shape the program itself. The means forecast the end. Here and now we must insist on true civil liberty everywhere: freedom of speech and assembly for fascists and communists, for college professors and labor leaders; for Negroes, the right to vote and to undergo fair trial.

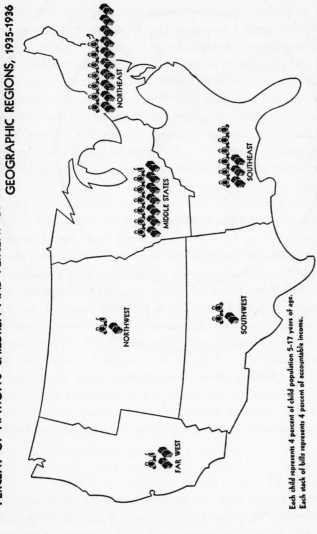

PERCENT OF NATION'S CHILDREN AND PERCENT OF NATION'S INCOME IN SIX GEOGRAPHIC REGIONS, 1935-1936

Each child represents 4 percent of child population 5-17 years of age.
Each stack of bills represents 4 percent of accountable income.

From "The Effect of Population Changes on American Education," copyrighted by the National Education Association

The South must educate one-third of the nation's children with one-sixth of the nation's income. According to conservative estimates the per capita ability of the richest state in the country to support education is six times as great as that of the poorest state.

PIONEER PSYCHOLOGY

"Why save when there is plenty more?"

Health and Education

Civil liberties imply and demand citizens capable of using them well. A national program for our democracy means raising the standards of health and of education throughout the nation. It means recognizing that the undernourished and undereducated children of the South are a national, not merely a regional responsibility, since they form a goodly group of our future citizens. It means recognizing that the income of the southern states is too low to provide adequate schools for their children. Moreover, it means supporting the *kind of education* that leads children to assess the present economic and social systems, not to accept them blindly, and raises to respectability any effort to make the country more truly democratic.

PLANNING PSYCHOLOGY

"Make the best use of what we have!"

Democratic Planning

In short, a program of national planning means extending the rights of democracy to all members of the United States. This democratic collectivism does not mean socialism, communism, or any other -ism as defined by present political parties here or in Europe. It does not mean doing away with the rugged individual but with the ragged individual. Here we may as well give our answers to two frequently heard questions. (1) Does national planning within a democracy involve abolishing private property? No. It does not. Private property becomes undemocratic and must be done away with only when it is used for the owners at the sacrifice of the national good and supported through the sacrifice of the good life of human beings. (2) Is public control of property and business enterprise dictatorial regimentation and therefore inconsistent with democracy? No. It is not. Otherwise our federal oil lands, the Post Office, the Interstate Commerce Commission, the Federal Reserve Board, and a thousand other federal activities and holdings would have turned the United States into a regimented nation. It becomes dictatorial only when public control is enforced by the denial of civil liberties and regardless of the way consumers, workers, and the public are served. Public good, the good of the majority, is the criterion in judging to what extent a particular property or business should be privately or governmentally controlled. We believe in democracy, which to us means the rights of the many, not of the few. Minority rights must be protected. But we believe that the claim to superiority by the minority who now control the majority is partly fallacious and, where true, is due to privileges rather than to inherent superiority. We look to greater and greater governmental control not merely because of frequent abuse to the public under private control, but because the government, and the government alone, is in a strategic position to bring about the sorely needed interplanning among industries.

A program of collectivism is a democratic planning and one which people of widely different political affiliation can join. Democratic planning forms a common denominator, as Max Lerner has said, in the strivings of socialists, progressives, trade unionists, professionals, and technicians, "who can identify themselves with an effort to give social meaning to technological advance and establish a basic social security;" and with those "who care about the richness of the culture that can be built on a stable economic base."

We believe there is evidence that more and more people are regarding the rights of the majority, their physical and economic and social health, as the basis of future national health. (The evidence lies not only in the torrent of panic utterances appearing everywhere—"Democracy is threatened"—"Capitalism is tottering"—etc. The evidence lies also in presidential slogans.) Hoover talked about the "full dinner pail." His successor, who disagreed with almost all of President Hoover's policies, spoke thus:

Every man has a right to life; and this means that he has also a right to make a comfortable living. He may by sloth or crime decline to exercise that right; but it may not be denied him. We have no actual famine or dearth; our industrial and agricultural mechanism can produce enough and to spare. Our government, formal and informal, political and economic, owes to everyone an avenue to possess himself of a portion of that plenty sufficient for his needs through his own work.

Words mean little, that we know, particularly in a campaign address. But the actions of Congress, yes, and even of the Supreme Court within the last few years, show that the government is taking a new role and in some measure assuming the responsibility for the effects of our present business economy upon the workers and the present public and the future public. Conservation of physical resources naturally came first as a government activity. A significant change from the pioneer psychology of "Why save when there is plenty more?" Conservation of human resources has begun—an even more significant change from the psychology of rugged individualism. Both changes are the beginning of a new interpretation of democratic planning which was so evident in our eloquent birth as a nation. They indicate an approaching maturity in economic and social thinking adapted to the present culture of a mature nation. We believe both lines should be pushed and pushed militantly by all who believe in democracy irrespective of group or political affiliations.

And finally, a democratic national planning is not only what we desire for our country. We believe it is what is going to happen here. If there is any place on this disturbed globe of which we still have hope,

My country, 'tis of thee.

AMERICAN STRIDE*

I. FLASH

Carefree America! Pep-it-up America!
The greatest show on earth
was our gift to the world.
Fire-eating sword-swallowing elephant-dancing America,
ball-batting line-plunging cheer-whooping nation!
We'll dance a new dance and make it a marathon—
never-wear-down
never-play-out
will-not-be-stopped
America!

II. BONE

We play hard.
We do everything hard.
We are a hard people,
stubborn, strong-framed, bony.
We hardened a long time gone.

1607
1620
so long ago we were born
on the wilderness edge of a hard land
in a hard winter.

For every foot of rocky soil
for every wall against the wind
stroke upon stroke of the ax
into stubborn wood.
The bones of a people hardened.

* Written for a production in choral speech and dance. The concluding dialogue quotes
John Wise, an Italian tyrant, the Declaration of Independence, Alexander Stephens, a New
England letter of about 1860, Abraham Lincoln, and current talk.

There is that in us all
hard as the stumps of the old Appalachians
stiff as the frame of a Puritan church
heavy as an ax-head, tough as wood
hard as the stock of a flint-lock gun.

III. STRIDE

Open-road Americans! Free-and-easy walkers!
Where did we learn that long strong stride?
We were all bone and muscle
and hungry for land.
We were learning to tread
—like the Indians—strong and clever.
We broke a mountain wall.
We pushed through the forest.
We came to a
long
trail.

The set of the head on the shoulders
the pace and the measure of our walk
and the deepness of breathing
opened
lengthened
opened
to a thousand miles of plains.

A man alone
on his own broad acres
farming the richest soil the wide earth offers
has a certain way of looking
a certain way of walking
a certain way of resting
with thanks and pride.

There is nothing for a thousand miles
to break the wind's blowing.
What should there be to break
America's stride?

IV. GRAB BAG

Prodigal America! Lucky-strike Americans,
nervous of gesture, nervy of speech!
Yes! we want Plenty.
We want it in a Hurry.
There's more where this came from.
Sure. Sure.

Gold in California—
stake yourself a claim!
Wheat will grow to gold.
Vote yourself a farm!
Trees cut up are gold;
oil spurts up, black gold;
copper, iron, coal—
buy yourself some stock!
Cut yourself a slice!
Hurry up, America, we'll all go West!

We'll dig the golden West.
We'll build a fabulous nation—
roads rails bridges towers
wings power speed light . . .

Of course
maybe we hurried it up too fast.
We got a lot we didn't count on.
Fortunes in wheat and beef; also a Dust Bowl.
Lumber kings; and flood after flood.
Coal barons; and ghost towns.
And we've learned more than is good for us
about hush money
dollar diplomacy
a certain way of making one's way:
"subtraction, division, silence."

V. PROMISE

The truth about America!
. . . What *is* the deep truth—
the life that animates these bones,
the breath impelling open strides,
the heart much finer than a "heart of gold,"
the truth not fact
but a faith to come up to?

1700
John Wise
free son of an indentured servant
spoke words for the future:
All power
is originally in the people.
The only end of government
is the good of every man
in all his rights
his life
liberty
estate
honor.

The people? A numbskull mob.
Feed them, amuse them,
and you can always force them.
Forza, fiesta, farina. Forza!

We hold *these* truths
to be self-evident:
that all men are created equal
endowed by their Creator with certain inalienable rights
among them life
liberty
the pursuit of happiness.
All power
is originally in the people!

320

1850
Plantations in the South.
The Negro is not equal to the white man.
Slavery—
subordination to the superior race—
is his natural and normal condition.

1850
Textile mills in the North.
A long low black wagon,
termed a "slaver,"
makes trips to the north of Massachusetts,
cruising around Vermont and New Hampshire,
with a commander
who is paid one dollar a head
for all the girls he brings to the mills.

Familiarize yourself with the chains of bondage
and you prepare your own limbs
to wear them.
Accustomed to trample on the rights of others,
you have lost the genius
of your own independence!
Shall government of the people
by the people
and for the people
perish from the earth?

1940
Troubled America.
Those farmers? Shiftless!
Others get along.
Those miners? Degenerate!
Others get along.
Why send good money
after bad people?

The only end of government
is the good of every man.
We hold *these* truths.

We promise here
every man his chance.
We promise a land
where a man can think and speak.
We promise a land
where men can meet and act.
We promise a new frontier
a new spaciousness
new Great Plains
not of land but of living.
We call upon that power
deep in the people.
The truth of America
will yet be lived!

M.P.

BIBLIOGRAPHY

This reading list serves two purposes: acknowledging works on which we have depended and suggesting material through which readers may make further study. In both respects it is selective rather than complete. The accent is on source materials, and we have had to omit many challenging interpretative books. We are also unable to include works of fiction that illuminate our problem. However, Lucy Sprague Mitchell's article, "Natural Regions in the United States," in *Progressive Education* magazine, April, 1938, contains a list of regional novels.

GENERAL

National Resources Board, *Report,* 1934.
   The first thorough study of all our land, water and mineral resources, with recommendations towards conserving them.
Census of the United States, 1910, 1920, 1930, and current releases from 1935 data.
Statistical Abstract of the United States.
   This desk-size compilation of statistics from the Census and from data collected by various government departments is invaluable for the study of state and national problems. Published annually. $1.50
National Resources Committee: *Technological Trends and National Policy,* 1937, $1.00; *Consumer Incomes in the United States,* 1938, $ .30; *Consumer Expenditures in the United States,* 1939, $ .50; *The Structure of the American Economy,* 1939, $1.00.
   The National Resources Committee, successor to the National Resources Board, continues in these and other studies to lay a groundwork for intelligent national planning.
(All books listed so far can be obtained from the Superintendent of Documents, Washington, D. C.)

Encyclopedia of the Social Sciences, 1935.
   Contains authoritative readable articles on nearly every subject relevant to social and economic problems here and throughout the world. Every library should own these volumes.
The World Almanac.
   Another desk-size reference book, published annually by the *New York World Telegram.* Includes facts on industries and trade in foreign countries as well as in the United States. Gives main provisions of important legislation and describes work of government agencies. $ .60.

PERIODICALS

The New York Times.

Fortune.

Survey Graphic.

(All three are valuable for reporting current developments.)

SOIL

Embree, E. R., Johnson, C. S., and Alexander, W. W., *The Collapse of Cotton Tenancy,* 1935.

Hacker, Louis, and Kendrick, Benjamin B., *The United States since 1865,* 1932.

Hacker, Louis, Modley, Rudolf, and Taylor, George B., *The United States: A Graphic History,* 1937.

Hulbert, Archer B., *The Paths of Inland Commerce,* 1920.

Nourse, E. G., Davis, J. S., and Black, J. D., *Three Years of the Agricultural Adjustment Administration,* 1937.

Odum, Howard W., *Southern Regions of the United States,* 1936.

Paullin, Charles O., *Atlas of the Historical Geography of the United States,* 1932.

Sears, Paul B., *Deserts on the March,* 1935.

Semple, Ellen C., *American History and Its Geographic Conditions,* 1903.

Smith, J. Russell, *North America,* 1925.

Vance, Rupert B., *Human Geography of the South,* 1932.

Willcox, O. W., *Reshaping Agriculture,* 1934.

Wood, Edith Elmer, *Recent Trends in American Housing,* 1931.

GOVERNMENT PUBLICATIONS

Agriculture Yearbooks, published annually.
    These contain, besides technical articles, tables of statistics and the annual report of the Secretary of Agriculture. The latter section is now published separately.

Baker, O. E., *A Graphic Summary of Physical Features and Land Utilization in the United States,* 1937.

Beck, P. G., and Forster, M. C., *Six Rural Problem Areas,* 1935.

Bureau of Agricultural Economics, *Report,* 1938.

Consumers' Counsel of the Agricultural Adjustment Administration, *Consumers' Guide,* published weekly.

Ezekiel, Mordecai, and Bean, Louis H., *Economic Bases for the Agricultural Adjustment Act,* 1933.

Farm Tenancy, the Report of the President's Committee, 1937.

Great Plains Committee, *Report,* 1937.

Great Plains Drought Area Committee, *Report,* 1936.

Lord, Russell, *To Hold This Soil,* 1938.

Mississippi Valley Committee of the Public Works Administration, *Report,* 1934.

Person, H. S., *Little Waters,* 1935.

Turner, H. A., *A Graphic Summary of Farm Tenure,* 1936.

COAL

Berquist, F. E., and others, *Economic Survey of the Bituminous Coal Industry under Free Competition and Code Regulation,* 1936.

Gilbert, C. G., and Pogue, J. E., *America's Power Resources: the Economic Significance of Coal, Oil and Water Power,* 1921.

Hamilton, Walton H., and Wright, Helen R., *The Case of Bituminous Coal,* 1925.

The History of the Consolidation Coal Company, 1934.

Jones, Eliot, *The Anthracite Coal Combination in the United States,* 1914.

Leighton, George R., *Five Cities: the Story of Their Youth and Old Age,* 1939. (Chapter on Shenandoah, Pa.)

Lubin, Isador, "The Coal Industry," in the *Encyclopedia of the Social Sciences.*

Morris, H. S., *The Plight of the Bituminous Coal Miner,* 1934.

National Industrial Conference Board, *The Competitive Position of Coal in the United States,* 1931.

Nicolls, William J., *The Story of American Coals,* 1897.

The Story of Blue Coal, Delaware, Lackawanna and Western Coal Company.

Van Kleek, Mary, *Miners and Management,* 1934.

Yellen, Samuel, *America's Labor Struggles,* 1936.

STATE OF PENNSYLVANIA PUBLICATIONS

Anthracite Coal Industry Commission of Pennsylvania, *Bootlegging or Illegal Mining of Anthracite Coal in Pennsylvania,* 1937.

Anthracite Coal Industry Commission, *Report and Final Recommendations,* 1938.

STATE OF KENTUCKY PUBLICATIONS

Governor Laffoon's Investigation Commission, *Report,* June, 1935.

GOVERNMENT PUBLICATIONS

Minerals Yearbooks, published annually.

Bureau of Labor Statistics, *Labor Information Bulletin,* monthly.

National Bituminous Coal Commission, *Annual Report of the Consumers' Counsel,* 1938.

National Labor Relations Board, *The Effect of Labor Relations in the Bituminous Coal Industry upon Interstate Commerce*, 1938.

Sachs, Dr. Alexander, statement in *Transcript of Proceedings, NRA Coal Code Hearings*, August 12, 1933.

Senate Committee on Education and Labor (La Follette Committee), 74th Congress, *Report*, February, 1939.

Senate Committee on Interstate Commerce, 74th Congress, *Stabilization of the Bituminous Coal Mining Industry*, 1935.

U. S. Anthracite Coal Commission, *Report No. 3*, 1923.

U. S. Coal Commission *Reports*, 1923–25. (This material is summarized in *What the Coal Commission Found*, edited by E. E. Hunt, 1925.)

U. S. Public Health Service, *Bulletin*, 1933.

OIL

Arnold, Ralph, and Kemnitzer, W. J., *Petroleum in the United States and Possessions*, 1931.

Berle, A. A., and Means, Gardiner C., "Trusts," in the *Encyclopedia of the Social Sciences*.

Chambers, William T., "Kilgore, Texas: an Oil Boom Town," in *Economic Geography* magazine, January, 1933.

Flynn, John T., *God's Gold*, 1932.

Ise, John, *The United States Oil Policy*, 1926.

Kemnitzer, W. J., *The Rebirth of Monopoly*, 1938.

Snider, L. S., and Brooks, B. T., *Petroleum Shortage and Its Alleviation*, pamphlet of the Chemical Foundation, New York.

Stocking, George Ward, "The Oil Industry," in the *Encyclopedia of the Social Sciences*.

Stocking, George Ward, *The Oil Industry and the Competitive System*, 1928.

Tarbell, Ida W., *The History of the Standard Oil Company*, 1904.

Watkins, Myron W., "Corporation," in the *Encyclopedia of the Social Sciences*.

Watkins, Myron W., *Oil: Stabilization or Conservation?* 1937.

Winkler, John K., *John D.*, 1929.

Petroleum Facts and Figures, American Petroleum Institute, 1939.

GOVERNMENT PUBLICATIONS

Minerals Yearbooks, published annually.

Federal Oil Conservation Board: Reports to the President, 1926–1932.

House Committee on Interstate and Foreign Commerce, 72nd Congress, 2nd Session, *Report on Pipe Lines*, 1933.

House Committee on Interstate and Foreign Commerce, 73rd Congress, *Petroleum Investigation*, 1934.

U. S. Federal Trade Commission Reports: *Pipe-Line Transportation of Petroleum*, 1916; *The Price of Gasoline in 1915*, 1917; *The Petroleum Industry: Prices, Profits and Competition*, 1928.

GEOLOGY

Lobeck, A. K., *Airways of America*, 1933.

Lobeck, A. K., *Atlas of American Geology*.

Loomis, Frederic B., *Physiography of the United States*, 1937.

Pirsson, Louis V., and Schuchert, Charles, *Introductory Geology*, 1924.

Price, Paul H., "The Appalachian Structural Front," *Journal of Geology*, January–February, 1931.

A Resumé of the Geology and Occurrence of Petroleum in the United States, by members of the U. S. Geological Survey, published in the Report of the Petroleum Investigation by the House Committee on Interstate and Foreign Commerce, 73rd Congress, 1934.

Whitney, Milton, *The Soil and Civilization*, 1925.

LAST CHAPTER

Leven, Maurice, and others, *America's Capacity to Consume*, 1934.

Loeb, Harold, and others, *The Chart of Plenty*, 1935.

Mackenzie, Findlay, editor, *Planned Society*, containing essays by thirty-five economists, sociologists and statesmen, 1937.

Nourse, E. G., and others, *America's Capacity to Produce*, 1934.

Zimmerman, Erich W., "Natural Resources," an article in the *Encyclopedia of the Social Sciences*.

INDEX